Women Poets in Pre-Revolutionary America

For Gene and Evalyn

Women Poets in Pre-Revolutionary America

1650 – 1775

An Anthology

by

Pattie Cowell

The Whitston Publishing Company
Troy, New York
1981

mno 2-19-82

Acknowledgments

Mr. and Mrs. Douglas C. Turnbull, Jr. and the Dickinson College Library—for permission to print Anna Young Smith's "Ode to Gratitude," "Occasional Verses on the Anniversary of the Death of My Grandfather, Dr. Thomas Graeme," "Ode to Sensibility," and "A Song."

Harvard University Press—for permission to reprint Anna Hayden's "Upon the Death of. . .Elizabeth Tompson" and "Verses on Benjamin Tompson" from *Handkerchiefs from Paul,* ed. Kenneth B. Murdock (1927).

The Historical Society of Pennsylvania—for permission to print Susanna Wright's "My Own Birthday, August, 1761" and "On the Death of a Young Girl, 1737"; Hannah Griffitts's "Verses, 1737," "An Ode on the State Peace, 1763," "On the 13th February of 1765, A Day in Which I First Drank of the Cup of Sorrow, in the Death of My Beloved Parent," "The Storm, 1765," "To the Memory of Our Valued Friend, Samuel Fothergill," " 'Beware of the Ides of March'. . . ," "Inscription on a Curious Chamberstove," "Wrote on Reading Some Paragraphs in 'The Crisis,' " "On the Death of John Roberts and Abraham Carlisle," and "To the Memory of My Late Valuable Friend, Susannah Wright"; Elizabeth Drinker's "I Stay Much at Home . . . " and "Lines Verging Somewhat on the Bath(os) . . ."; Elizabeth Fergusson's "Hymn on the Charms of Creation" and "Upon the Discovery of the Planet By Mr. Herschel . . . "; Phillis Wheatley's "America." Permission to quote from other poems and correspondence of Hannah Griffitts, Annis Stockton and Elizabeth Fergusson has also been granted. All of the Hannah Griffitts poems except "To the Memory of . . . Samuel Fothergill" are owned by the Library Company of Philadelphia, which has placed them in the Historical Society of Pennsylvania.

The Houghton Library of Harvard University—for permission to print Phillis Wheatley's "A Poem on the Death of Charles Eliot."

The Huntington Library, San Marino, California—for permission to print Sarah Morton's "Stanzas to a Husband Recently United."

The Massachusetts Historical Society—for permission to print Mercy Warren's "A Thought on the Inestimable Blessing of Reason" and "To the Hon[ora]ble James Warren, Esq . . . ." Permission to quote from the correspondence of Mercy Warren and of Judith Sargent Murray has also been granted.

The Princeton University Library—for permission to print Annis Stockton's "Epistle to Mr. S[tockton]," "On Hearing that General Warren Was Killed on Bunker Hill . . . ," "Addressed to General Washington in the Year 1777," "To Laura," "To the Same," and "Elegy on the Destruction of the Trees by the Icicles"; Elizabeth Fergusson's "Lines Written on Reading Dr. More's Journal in France." Permission to quote from other poems and correspondence of Annis Stockton has also been granted.

The University of North Carolina Press—for permission to reprint from *The Poems of Phillis Wheatley,* edited by Julian D. Mason, Jr. (1966).

Articles based on research for parts of this collection have been published in *13th Moon, Seventeenth-Century News* and the *Bulletin of Bibliography and Magazine Notes.*

Contents

Illustrations
(following p. 26)

Mercy Otis Warren
by John Singleton Copley
Reproduced by the courtesy of
Boston Museum of Fine Arts

Annis Boudinot Stockton
(artist unknown)
Reproduced by the courtesy of
Princeton University

Elizabeth Graeme Fergusson
(artist unknown)
Reproduced by the courtesy of the
Historical Society of Pennsylvania

Judith Sargent Murray
by John Singleton Copley
Reproduced by the courtesy of the
Sargent-Murray-Gilman-Hough House Association
Gloucester, Massachusetts

Ann Eliza Bleecker
by Tiebout
from *The Posthumous Works of Ann Eliza Bleecker,*
Reproduced by the courtesy of the
University of Colorado at Boulder

Phillis Wheatley
(artist unknown)
from *Poems on Various Subjects, Religious and Moral,*
Reproduced by the courtesy of the
Library of Congress

Sarah Wentworth Apthorp Morton
by Gilbert Stuart
Reproduced by the courtesy of the
Worcester Art Museum

Introduction

Unlike that of most other nations, all of American history has been written within the eras of printing and relatively high standards of literacy. As scholars are just beginning to recognize, early American history can be explored not only in the official records of an evolving government or in the writings of a Franklin or an Edwards, a Byles or a Wigglesworth, but also in the manuscripts and publications of forgotten women. Many such materials exist, for literature was the first of the fine arts to be cultivated by a significant number of women in colonial America.

That colonial women turned first to literature should come as no surprise. In the context of her own initial attempts at writing, Virginia Woolf identified (perhaps facetiously, but no less accurately) the factors which allow even socially and economically dependent persons to write:

> The family peace was not broken by the scratching of a pen. No demand was made upon the family purse. . . . Pianos and models, Paris, Vienna and Berlin, masters and mistresses, are not needed by a writer. The cheapness of writing paper is, of course, the reason why women have succeeded as writers before they have succeeded in the other professions. [1]

Perhaps because the barriers to literature were (relatively speaking) easier to overcome than those for the other arts, more than fifty colonial women, some of them anonymous, have left records of their poetic endeavors.

Although colonial Boston and Philadelphia produced (or at least preserved the records of) larger concentrations of women poets than elsewhere, women were writing and occasionally publishing their verses throughout the colonies. Their devotion to their craft varied enormously, of course. Some women produced only a single poem while others published several volumes; some embroidered sampler verses or wrote metrical accounts of battles and Indian captivities while others created more polished lines of genuine literary merit.

More surprising than the numbers of women who turned to poetry or the variety of verse they produced is contemporary ignorance of the results of their efforts: the verse of colonial women is almost totally unavailable to readers today.[2] As early as 1712, Cotton Mather had noted that many women "have wrote such things as have been very valuable; especially relating to their own experiences. . . .[but] they have been patterns of humility. They have made no noise; they have sought no fame . . . ."[3] More than 250 years later, their "valuable" writings are still unknown. To assist these poets in making some long overdue "noise," *Women Poets in Pre-Revolutionary America, 1650-1775* makes accessible many long out-of-print or unpublished poems in a collected edition. Certainly all the poets considered here were minor figures, with few exceptions obscure even in their own day. None were so professional as Anne Bradstreet, the earliest of them for whom we have existing poems and herself a minor figure in American poetry. Yet taken together, these lesser poets have a greater statement to make than any of them can make individually. Examining who they were, what and why they wrote, may more fully develop our partial view of America's literary achievement. Not merely curiosities, their poems are pages for the history of an America engaged, once again, in reviewing and rewriting its past.

I

Women Poets and Colonial Society: Opportunities

A selected gathering of colonial women's poetry such as this almost compels us to ask who these "lost women" were. Did they share common experiences that turned them to writing poetry? Did their activities as poets affect their relationships with their families? With their communities? Did it matter to the society at large that so many women were writing poetry? Answers to these questions are difficult at best for such a diverse group of poets. The obvious similarities of sex, geography and time will determine much regarding their poetic materials and forms. But they reveal little about these poets' relationships with colonial society, about their status, their opportunities, their frustrations.

Pursuing a collective sense of who America's early women poets were leads immediately to one overwhelming generalization: with regard to their educational advantages, these women were unrepresentative of the female populace at large. With few exceptions, America's early women poets profited from unusually extensive opportunities for learning. The uniqueness of these opportunities is most clearly apparent in contrast with standard instructional practices in the colonies.

Cotton Mather's *Ornaments for the Daughters of Zion* (1692) had detailed the kind of education considered appropriate for young women in seventeenth-century America:

> Such is her industry, that she betimes applies herself to learn all the affairs of housewifry, and besides a good skill at her needle, as well as in the kitchen, she acquaints herself with arithmetic and accomptantship (perhaps also chiurgery) and such other arts relating to business as may enable her to do the man whom she may hereafter have, good and not evil all the days of her life. If she have any time after this to learn music and language, she will not lose her time, and yet she will not be proud of her skill. . . .[4]

Largely directed toward areas of practical domestic economy, this conventional education for women provided few skills useful to a writer. Even well into the eighteenth century, most women's educations were scanty and ill-planned.

> Dress, pleasantry, and show
> Is all they're taught, and all they know:
>
> . . . .
>
> 'Tis question whether one in ten
> Knows how to spell her name:—what then![5]

And such unconcern with the development of the female intellect was not limited to the southern colonies, where this verse was published. In Philadelphia, where educational opportunities for women were relatively high, most women with access to schooling barely achieved literacy. Though by 1647 New England required each community to establish a public school, girls seldom received full benefit. At first they were allowed to attend only during the summer months when boys were doing farm work. Since conventional women's activities demanded little formal study, scanty educational resources in the colonies were directed primarily to men. This is not to suggest that formal education was freely available for all colonial men who wished it: schooling was certainly more accessible for boys of well-to-do, urban families than for sons of laborers or farmers. But cultural assumptions about the future roles of sons and daughters led colonists to structure substantially different curricula for girls than for boys, even for girls from middle and upper class backgrounds.

It was not until very late in the eighteenth century that theorists began to attribute women's intellectual inferiority to their education rather than to their biology. Benjamin Rush reflected the changing attitudes in his *Thoughts Upon Female Education* (1787): "I know that the elevation of the female mind . . . is considered by some men as unfriendly to the domestic character of a woman. But this is the prejudice of little minds . . . . for a weak and ignorant woman will always be governed with the greatest difficulty."[6] Pressing for greater educational opportunities for women, Rush made it clear that the primary beneficiaries would be men. But whatever his motives, he was proposing a radical change in education for women, a change more conducive to intellectual activities among them. As early as 1706, British feminist Mary Astell had lamented that the practical focus of the meagre education available to women "beat [them] not *for* but *from* the Muses."[7] Except for the accidents of birth which allowed the women represented here to obtain unusual cultivation, there would be many fewer colonial women poets.

Though refinement of the intellect was a secondary concern in a woman's eduation, America's literary women sought such development aggressively. The means by which they acquired their educations vary from case to case, but often these women benefited from proximity to educated fathers and brothers. Anne Bradstreet was solidly grounded in classical learning before she left England because her father, as steward to the Earl of Lincoln, had access to his large private library. Jane Turell was tutored and encouraged in her writing by her father, Benjamin Colman. Phillis Wheatley was instructed by her owner's twin children, Nathaniel and Mary Wheatley. Mercy Warren shared her brother's tutors as he prepared for Harvard; though she could not accompany James Otis to college, their close relationship facilitated her participation in some of his studies.

Other women combined family advantages with more formal schooling or with travel. Anthony Benezet, noted abolitionist and feminist, briefly directed a Quaker school for girls in Philadelphia that provided a curriculum the equivalent of that available to boys. Deborah Logan, Sarah Wister and Hannah Griffitts, all of whom later wrote poetry (though Logan's and Wister's verse was written too late for inclusion here), were among his students. Extensive reading and travel gave Elizabeth Graeme Fergusson an educational breadth beyond that of most of her contemporaries, female or male. And the list could well continue. Few poets represented here did not benefit from an intellectual cultivation rare among colonial women. Though not at an educational parity with their male counterparts, these women collectively represent a remarkable achievement. At a time when even basic literacy was noteworthy, many women poets were among the best educated minds in the colonies.[8]

Generally from well-to-do families, several of these poets shared another advantage rare for colonial women: leisure for study and writing. Few of them seemed cognizant of their relative good fortune, a common lament being their lack of time for pursuing intellectual or literary activities.

> ... Amidst domestic cares to rhyme
> I find no pleasure, and I find no time,[9]

wrote Ann Bleecker of her experience juggling familial responsibilities with her verse. Household tasks, family duties and social obligations frequently encroached on the writing and study time of even the most wealthy colonial women poets. But despite their disclaimers, many of them were sufficiently secure financially to allow time for their writing.

Able to support the luxury of a literary woman (so long as she didn't neglect her primary responsibilities or damage her health), the men of prosperous families frequently took pride in the public success of wives, sisters and daughters. Anne Bradstreet's poems were first published through the efforts of her brother-in-law, John Woodbridge. Sarah Morton brought favorable notice to her family with her numerous publications. Phillis Wheatley, despite her slave status, received encouragement from the Wheatleys. Other examples of family support for a woman poet can be found throughout this collection. Partially insulated by their status from negative social opinion of women writers, these poets from distinguished families were able to pursue their writing more easily than were their less well-to-do contemporaries. Education, financial security and social circumstances combined, if not to make a literary avocation easy, at least to make it possible.

Though clearly subordinate figures in a patriarchal society, colonial American women—poets and non-poets alike—achieved a status unknown to their British counterparts at least until the mid-eighteenth century. Their greater economic value in a situation of labor shortage made it possible for women to seek employment in a wider range of fields. Although most women continued to work at home, women printers, tavern-keepers, school teachers, blacksmiths, plantation managers, even soldiers and pirates were not unknown. Favorable sex ratios—fewer women than men—further increased the status of American women in the seventeenth and early eighteenth centuries. The popular proverb "houses where no women be are like deserts or untilled land"[10] reflects the importance of a woman-centered family to the English colonists. Additionally, the religious base of colonial life, particularly in Puritan and Quaker societies, assured women of spiritual (if not practical) equality, providing theological sanction for the inherent value of women's lives regardless of their subordinate functions. These early conditions of colonial life, given further impetus by greater prosperity, growing urbanism and the political liberalism of the eighteenth century, provided opportunities for American women that had been unavailable to their English contemporaries since the reign of Elizabeth. Though not without hazard to those who chose to take advantage of them, these opportunities were seized by many American women who became poets.

II

Women Poets and Colonial Society: Obstacles

The frequency with which colonial women tried their skills at poetry should not suggest that the pursuit of a literary avocation (more would hardly be thinkable) was without difficulty. Hampered by rigid role definitions and social expectations, most women colonists were neither expected nor encouraged to develop an interest in the arts. While students of colonial history have demonstrated the relative advantages possessed by American women in comparison with their British peers,[11] and even in comparison with nineteenth-century American women,[12] such advantages must be qualified. Women's status in such comparisons is measured almost solely in terms of the economic and social value of their work.[13] The individual toll of that work (often not freely chosen) and of continuous child-bearing, including the lack of leisure for education and for the arts, counts for little in these studies.

> Seek to be good, but aim not to be great,
> A woman's noblest station is retreat . . .[14]

wrote an anonymous poet in the *American Magazine, or General Repository* for July, 1769. Though the American woman's retreat may have been less precipitous than that of her British contemporary, the colonial woman took a considerable risk when she stepped outside her carefully defined role. The writing of poetry involved such a risk.

The earliest known woman writer in America, Anne Yale Hopkins, illustrated (at their worst extreme) the hazards of literature for women. She is chiefly remembered through John Winthrop's journal reference of April 13, 1645:

> Mr. Hopkins, the governor of Hartford upon Connecticut, came to Boston, and brought his wife with him (a godly young woman, and of special parts) who was fallen into a sad infirmity, the loss of her understanding and reason, which had been growing upon her divers years, by occasion of her giving herself wholly to reading and writing, and had written many books . . . . if she had attended her household affairs, and such things as belong to women, and not gone out of her way and calling to meddle in such things as are proper for men, whose minds are stronger, etc., she had kept her wits, and might have improved them usefully and honorably in the place God had set her.[15]

None of her "many books" have survived for modern perusal, perhaps a sign of the low esteem in which women's writings were held. Certainly Winthrop provides evidence of strong attitudinal barriers to literary occupations for women. He explained Hopkins' apparent insanity in accord with contemporary assumptions regarding women's intellectual capacities. Even late in the eighteenth century, James Fordyce, a theorist who favored wider educational opportunities for women, cautioned that such studies should only be pursued "to every prudent length," for fear of impairing women's "more tender health."[16] Is it any wonder that many fathers were careful to guard their daughters from the rigors of education?

Such views regarding the deleterious effects of education for women were not the only attitudinal barriers to literary women. The social risks were compounded by the very real possibility that a woman author's personal reputation would be damaged by her presumptuousness in appearing in print. Thomas Parker, minister of Newbury, Massachusetts, forcefully clarified seventeenth-century attitudes in an open letter to his sister, Elizabeth Avery, in England: "your printing of a book, beyond the custom of your sex, doth rankly smell."[17] An anonymous writer in the *Boston Weekly Magazine* for March 2, 1743, explained "to a poetical lady" the social consequences of a woman's insistence on writing poetry:

> What's beauty, wealth and wit beside?
> Nor God, nor man will love her. . . .[18]

Many women poets refused to allow publication of their work to avoid such censure.

Women who dared seek publication frequently did so anonymously; others frankly acknowledged their fears. Bathsheba Bowers prefaced her spiritual autobiography, *An Alarm Sounded to Prepare . . . the World to Meet the Lord* (1709), by noting that "it was . . . a secret terror to me to think of making a contemptible appearance in the world. . . . [but] now I can hear my reputation called in question, without being stung to the heart."[19] Steeling herself to public disapproval, Bowers was regarded as an eccentric in her native Philadelphia. In the *Pennsylvania Chronicle* for March 7-14, 1768, a "circle of ladies" responded to public ridicule of learned women by noting that women's intellectual endeavors might well be greater

> But that the odium of "a bookish fair,"
> Or "female pedant," or "they quit their sphere,"
> Damps all their views, and they must drag the chain,
> And sigh for sweet instruction's page in vain.[20]

Even those colonial women fortunate enough to obtain "sweet instruction's page" found that they must "drag the chain" of social disapprobation.

Public encouragement from essays like the unsigned piece in the *American Weekly Mercury* for April 8-15, 1736, protesting the linguistic exclusion of women from discussions about the dependence of their "fellow-men" on one another,[21] or "An Occasional Letter on the Female Sex" from the *Pennsylvania Magazine* for August, 1775,[22] must have buoyed the spirits of eighteenth-century women poets who continued to write despite wide-spread skepticism regarding the propriety of their efforts. Still they probably recognized that the anonymous writer of "To a Poetical Lady" in the *Boston Weekly Magazine* for March 2, 1743, spoke for their culture:

> Yet still, to rule her house aright
> Would better far become her,
> Than to surpass the noblest flight
> In Milton or in Homer.[23]

It was to be a long time before women would be allowed to "employ by turns the needle and the pen"[24] with impunity.

The attitudes of a colonial patriarchy provided more subtle obstacles than damaged reputations to women poets. Living among male leaders who spoke of "silly women laden with diverse lusts," "phantastical madness,"[25] and "squirrel's brains"[26] inevitably influenced women's perceptions of themselves and their abilities. The condescension of Benjamin Tompson's "On a Fortification at Boston begun by Women" or Nathaniel Ward's commendatory poem on Anne Bradstreet's *Tenth Muse* was representative:

> It half revives my chill frost-bitten blood,
> To see a woman once do ought that's good.[27]

How many self-fulfilling prophecies of failure women writers accepted is impossible to determine, but evidence abounds of the hesitancy they felt when attempting intellectual tasks.

Women's writings indicate that many of them had fully internalized their prescribed roles. While detailing the effects of inequitable educations in which "one [sex] is taught to aspire, and the other is early confined and limited," Judith Sargent Murray pointed to the psychological consequences for women:

> At length arrived at womanhood, the uncultivated fair one feels a void, which the employments allotted her are by no means capable of filling .... she herself is most unhappy; she feels the want of a cultivated mind .... She experiences a mortifying consciousness of inferiority, which embitters every enjoyment.[28]

This culturally induced sense of limited potential must have frustrated the intellectual development of countless women. Jane Turell, for example, cautioned her sister Abigail Dennie in 1727 "not to spend any part of [her] precious time in reading romances or idle poems."[29] Women frequently expressed guilt at spending time reading any material other than the Bible. Apologies for presuming to publish seem ubiquitous; protestations of the inferiority of their work introduce many women's writings. The preface to Bridget

Fletcher's posthumous collection of *Hymns and Spiritual Songs* (1773) is typical:

> In as much as this small collection of hymns and spiritual songs is about to appear in public, it is expected that every candid reader will be ready to make allowances for the many inaccuracies of a female pen, when he considers that the advantages of females in general are but small, in comparison of those of the other sex, in point of polite learning.[30]

Implying regret at Fletcher's lesser "advantages" and lamenting that she had no opportunity for revision of her work, the anonymous editor pursued an apology that echoes in substance the expressions of numerous colonial women writers. Even a writer as popular as Sarah Morton felt a need to justify herself. She prefaced her first book *Ouâbi* (1790) with a plea that the reader "make many allowances for the various imperfections of the work, from a consideration of [her] sex and situation; the one by education incident to weakness, the other from duty devoted to domestic avocations."[31] Even partly discounting such self-deprecatory remarks as a pose of modesty, the frequency and clarity of these statements from women writers indicate the high degree to which their station had been internalized.

Additional obstacles, more practical than the social and psychological barriers already discussed, faced colonial women poets in their writing and in their publishing. Women's roles were prescriptive as well as proscriptive, and the quantity of work allotted to women, particularly married women, left little time for activities other than household management, child-bearing and child-rearing.[32] Except among the fairly wealthy (as was noted before), working long hours for their families was an economic necessity for colonial women. The slighting of family duties and traditional feminine activities for poetry was a scandalous offense. Anne Bradstreet's brother-in-law John Woodbridge was careful to point out to her readers that her poems were "the fruit but of some few hours, curtailed from her sleep and other refreshments,"[33] not written through neglect of her family duties. Nearly 150 years later, Sarah Morton closed her preface to *Beacon Hill* (1797) by explaining that "it is only amid the leisure and retirement, to which the sultry season is devoted, that I permit myself to hold converse with the Muses; nor does their enchantment ever allure me from one personal occupation, which my station renders obligatory. . . ."[34] Even those women who made time for their poetry felt the need to clarify its subordinate place in their lives.

The difficulty of obtaining a publisher presented another fundamental problem for colonial women poets who sought a wider audience. The development of periodicals, especially magazines, in the eighteenth century provided an outlet for the occasional dabbler in verse (though even here southern women faced difficulty, since magazines were slower to develop south of Philadelphia). But the woman with a volume of writing faced greater problems. Judith Sargent Murray and Ann Bleecker had their books published by subscription, thus assuring a printer of sufficient sales before an investment had to be made. But before that practice was established, editors chose their publications based on their perceptions of an audience. Bathsheba Bowers frankly acknowledged her difficutly in finding a printer for *An Alarm*. . . . Her preface mentions her "meeting with repulses in . . . proceeding to print," a circumstance which may explain why her book was printed in New York rather than in her native Philadelphia. How many colonial women writers had similar difficulties we may never know, but the combination of social, psychological and practical pressures was sufficient to discourage all but the most hardy.

III

Colonial Literary Women: A Subculture

The numbers of women poets in colonial America seemed to increase exponentially in the eighteenth century. That so many women continued to write poetry in an environment so little conducive to their efforts invites speculation regarding their motives and rewards. Perhaps, as Ellen Moers suggests for British women writers of the nineteenth century, the drive to some form of expression, public or private, was so great that in a culture with rigid proscriptions on their political and social activities, educated women were impelled to turn to literature for an outlet.[35] Perhaps this was the only avenue to recognition for women who felt the need to leave something of themselves besides children to ensuing generations. Or perhaps the availability of earlier publications by women encouraged other women's emulation. Facing enormous obstacles, why did these women write at all?

Though colonial society at large seldom supported their work, much of the available evidence suggests that women poets encouraged one another. Indirect support from reading the published works of other women, British and American, was available to some, though it is difficult to discover how many. Records documenting the accessibility of Anne Bradstreet's early volume, for example, are virtually non-existent. Still, the dedicatory poems to the 1650 edition indicate the immediate success of *The Tenth Muse*. Two Boston editions, in 1678 and 1758, testify to its long-lived appeal, at least in New England. The only volume of English poetry in Edward Taylor's library was Bradstreet's.[36] Cotton Mather's *Magnalia Christi Americana* referred to Bradstreet's poems as "a monument for her memory beyond the statliest marbles."[37] The private library of Thomas Prince contained a copy of the 1678 edition,[38] making it accessible to poets Deborah Prince and Sarah Gill, his daughters. (Unfortunately few of their works have survived for investigating influences.) Martha Brewster's *Poems on Divers Subjects* (1757), including a long piece "On the Four Ages of Man" and several personal verses, seems deliberately patterned after Bradstreet's collection. Well-regarded in England and in New England, Bradstreet's poetry may have made it easier for subsequent colonial women to consider writing poetry themselves.

Whether they read Bradstreet or not, American women were reading the productions of other women. Ann Bolton, niece of Bathsheba Bowers of Philadelphia, noted in her diary that her aunt owned "several [books] wrote by a female hand."[39] Bowers' books are not identified, but it is possible to determine some of the verse by women available to Americans later in the eighteenth century. Since it is probably safe to assume that British publications reprinted in the colonies were among the most popular reading, a list of these reprints can indicate possible influences by British women writers.[40] Elizabeth Carter's "Ode to Wisdom," for example, was reprinted anonymously in New Jersey by the *New American Magazine* for February, 1760. One of Susanna Centlivre's plays, *The Basset-Table: A Comedy*, was published in New York in 1761. *The Poetical Works of Lady Mary Wortley Montagu* was reprinted in Philadelphia in 1769; separate poems by Montagu appeared sporadically, as in the case of "The Lady's Resolve," included in the *Virginia Gazette* (ed. William Parks) for July 22, 1737, and again later in the *Virginia Gazette* (ed. Purdie and Dixon) for January 18, 1770. Four editions of Mary Southworth Mollineux's verse meditations appeared in America before 1800, as did more than a dozen editions of works by Elizabeth Singer Rowe, a poet particularly admired by Jane Turell and Elizabeth Fergusson. Two of Hannah More's plays, *The Inflexible Captive* and *Search for Happiness*, were reprinted in Philadelphia before the Revolution. And still the catalog of American reprints of British women could continue.[41]

The number of volumes by English women that were available to American women yet not reprinted in America is more difficult to determine. Judith Sargent Murray's "Observations on Female Abilities," published in 1798, listed dozens of British, European and American women writers and scholars known at least by reputation in America's early national period; we are probably safe in assuming that many of them were known earlier as well. Murray's catalog of well-known women included the Duchess of Newcastle, Mary Astell, Lady Chudleigh, Anne Killigrew, Lady Winchelsea, Anna Maria Schurman, Lady Montagu and Catherine Macauley. Jane Turell alluded to Katherine Philips in her verse; Mercy Warren addressed one of her poems to Elizabeth Montagu. But even for these British and European women of reputation, the ease with which an American could obtain their publications is unclear. Did copies of Lady Chudleigh's *Poems on Several Occasions* (1703), explicitly addressed to a female audience, circulate in America? Her "Caveat to the Fair Sex" was excerpted from that volume by the *Pennsylvania Evening Post* in 1775, giving colonial women an opportunity to read at least of her sentiments on marriage:

> Wife and servant are the same,
> But only differ in the name:
>
> . . . .

> Value yourselves, and men despise,
> You must be proud, if you'll be wise.[42]

Were Lady Chudleigh's other verses available? Were the early feminist writings of Mary Astell accessible in the colonies? Was Anna Maria Schurman's *The Learned Maid; or, Whether a Maid May be a Scholar . . .* (Leyden, 1641; trans., 1659) known to American women? Precise answers to such questions are difficult to obtain for books not reprinted in the colonies. Certainly the ideas and positions of these women were not unknown.

Such indirect, perhaps unintentional, encouragements among women writers were not the only supports available to them. Many colonial women poets knew one another personally, corresponded and exchanged their poems. Hannah Griffitts' letters to Susanna Wright often speak of their poetry. Griffitts' correspondence with Deborah Logan and Elizabeth Graeme Fergusson, while more formal, indicates a wide circle of acquaintance among women poets. One of Fergusson's extant commonplace books was apparently written for the New Jersey poet Annis Stockton. Anna Young Smith, Fergusson's niece and ward, occasionally wrote verse and Anne Wharton suggests that Fergusson's mother, Ann Graeme, was also a poet (though I have located none of her work).[43] Ann Bleecker's verse was published posthumously by her daughter Margaretta Faugeres, herself a poet. Abigail Dennie almost certainly read her sister Jane Turell's verse, and her only extant piece is a verse letter sent to Turell. Other occasions for intellectual and literary contact were fostered when Elizabeth Fergusson followed the tradition of the European salon by initiating regular gatherings of talented women and men at Graeme Park, north of Philadelphia.

As further evidence of this direct contact among women poets, verses by one poet to another appeared frequently. Hannah Griffitts' eulogy to Susanna Wright is included here,[44] as is Sarah Morton's ode to Mercy Warren.[45] Judith Murray and Sarah Morton exchanged poems in the *Massachusetts Magazine* to explain a misunderstanding regarding their choices of identical pseudonyms.[46] Even those women who did not seek publication for their verse

circulated their manuscripts among friends. Annis Stockton addressed at least two poems to "Laura," pseudonym for poet-friend
Elizabeth Fergusson.[47] Such networks allowed women to encourage
one another in an activity unfavorably regarded by the society at
large.

Nor were these circles of women writers entirely underground
operations; occasionally they sparked public controversy. The
Pennsylvania Chronicle in 1772 published a running argument between a denigrator and various supporters of Philadelphia's literary
women. "Misericordis" complained that "among ladies of high and
low degree, many are more eager to mix the ingredients of a little
piece of [poetry], than to mix the ingredients of a pudding."[48]
Evidently "Miss Sappho Hexameter" was more than he could tol-
erate. Various pseudonymous defenders (e.g., "Amicus Musarum"
and "Iambicus") of Philadelphia's women poets carried on a dialogue with "Misericordis," none of which seemed to discourage the
efforts of the women being discussed.

IV

Poetic Materials: Forms, Themes, Motifs

A diverse group of colonial women adopted literary avocations, some frivolously, some seriously, a few more successfully than
others. As a result, the extant work of colonial women encompasses
a broad range of forms and materials. Verse letters, plays and journal
entries, elegies and odes to friends or prominent figures, religious
meditations, love poems, historical narratives, hymns, social and
political satires, translations and paraphrases of the classics and the
Bible, poetic dialogues—colonial women attempted them all. Often
writing only for themselves or their close friends, occasionally for
the general public, they wrote in the forms available to the literate
populace of the day.

In keeping with those conventional poetic forms, women
poets frequently adopted popular concerns as their subject matter.

The seventeenth-century verses of an Edward Johnson or a Jonathan Mitchell, for example, derive from an environment that created similar preoccupations for women: sin, salvation, eternity. Lora Standish's sampler provides an illustration of the pious verse sometimes originated, sometimes borrowed by girls as they learned needlework:

> Lora Standish is my name.
> Lord guide my heart that I may do thy Will;
> Also fill my hands with such convenient skill
> As will conduce to virtue void of shame,
> And I will give the glory to Thy Name.[49]

The simplicity and religious devotion of Standish's rough verse prayer marks much of the extant poetry by women of the seventeenth and early eighteenth centuries. Sarah Goodhue and Mercy Wheeler directed their verses to the spiritual edification of young people, in Goodhue's case to her own children. Anna Hayden and Jane Turell drew divine messages from the deaths of family members. Mary English and Bathsheba Bowers formed poems into prayers. Anne Bradstreet's posthumous *Several Poems* (1678), with its political, religious and personal pieces, offered a range unusual until a century later (and quality unique even longer). Religious themes predominate among seventeenth-century women as among men.

But by the mid-eighteenth century, a fuller range of materials was common. Women moved easily from religious meditations to political satire, from light occasional pieces about social events to elegies for prominent figures. Hannah Griffitts, for example, touched on political issues when she poetically accused Thomas Paine of opportunism:

> Pane—though thy tongue may now run glibber,
> Warm'd with thy independent glow,
> Thou art indeed the coldest fibber,
> I ever knew, or wish to know.[50]

But Griffitts turned as easily to social and religious themes for a satire of Philadelphia women dancing with British officers during the

occupation in 1778 or for a somber anniversary poem on her mother's death. Ann Bleecker's poems often used pastoral images to reveal at once her sense of loneliness and isolation in upstate New York
and her joy in "the rural scene"; her narrative verses conveyed the
terror of her flight from Indians and an invitation to friends to join
her in the country, seemingly without contradiction. Such eclecticism was not unusual among eighteenth-century writers. Drawing
on easily accessible British and classical models, colonial women
poets attempted a wide range of popular modes.

Forceful British influences are not difficult to trace in pre-
Revolutionary American poetry. Annis Stockton's verses were as
carefully imitative of Pope's work as her garden was of his land-
scaped grotto. Ann Bleecker mourned her daughter's death during
their flight from Indians by comparing the death to Aeneas' loss of
Creusa: Bleecker had been reading Dryden's Virgil. Protesting Jonathan Swift's "vengeful satire" of women, Anna Smith addressed him
directly:

> Say, when thou dipp'st thy keenest pen in gall,
> Why must it still on helpless woman fall?[51]

Allusions to Spenser, Swift and Sidney, Milton, Dryden and Pope
occur again and again, complemented by references to Edmund
Waller, Richard Blackmore, Elizabeth Singer Rowe, Katherine
Philips, Francis Quarles, Edward Young, Thomas Gray, John Donne
and a host of others. The use of classical materials by colonial women poets reveals their acquaintance (via British translations) with
Ovid, Sappho, Plutarch and Horace; Dryden's Virgil and Pope's
Homer were widely known. Not surprisingly, given America's cultural ties with England, British influences pervade colonial poetry.

But after recognizing these powerful links with England, a
caveat seems appropriate. Materials native to the colonies, or to the
European immigrants' attempts to relate to the New World, were
irrepressible. Ann Bleecker, for example, often used the elevated
diction popular in eighteenth-century England: the moon becomes
"Cynthia's crescent," Nature possesses a "teeming womb." But she
also turned to simpler descriptions of rural New York and its (to her)

presumptuous laborers:

> What though the spiral pines around us rise,
> And airy mountains intercept the skies,
> Faction has chas'd away the warbling Muse,
> And Echo only learns to tattle news;
> Each clown commences politician here,
> And calculates th' expenses of the year;
> He quits his plow, and throws aside his spade,
> To talk with 'squire about decrease of trade.[52]

Ann Bleecker was not alone in combining the influences of her British models with native materials. Anne Bradstreet's gradually increasing sensitivity to her colonial environment has been carefully traced.[53] Sarah Knight's verse description of rural poverty approached realism. Often thoroughly acquainted with the British literary scene, colonial women poets nevertheless wrote from experiences for which those models were only partly satisfactory.

Despite diversity in form and theme, certain tensions and motifs appear repeatedly in the poetry of colonial women. Derived perhaps from shared pressures and experiences as well as from common models and influences, recurrent themes provide clues to these poets' perceptions of themselves in relation to cultural expectations. Not surprisingly, one such recurring motif is the conflict between a desire for personal recognition and the modesty necessitated by conventional female roles. Judith Sargent Murry published a rare admission of one of her driving forces in the first volume of *The Gleaner:*

> Yes, I confess I love the paths of fame,
> And ardent wish to glean a brightening name.[54]

(Ironically, most of her unpublished manuscripts have been destroyed by mildew.) Bathsheba Bowers also took few pains to hide her desire for reputation. But most colonial women felt compelled to disguise their pride in their work behind apologies or silence. A more representative expression of this tension between a desire for recognition and a self-effacing modesty can be found in the preface to Martha Brewster's *Poems on Divers Subjects* (1757). Protesting (for

the record, anyway) that her verses should never have been published, Brewster asked her readers to

> Pardon her bold attempt who has reveal'd
> Her thoughts to view, more fit to be conceal'd;
> Since thus to do was urged vehemently,
> Yet most no doubt will call it vanity. . . .[55]

The (necessarily) quiet pride of these women in their work can only
be surmised, but the circulation of their verse among family and
friends, and its occasional publication (more frequent after the development of colonial periodicals), indicates the intensity of their
desire for recognition.

Writing personal accounts of child-bearing and rearing, the
deaths of children, loving (and not-so-loving) husbands, parents,
domestic routines and home life, colonial women poets sometimes
adapted a range of image and metaphor less available to their male
contemporaries. Anne Bradstreet, for example, compared her poetic
skill to that of DuBartas in a metaphor that required her persona to
see with a child's wonder: DuBartas' works became riches that to a
child seemed unattainable, even indescribable.[56] Jane Turell charac-
terized her first pregnancy as "the pleasing strife,/In the first struggles of my infant's life," but focused on her pain in an account of
her second delivery:

> Again in travail pains my nerves are wreck'd,
> My eye balls start, my heart strings almost crack' d.[57]

Annis Stockton concealed her failing energy as she watched by her
husband's deathbed, after his prolonged illness:

> But vain is prophecy when death's approach,
> Through years of pain, has sapp'd a dearer life,
> And makes me, coward like, myself reproach,
> That e'er I knew the tender name of wife.[58]

Family deaths and childhood perspectives were not, of course, the
exclusive province of women: Edward Taylor wrote of the deaths of

two of his children in "Upon Wedlock, and Death of Children";
John Saffin left a manuscript "Lamentation on my Dear Son Simon
Who Died of the Smallpox. . . ." But even in sharing much of their
poetic material with men, colonial women poets occasionally raised
discernibly female voices.

A number of women wrote directly of women's experiences,
developing a personal poetry interesting for its conflict between
internalized roles and evolving feminism. The cover of anonymity
encouraged a few women to confront their political status directly
in colonial periodicals; one such poet as early as 1736 suggested
(with little success) that lawmakers

> Then equal laws let custom find,
>   And neither sex oppress;
> More freedom give to womankind,
>   Or give to mankind less.[59]

Judith Sargent Murray's essay "On the Equality of the Sexes"
(written in 1779, though not published until 1790) reveals her as
an early American feminist protesting the automatic designation of
abilities by sex,

> As if a woman's form must needs enroll,
> A weak, a servile, an inferior soul;
> And that the guise of man must still proclaim,
> Greatness of mind, and him, to be the same:
>   .   .   .   .
> They rob us of the power t' improve,
> And then declare we only trifles love.[60]

Most of Murray's fellow writers were less direct. Anne Bradstreet
clearly granted that "men have precedency and still excell," yet
vented her anger that

> . . . such despite they cast on female wits:
> If what I do prove well, it won't advance,
> They'll say it's stol'n, or else it was by chance.[61]

Such frustrations, disguised thinly or not at all, appear in example after example of colonial women's poetry, delineating a tension between socially-defined duty and personally-defined desires. Hannah Griffitts acknowledges that conflict directly: though she wrote prolifically and refused to accept male superiority, she still hoped that she hadn't been guilty of "studying for verse when the stockin' ball was so much more necessary."[62] Pre-revolutionary women poets, for the most part, assumed their culturally defined responsibilities without question; seldom did their poetry interfere with those primary obligations of home and family. But occasionally, the personal costs of subordinating their intellectual acitivity surfaced in their verse.

The conflicts and tensions, experiences and aspirations, of colonial women are nowhere so clearly articulated as in their poetry. However derivative their diction, however rough their technique, colonial women poets produced a body of work that deserves our attention. Despite educational handicaps and social limitations, American women began writing early, shaping their experiences and creating meaning in an environment that did little to encourage their activities. If they were willing to devote hours to writing (for some even at the expense of sleep), presumably that work filled a necessary function for them. Jane Turell's verse, for example, belies her husband's observation that "she made the writing of poetry a recreation and not a business."

> Come, gentle muse, and once more lend thine aid,
> O bring thy succor to a humble maid!
>
> .   .   .   .
>
> Come now, fair muse, and fill my empty mind,
> With rich ideas, great and unconfin'd.
> Instruct me in those secret arts that lie
> Unseen to all but to a poet's eye.
> O let me burn with Sappho's noble fire,
> But not like her for faithless man expire.
> And let me rival great Orinda's[63] fame,
> Or like sweet Philomela's[64] be my name.
> Go lead the way, my muse, nor must you stop,
> 'Till we have gain'd Parnassus' shady top:
> 'Till I have view'd those fragrant soft retreats,
> Those fields of bliss, the muses' sacred seats.
> I'll then devote thee to fair virtue's fame,
> And so be worthy of a poet's name.[65]

The conventionality and didactic assumptions behind these lines do not mask the genuiness of her commitment to poetry. Perhaps "a poet's name" was more frequently and more seriously sought by colonial women than we have believed.

To thank everyone who has given aid to this project would be an impossible task. But let me acknowledge at least a few of my debts. Staff members for the Library Company of Philadelphia, Brown University's John Hay Library, Harvard University's Houghton Library, Yale University's Beinecke Library, the New York and Boston Public Libraries, and the American Antiquarian Society were unfailingly cooperative, frequently suggesting avenues of research that might otherwise have been left unexplored. Katherine Emerson and Melinda McIntosh of the University of Massachusetts/ Amherst Library, Peter Parker of the Historical Society of Pennsylvania, and Martha Slotten of the Dickinson College Library made special efforts to facilitate my work on several occasions. Valuable research leads were supplied by Harrison Meserole, Emily Stipes Watts, Ann Stanford, Roger Stoddard and Kenneth Silverman. George Vaught put aside a busy schedule to provide the new translation of Barbara Leininger's poem included here. Special thanks are due Everett Emerson, at whose suggestion I began this collection, for his consistently valuable criticism and continued encouragement. Finally, let me thank my husband, Wayne Ude, for a critical proofreading of the final manuscript and for his constant support of my work.

Pattie Cowell
Colorado State University

A Note on the Selection and Presentation of the Texts

Women Poets in Pre-Revolutionary America, 1650-1775 collects works only from those women who began writing before 1775 within what became the continental United States. Even women who wrote only a few lines not intended for publication are represented, not for their contribution to literature, but toward a more complete picture of the kinds of writing being attempted by colonial women. Sampler verses and hatchments have been excluded, however, as have those poets whose mature writing was produced in another country. Anne Grant (1755-1838), for example, who spent eleven years of her childhood in Vermont before returning to Scotland where she had been born, wrote verses (including an imitation of Milton) while she lived in New England. She is not included here because her adult writing began only after she had left America. Charlotte Ramsey (or Rumsay) Lennox (1720-1804), better known for her prolific novels, plays and translations than for her poetry, had traveled to America as a child with her father, Colonel James Ramsey, the Lieutenant Governor of New York. Though she became New York's first woman poet, she is excluded here because she went back to England at age fifteen to finish her education and never returned to America. The broadside verse "Dialogue Between Elizabeth Smith and John Sennet..." is omitted because it was probably written by a third party. Hymn writer Anastasia Thome (1720-1778) of Pennsylvania's Ephrata Cloister apparently refrained from acknowledging her pieces, preferring that they achieve a communal identity; her work has been impossible to separate from that of her colleagues. Other American women, among them Lydia Learned (1730-1792), Elizabeth Whitman (1752-1788), Grizzell Hawkshaw (1756-1799), Deborah Logan (1761-1839), and Sarah Wister (1761-1804), have left poems written during or soon after the Revolution. No doubt they wrote earlier pieces as well, but those poets for whom I could find no record of pre-1775 work have been excluded. Presumably more poems by women remain to be found, chiefly in periodicals and diaries, but this collection is as complete as I could make it with over a year of searching.

In selecting material, my primary goal has been to suggest the range of style, theme and skill for each poet. Early materials are emphasized wherever possible for those poets whose work extends beyond the Revolution into the national period, but in every case I have attempted to include material from the full span of a poet's career. The poetry is presented in three sections: poets who left large bodies of work are grouped together in Part I; those who wrote infrequently, often leaving only a single poem, are grouped in Part II; anonymous poets comprise Part III. Within each section, the arrangement is chronological.

The only textual changes were made to facilitate reading of the poems for a twentieth-century audience. All of the texts have been presented with modern English usage as to capitalization, punctuation, spelling and typography, but I have tried to respect the language of the poets by leaving grammar, syntax, vocabulary, proper names and stanzaic structure intact. Contractions and abbreviations, especially common in manuscripts, have been spelled out except when the contraction is a clue to pronunciation or rhythm. Years are presented in new style, days and months as the poet used them. Manuscript originals, colonial publications and modern scholarly editions were used to establish texts wherever possible, but where the only extant version of a poem is located in a nineteenth-century local history or periodical, I have used the reprint.

Mercy Otis Warren
by John Singleton Copley
Reproduced by the couresty of
Boston Museum of Fine Arts
(Bequest of Winslow Warren)

Annis Boudinot Stockton
(artist unknown)
Reproduced by the courtesy of
Princeton University

Elizabeth Graeme Fergusson
(artist unknown)
Reproduced by the courtesy of the
Historical Society of Pennsylvania

Judith Sargent Murray
by John Singleton Copley
Reproduced by the courtesy of the
Sargent-Murray-Gilman-Hough House Association
Gloucester, Massachusetts

Ann Eliza Bleecker
by Tiebout
from *The Posthumous Works of Ann Eliza Bleecker,*
Reproduced by the courtesy of the
University of Colorado at Boulder

PHILLIS WHEATLEY NEGRO SERVANT to Mr JOHN WHEATLEY, of BOSTON.

Published according to Act of Parliament, Sept.r 1, 1773 by Arch.d Bell, Bookseller No 8 near the Saracens Head Aldgate.

Phillis Wheatley
(artist unknown)
from *Poems on Various Subjects, Religious and Moral,*
Reproduced by the courtesy of the
Library of Congress

Sarah Wentworth Apthorp Morton
by Gilbert Stuart
Reproduced by the courtesy of the
Worcester Art Museum

Part One

Prolific Poets

Anne Bradstreet

(1612?-September 16, 1672)

Publishing a small body of poetry that spans most of her adult life, Anne Dudley Bradstreet has become the only well-known exception to the assumption that colonial women wrote no poetry. Born in England to Thomas Dudley, steward for the Earl of Lincoln, and Dorothy Yorke, "a gentlewoman whose extract and estate were considerable,"[1] she had access as a child to private tutors and the Earl's library. Part of a Nonconformist family that actively participated in the planning for Massachusetts Bay colony, she was caught up in the Puritan emigration. She married Simon Bradstreet (also Nonconformist) in 1628, and in 1630 she arrived with her husband and her parents in Massachusetts, "where [she] found a new world and new manners, at which [her] heart rose. But after [she] was convinced it was the way of God, [she] submitted to it and joined to the church at Boston."[2] A simple statement of rebellion and acquiescence, it marks a cycle which recurs in Bradstreet's poetry as in her life.

The Bradstreets soon moved from Boston to Ipswich, and after 1644 to North Andover, where Anne remained until her death in 1672. While her husband and her father began long careers as public officials in the new colony, she raised eight children in a frontier environment and wrote her poetry. Committed to Puritan ideals (though not without questions and doubt), she accepted the New England wilderness as her home and struggled to adapt it to her needs.

The Tenth Muse Lately Sprung Up in America. Or Severall Poems, Compiled with Great Variety of Wit and Learning . . . . By a Gentlewoman in Those Parts was published in London in 1650 at the insistence of John Woodbridge, Bradstreet's brother-in-law. (His wife, Mercy Dudley Woodbridge, apparently wrote a verse epistle to her sister on the occasion of this publication, but it has disappeared since Samuel Kettell saw it in 1829.[3]) The poems had evidently circulated among various members of Bradstreet's family. Taking a manuscript copy to London without her knowledge, Woodbridge inserted a preface in the first edition to assure readers of the book's authenticity:

> the worst effect of his [the reader's] reading will be unbelief, which will make him question whether it be a woman's work, and ask, is it possible? If any do, take this as an answer from him that dares avow it; it is the work of a woman, honored, and esteemed where she lives, for her gracious demeanor, her eminent parts, her pious conversation, her courteous disposition, her exact diligence in her place, and discreet managing of her family occasions, and more than so, these poems are the fruit but of some few hours, curtailed from her sleep and other refreshments.[4]

Woodbridge's care to point out that Bradstreet's poems were not written through neglect of family duties says much about colonial suspicions regarding literary women.

Even in a milieu by turns hostile and condescending, Anne Bradstreet continued to write. The 1650 edition of her poems contains her early conventional verse: quaternions, elegies and dialogues that reveal more about her literary influences (Quarles, DuBartas, Sylvester, Sidney, Spenser, Thomas Dudley) than about her human environment. Despite opposition from "carping tongues" who said "[her] hand a needle better fits" than a poet's pen, she continued to compose new pieces and to revise her already published compositions. A Boston edition of her poems appeared posthumously in 1678 with a substantial quantity of new material, much of it her finest work. Too long to include here, the 231 lines of "Contemplations" from that edition is perhaps her best poem. Bradstreet has produced among these mature poems several that will be remembered for aesthetic as well as for historical reasons.

This later work, from which most of the selections included here are taken,[5] develops from the conventional public verse of the first edition to more private themes of family, love, sorrow, religious tension, nature, and resignation. The qualified feminism of her public pieces, notably "The Prologue" and "In Honor of Queen Elizabeth," grows into an uninhibitied use of images drawn from women's experiences, particularly her own. Suppressing an urge "to sing of wars, of captains, and of kings" because such subjects are "too superior things" for her "mean pen," Bradstreet seeks less conventional materials. In her mature poems, as in the meditations she left to her children, she "avoided encroaching upon other's conceptions, because [she] would leave [them] nothing but [her] own."[6] The poet's voice becomes distinct and individual, less imitative of her British predecessors. While her didactic motives sometimes remain, they are submerged, implicit. She intends no moralizing in verse, but a simpler end: to react to her own experience. With those personal reactions, she occasionally makes the Puritan aesthetic within which she worked satisfy a larger aesthetic, one more acceptable to modern readers. As the first widely-recognized woman poet in a literature not known for its attention to women writers, Anne Bradstreet may have become a model for future generations of women.

Three editions of Bradstreet's poems were published in colonial times: in London in 1650, and in Boston in 1678 and 1758. The standard edition of her complete canon is *The Works of Anne Bradstreet in Prose and Verse*, edited by John Harvard Ellis (Charlestown, Mass., 1867; rpt. New York, 1932, and Gloucester, Mass., 1962), though *The Works of Anne Bradstreet*, edited by Jeannine Hensley (Cambridge, Mass., 1967) provides a modernized text. Josephine K. Piercy edited a facsimile of *The Tenth Muse* (Gainsville, Fla., 1965) that also reproduces the Bradstreet manuscripts in the Stevens Memorial Library in North Andover, Massachusetts.

Secondary materials on Anne Bradstreet have proliferated recently. A useful guide to earlier materials is available in Ann Stanford's "Anne Bradstreet: An Annotated Checklist," *Early American Literature*, 3 (Winter, 1968-69), 217-228. Perhaps the best full treatment is Ann Stanford's *Anne Bradstreet: The Worldly Puritan* (New York, 1974), but Stanford provides a useful shorter introduction in "Anne Bradstreet," *Major Writers of Early American Literature*, ed. Everett Emerson (Madison, Wisc., 1972), pp. 33-58. While Stanford focuses on Bradstreet's personal "struggle between the visible and the invisible worlds,"[7] Robert D. Richardson, Jr., studies her verse in terms of its theology in "The Puritan Poetry of Anne Bradstreet," *The American Puritan Imagination*, ed. Sacvan Bercovitch (New York, 1974), pp. 105-122. Elizabeth Wade White's *Anne Bradstreet: The Tenth Muse* (New York, 1971) furnishes a complete biographical study.

The Prologue [To Her Book]

1

To sing of wars, of captains, and of kings,
Of cities founded, commonwealths begun,
For my mean pen are too superior things:
Or how they all or each their dates have run,
Let poets and historians set these forth,
My obscure lines shall not so dim their worth.

2

But when my wond'ring eyes and envious heart
Great Bartas' sugar'd lines do but read o'er
Fool I do grudge the Muses did not part
'Twixt him and me that overfluent store;
A Bartas can do what a Bartas will,
But simple I according to my skill.

3

From schoolboy's tongue no rhet'ric we expect,
Nor yet a sweet consort from broken strings,
Nor perfect beauty where's a main defect:
My foolish, broken, blemish'd Muse so sings,
And this to mend, alas, no art is able,
'Cause nature made it so irreparable.

4

Nor can I, like that fluent sweet tongu'd Greek,
Who lisp'd at first, in future times speak plain;
By art he gladly found what he did seek,
A full requital of his striving pain.
Art can do much, but this maxim's most sure:
A weak or wounded brain admits no cure.

5

I am obnoxious to each carping tongue
Who says my hand a needle better fits,
A poet's pen all scorn I should thus wrong,

For such despite they cast on female wits:
If what I do prove well, it won't advance,
They'll say it's stol'n, or else it was by chance.

6

But sure the antique Greeks were far more mild,
Else of our sex, why feigned they those Nine,
And poesy made Calliope's own child;
So 'mongst the rest they placed the arts divine,
But this weak knot, they will full soon untie,
The Greeks did nought, but play the fools and lie.

7

Let Greeks be Greeks, and women what they are,
Men have precedency and still excel,
It is but vain unjustly to wage war;
Men can do best, and women know it well.
Preeminence in all and each is yours;
Yet grant some small acknowledgment of ours.

8

And oh ye high flown quills that soar the skies,
And ever with your prey still catch your praise,
If e'er you deign these lowly lines your eyes,
Give thyme or parsley wreath, I ask no bays;
This mean and unrefined ore of mine
Will make your glist'ring gold but more to shine.

The Author to Her Book

Thou ill-form'd offspring of my feeble brain,
Who after birth did'st by my side remain,
Till snatcht from thence by friends, less wise than true,
Who thee abroad expos'd to public view,
Made thee in rags halting to th' press to trudge,
Where errors were not lessened (all may judge).
At thy return my blushing was not small,
My rambling brat (in print) should mother call;

I cast thee by as one unfit for light,
Thy visage was so irksome in my sight;
Yet being mine own, at length affection would
Thy blemishes amend, if so I could:
I wash'd thy face, but more defects I saw,
And rubbing off a spot, still made a flaw.
I stretcht thy joints to make thee even feet,
Yet still thou run'st more hobbling than is meet;
In better dress to trim thee was my mind,
But nought save homespun cloth i' th' house I find;
In this array, 'mongst vulgars may'st thou roam,
In critic's hands, beware thou dost not come;
And take thy way where yet thou art not known,
If for thy father asked, say thou had'st none:
And for thy mother, she alas is poor,
Which caus'd her thus to send thee out of door.

Before the Birth of One of Her Children

All things within this fading world hath end,
Adversity doth still our joys attend;
No ties so strong, no friends so dear and sweet,
But with death's parting blow is sure to meet.
The sentence past is most irrevocable,
A common thing, yet oh inevitable;
How soon, my dear, death may my steps attend,
How soon't may be thy lot to lose thy friend,
We both are ignorant, yet love bids me
These farewell lines to recommend to thee,
That when that knot's untied that made us one,
I may seem thine, who in effect am none.
And if I see not half my days that's due,
What nature would, God grant to yours and you;
The many faults that well you know I have,
Let be interr'd in my oblivion's grave;
If any worth or virtue were in me,
Let that live freshly in thy memory,
And when thou feel'st no grief, as I no harms,

Yet love thy dead, who long lay in thine arms:
And when thy loss shall be repaid with gains,
Look to my little babes, my dear remains.
And if thou love thy self, or loved'st me,
These O protect from step-dame's injury.
And if chance to thine eyes shall bring this verse,
With some sad sighs honor my absent hearse;
And kiss this paper for thy love's dear sake,
Who with salt tears this last farewell did take.

A Letter to Her Husband, Absent Upon Public Employment

My head, my heart, mine eyes, my life, nay more,
My joy, my magazine of earthly store,
If two be one, as surely thou and I,
How stayest thou there, whilst I at Ipswich lie?
So many steps, head from the heart to sever,
If but a neck, soon should we be together:
I, like the earth this season, mourn in black,
My sun is gone so far in's zodiac,
Whom whilst I 'joy'd, nor storms, nor frosts I felt,
His warmth such frigid colds did cause to melt.
My chilled limbs now numbed lie forlorn;
Return, return sweet Sol from Capricorn;
In this dead time, alas, what can I more
Then view those fruits which through thy heat I bore?
Which sweet contentment yield me for a space,
True living pictures of their father's face.
O strange effect! now thou art southward gone,
I weary grow, the tedious day so long;
But when thou northward to me shalt return,
I wish my sun may never set, but burn
Within the Cancer of my glowing breast,
The welcome house of him my dearest guest.
Where ever, ever stay, and go not thence,
Till nature's sad decree shall call thee hence;
Flesh of thy flesh, bone of thy bone,
I here, thou there, yet both but one.

To Her Father With Some Verses

Most truly honored, and as truly dear,
If worth in me, or ought I do appear,
Who can of right better demand the fame,
Then may your worthy self from whom it came?
The principle might yield a greater sum,
Yet handled ill, amounts but to this crumb;
My stock's so small, I know not how to pay,
My bond remains in force unto this day;
Yet for part payment take this simple mite,
Where nothing's to be had kings loose their right;
Such is my debt, I may not say forgive,
But as I can, I'll pay it while I live:
Such is my bond, none can discharge but I,
Yet paying is not paid until I die.

In Reference to Her Children, 23 June 1656[8]

I had eight birds hatcht in one nest,
Four cocks there were, and hens the rest,
I nurst them up with pain and care,
Nor cost, nor labor did I spare,
Till at the last they felt their wing,
Mounted the trees, and learn'd to sing;
Chief of the brood[9] then took his flight,
To regions far, and left me quite.
My mournful chirps I after send,
Till he return, or I do end:
Leave not thy nest, thy dam and sire,
Fly back and sing amidst this choir.
My second bird[10] did take her flight,
And with her mate flew out of sight;
Southward they both their course did bend,
And seasons twain they there did spend:
Till after blown by southern gales,
They norward steer'd with filled sails.
A prettier bird was no where seen,

Along the beach among the treen.
I have a third of color white,[11]
On whom I plac'd no small delight;
Coupled with mate loving and true,
Hath also bid her dam adieu:
And where Aurora first appears,
She now hath percht to spend her years;
One[12] to the academy flew
To chat among that learned crew:
Ambition moves still in his breast
That he might chant above the rest,
Striving for more than to do well,
That nightingales he might excel.
My fifth,[13] whose down is yet scarce gone,
Is 'mongst the shrubs and bushes flown,
And as his wings increase in strength,
On higher boughs he'll perch at length.
My other three,[14] still with me nest,
Until they're grown, then as the rest,
Or here or there, they'll take their flight,
As is ordain'd, so shall they light.
If birds could weep, then would my tears
Let others know what are my fears
Lest this my brood some harm should catch,
And be surpris'd for want of watch,
Whilst pecking corn, and void of care
They fall un'wares in fowler's snare:
Or whilst on trees they sit and sing,
Some untoward boy at them do fling:
Or whilst allur'd with bell and glass,
The net be spread, and caught, alas.
Or least by lime-twigs they be foil'd,
Or by some greedy hawks be spoil'd.
O would my young, ye saw my breast,
And knew what thoughts there sadly rest,
Great was my pain when I you bred,
Great was my care when I you fed,
Long did I keep you soft and warm,
And with my wings kept off all harm,
My cares are more, and fears than ever,
My throbs such now, as 'fore were never:
Alas my birds, you wisdom want,

Of perils you are ignorant,
Oft times in grass, on trees, in flight,
Sore accidents on you may light.
O to your safety have an eye,
So happy may you live and die:
Mean while my days in tunes I'll spend,
Till my weak lays with me shall end.
In shady woods I'll sit and sing,
And things that past, to mind I'll bring.
Once young and pleasant, as are you,
But former toys (no joys) adieu.
My age I will not once lament,
But sing, my time so near is spent.
And from the top bough take my flight,
Into a country beyond sight,
Where old ones instantly grow young,
And there with seraphims set song:
No seasons cold, nor storms they see,
But spring lasts to eternity.
When each of you shall in your nest
Among your young ones take your rest,
In chirping language, oft them tell,
You had a dam that lov'd you well,
That did what could be done for young,
And nurst you up till you were strong,
And 'fore she once would let you fly,
She show'd you joy and misery;
Taught what was good, and what was ill,
What would save life, and what would kill.
Thus gone, amongst you I may live,
And dead, yet speak, and counsel give:
Farewell, my birds, farewell adieu,
I happy am, if well with you.

Some Verses Upon the Burning of Our House, July 10th, 1666

In silent night when rest I took,
For sorrow near I did not look,

I waken'd was with thund'ring noise
And piteous shrieks of dreadful voice.
That fearful sound of fire and fire,
Let no man know is my desire.

I, starting up, the light did spy,
And to my God my heart did cry
To strengthen me in my distress
And not to leave me succorless.
Then coming out beheld a space,
The flame consume my dwelling place.

And, when I could no longer look,
I blest his Name that gave and took,
That laid my goods now in the dust:
Yea so it was, and so 'twas just.
It was his own: it was not mine;
Far be it that I should repine.

He might of all justly bereft,
But yet sufficient for us left.
When by the ruins oft I past,
My sorrowing eyes aside did cast,
And here and there the places spy
Where oft I sat, and long did lie.

Here stood that trunk, and there that chest;
There lay that store I counted best:
My pleasant things in ashes lie,
And them behold no more shall I.
Under thy roof no guest shall sit,
Nor at thy table eat a bit.

No pleasant tale shall e'er be told,
Nor things recounted done of old.
No candle e'er shall shine in thee,
Nor bridegroom's voice e'er heard shall be.
In silence ever shalt thou lie;
Adieu, adieu; all's vanity.

Then straight I 'gin my heart to chide,
And did thy wealth on earth abide?

Didst fix thy hope on mold'ring dust,
The arm of flesh didst make thy trust?
Raise up thy thoughts above the sky
That dunghill mists away may fly.

That hast an house on high erect,
Fram'd by that mighty Architect,
With glory richly furnished,
Stands permanent though this be fled.
It's purchased, and paid for too
By Him who hath enough to do.

A price so vast as is unknown,
Yet, by his gift, is made thine own.
There's wealth enough, I need no more;
Farewell my pelf, farewell my store.
The world no longer let me love,
My hope and treasure lies above.

["As Weary Pilgrim"]

As weary pilgrim, now at rest,
    Hugs with delight his silent nest,
His wasted limbs now lie full soft,
    That miry steps have trodden oft,
Blesses himself, to think upon
    His dangers past, and travails done:
The burning sun no more shall heat,
    Nor stormy rains on him shall beat.
The briars and thorns no more shall scratch,
    Nor hungry wolves at him shall catch;
He erring paths no more shall tread,
    Nor wild fruits eat instead of bread;
For waters cold he doth not long,
    For thirst no more shall parch his tongue;
No rugged stones his feet shall gall,
    Nor stumps nor rocks cause him to fall:
All cares and fears, he bids farewell,

And means in safety now to dwell.
A pilgrim I, on earth, perplext
    With sins, with cares and sorrows vext,
By age and pains brought to decay,
    And my clay house mold'ring away:
Oh how I long to be at rest,
    And soar on high among the blest.
This body shall in silence sleep,
    Mine eyes no more shall ever weep;
No fainting fits shall me assail,
    Nor grinding pains my body frail,
With cares and fears ne'er cumb'red be,
    Nor losses know, nor sorrows see.
What though my flesh shall there consume,
    It is the bed Christ did perfume;
And when a few years shall be gone,
    This mortal shall be cloth'd upon:
A corrupt carcass down it lies,
    A glorious body it shall rise;
In weakness and dishonor sown,
    In power 'tis rais'd by Christ alone.
Then soul and body shall unite,
    And of their maker have the sight;
Such lasting joys shall there behold,
    As ear ne'er heard nor tongue e'er told:
Lord make me ready for that day,
    Then come, dear Bridegroom, come away.

Aug[ust] 31, [16]69

Jane Colman Turell

(February 25, 1708-March 26, 1735)

Jane Colman Turell acquired almost from infancy a local reputation as a prodigy. The daughter of Jane Clark and Benjamin Colman, the liberal pastor of Boston's Brattle Street Church, she received an unusually extensive education from her father. She apparently began reading by age two; before she was four "she could say the greater part of the Assembly's Catechism, many of the Psalms, some hundred lines of the best poetry, read distinctly, and make pertinent remarks on many things she read."[1] Inclined by chronic ill health to sedentary occupations even as a child, she supplemented her father's instruction with constant reading. Access to Colman's large library enabled her to explore works of divinity, history and literature, an avocation for which "the leisure of the day did not suffice, but she spent whole nights in reading."[2] To improve her writing skills, Turell developed a regular correspondence with her father. Their epistolary dialogue frequently involved the exchange of verses, the earliest of which was apparently a hymn written before her tenth birthday. Emotionally and intellectually dependent upon her father throughout her short life, she customarily submitted samples of her verse to Benjamin Colman for correction. Perhaps sensing his daughter's need for his approval, Colman judiciously mingled his criticism with praise:

> Joy of my life! is this thy lovely voice?
> Sing on, and a fond father's heart rejoice.[3]

On August 11, 1726, Jane Colman married one of her father's former theology students, the Reverend Ebenezer Turell of Medford, Massachusetts. Though she saw much less of Colman after her move to Medford, Turell maintained close ties with him, frequently seeking his counsel in times of spiritual depression. She entered full communion with the church at Medford on October 29, 1727, after much hesitation regarding the certainty of her salvation. Her marriage resulted in four children, only one of whom survived his mother to live until six years of age. Several diary entries and a poem (reprinted here) describe her sorrow over her children:

> Thrice in my womb I've found the pleasing strife,
> In the first struggles of my infant's life:
> But O how soon by Heaven I'm call'd to mourn,
> While from my womb a lifeless babe is torn?

Perhaps the heavy physical toll of repeated childbearing combined with her "wonderful weak" constitution to hasten Turell's death. Attended by her only sister, Abigail Dennie (see pages 241-243), she died on March 26, 1735, deprived of time to achieve the maturity and independence that her diary and correspondence indicate she lacked.

Although Turell developed regular writing habits that made her a prolific poet, correspondent and diarist, only those works which her husband Ebenezer chose to include in *Some Memoirs of the Life and Death of Mrs. Jane Turell*, signatured with Benjamin Colman's *Reliquiae Turellae, et Lachrymae Paternae . . .* (Boston, 1735), have been preserved. He omitted her "pieces of wit and humor, which if published would give a brighter idea of her to some sort of readers" because "her heart was set on graver and better subjects, and her pen much oftener employ'd about them."[4] Consequently, moral preoccupations dominate Turell's extant work. Yet despite religious concerns that sometimes (by Ebenezer's account) bordered on fanaticism, she demonstrates an uncommon devotion to poetry for its "rich ideas, great and unconfin'd." Her poem "On the Incomparable Mr. Waller," for example, draws on the processes rather than the static images of nature. For Turell, Waller not only absorbs the gifts of the civilized world in his "capacious soul" but adds to its store

> As the fierce sun, by his meridian rays,
> Exhales the moisture from this lower earth;
> Again at night by dews the fields repays,
> That nature labors with a double birth . . . .

Themes of rural living, childbirth, local affairs, grief, praise for other poets and personal ambition supplement her biblical paraphrases, spiritual messages and hymns. Ebenezer Turell's unfortunate censorship deprives us of a fully balanced view of his wife's work, but he notes (for latter-day feminists I presume) that

> she was sometimes fir'd with a laudable ambition of raising the honor of her sex, who are therefore under obligations to her; and all will be ready to own she had a fine genius, and is to be placed among those who have excell'd.[5]

The major source for Turell's biographical and literary materials is the *Memoir* by Ebenezer Turell already mentioned; all subsequent studies trace their origin to that record. Several nineteenth-century anthologists have included Turell's verse among their offerings: Samuel Kettell, ed., *Specimens of American Poetry* (Boston, 1829; rpt. New York, 1967), I, 61-67; Caroline May, ed., *The American Female Poets* (Philadelphia, 1848), pp. 21-25; Evert A. Duyckinck and George L. Duyckinck, eds., *The Cyclopaedia of American Literature* (New York, 1855), I, 124-125; and Edmund C. Stedman and Ellen M. Hutchinson, eds., *A Library of American Literature* (New York, 1889-1890), II, 356-364. Brief biographical sketches are available in Charles Brooks' *History of the Town of Medford, Massachusetts 1630-1855* (Boston, 1855), pp. 319-324, and in an anonymous article on Jane Turell in the *North American Review*, 93 (July, 1861), 22-35. The most useful recent accounts are Clayton H. Chapman's "Benjamin Colman's Daughters," *New England Quarterly*, 26 (June, 1953), 169-192; Ola Elizabeth Winslow's "Jane Colman Turell," *Notable American Women*, ed. Edward T. James, Janet Wilson James and Paul Boyer (Cambridge, Mass., 1971), III, 483-484; and Pattie Cowell's "Jane Colman Turell: 'A Double Birth,' " *13th Moon*, 4 (n. d.), 59-70.

Psalm CXXXVII. Paraphras'd, August 5th, 1725. AETAT. 17.

As on the margin of Euphrate's flood
We wail'd our sins, and mourn'd an angry God:
For God provok'd, to strangers gave our land,
And by a righteous judge condemn'd we stand;
Deep were our groans, our griefs without compare,
With ardent cries, we rent the yielding air.
Born down with woes, no friend at hand was found,
No helper in the waste and barren ground;
Only a mournful willow wither'd there,
Its aged arms by winter storms made bare,
On this our lyres, now useless grown, we hung,
Our lyres by us forsaken and unstrung!
We sigh'd in chains, and sunk beneath our woe,
Whilst more insulting our proud tyrants grow.
From hearts opprest with grief they did require
A sacred anthem on the sounding lyre:
Come, now, they cry, regale us with a song,
Music and mirth the fleeting hours prolong.
Shall Babel's daughter hear that blessed sound?
Shall songs divine be sung in heathen ground?
No. Heaven forbid that we should tune our voice,
Or touch the lyre! whilst slaves we can't rejoice.
O Palestina! our once dear abode,
Thou once wert blest with peace, and lov'd by God,
But now art desolate, a barren waste,
Thy fruitful fields by thorns and weeds defac'd.
If I forget Judea's mournful land,
May nothing prosper that I take in hand!
Or if I string the lyre, or tune my voice,
Till thy deliverance cause me to rejoice,
O may my tongue forget her art to move,
And may I never more my speech improve!
Return O Lord! avenge us of our foes,
Destroy the men that up against us rose:
Let Eden's sons thy just displeasure know,
And like us serve some foreign conquering foe,
In distant realms, far from their native home,
To which dear seat O let them never come!
Thou Babel's daughter! Author of our woe,
Shalt feel the stroke of some revenging blow;

Thy walls and towers be level'd with the ground,
Sorrow and grief shall in each soul be found:
Thrice blest the man, who that auspicious night
Shall seize thy trembling infants in thy sight;
Regardless of thy flowing tears and moans,
And dash the tender babes against the stones.

On Reading the Warning By Mrs. Singer[6]

Surpris'd I view, wrote by a female pen,
Such a grave warning to the sons of men.
Bold was the attempt and worthy of your lays,
To strike at vice, and sinking virtue raise.
Each noble line a pleasing terror gives,
A secret force in every sentence lives.
Inspir'd by virtue you could safely stand
The fair reprover of a guilty land.
You vie with the fam'd prophetess[7] of old,
Burn with her fire, in the same cause grow bold.
Dauntless you undertake th' unequal strife,
And raise dead virtue by your verse to life.
A woman's pen strikes the curs'd serpent's head,
And lays the monster gasping, if not dead.

Part of the Fifth Chapter of Canticles Paraphras'd From the 8th Verse. Ent'red Sept[ember] 14th, 1725.

You beauteous dames, if that my love you see,
With eager steps conduct him here to me,
Tell him no joy to me you can impart,
And that no pain is like a bleeding heart.
Say I am sick of love, and moaning lie,
Whilst the sad echo to my groans reply,
    Who is thy love? the scornful maids reply,

And for what form waste you your bloom in sighs?
Let's know the man, if he be worth your care,
Or does deserve the tender love you bear.
 Whilst your request with pleasure I obey,
Your strict attention give to what I say.
My love excels all that's on earth call'd fair,
As the bright sun excels the meanest star.
His head is wisdom's spacious theatre,
Riches of grace and beauty there appear.
A down his shoulders with becoming pride
Falls his fine hair in beauteous ringlets tied.
His sparkling eyes in splendent luster vie
With the twin stars that grace the azure sky.
His cheeks excel the fragrant blushing rose
Which in the fruitful vale of Sharon grows.
His lips like lilies in their flow'ry bloom
Yield a sweet odor and a rich perfume.
His ivory arms more charming to behold
Than orient pearls, encas'd in shining gold.
His well turn'd legs like stately pillars stand
Of marble, polish'd by a curious hand.
His mien is noble and august his air,
His countenance as Lebanon does appear.

To My Muse, December 29, 1725

Come gentle muse, and once more lend thine aid,
O bring thy succor to a humble maid!
How often dost thou liberally dispense
To our dull breast thy quick'ning influence!
By thee inspir'd, I'll cheerful tune my voice,
And love and sacred friendship make my choice.
In my pleas'd bosom you can freely pour
A greater treasure than Jove's golden shower.
Come now, fair muse, and fill my empty mind
With rich ideas, great and unconfin'd.
Instruct me in those secret arts that lie
Unseen to all but to a poet's eye.

O let me burn with Sappho's noble fire,
But not like her for faithless man expire.
And let me rival great Orinda's[8] fame,
Or like sweet Philomela's[9] be my name.
Go lead the way, my muse, nor must you stop,
'Till we have gain'd Parnassus' shady top:
'Till I have view'd those fragrant soft retreats,
Those fields of bliss, the muses' sacred seats.
I'll then devote thee to fair virtue's fame,
And so be worthy of a poet's name.

An Invitation Into the Country, In Imitation of Horace

From the soft shades, and from the balmy sweets
Of Medford's flow'ry vales, and greet retreats,
Your absent Delia[10] to her father sends
And prays to see him ere the summer ends.

Now while the earth's with beauteous verdue dy'd,
And Flora paints the meads in all her pride;
While laden trees Pomonia's bounty own,
And Ceres' treasures do the fields adorn;
From the thick smokes, and noisy town, O come,
And in these plains a while forget your home.

Though my small incomes never can afford,
Like wealthy Celsus to regale a Lord;
No ivory tables groan beneath the weight
Of sumptuous dishes, serv'd in massy plate;
The forest ne'er was search'd for food for me,
Nor from my hounds the timorous hare does flee:
No leaden thunder strikes the fowl in air,
Nor from my shaft the winged death do fear:
With silken nets I ne'er the lake despoil,
Nor with my bait the larger fish beguile.
No luscious sweet-meats, by my servants plac'd
In curious order, e'er my table grac'd:
To please the taste, no rich Burgundian wine,

In crystal glasses on my side-board shine;
The luscious sweets of fair Canaries' Isle
Ne'er fill'd my casks, nor in my flagons smile:
No wine, but what does from my apples flow,
My frugal house on any can bestow:
Except when Cesar's birth-day does return,
And joyful fires throughout the village burn;
Then moderate each takes his cheerful glass,
And our good wishes to Augustus pass.

But though rich dainties never spread my board,
Nor my cool vaults Calabrian wines afford;
Yet what is neat and wholesome I can spread,
My good fat bacon, and our homely bread,
With which my healthful family is fed,
Milk from the cow, and butter newly churn'd,
And new fresh cheese, with curds and cream just turn'd.
For a dessert upon my table's seen
The golden apple, and the melon green;
The blushing peach and glossy plum there lies,
And with the mandrake tempt your hands and eyes.

This I can give, and if you'll here repair,
To slake your thirst a cask of autumn beer,
Reserv'd on purpose for your drinking here.

Under the spreading elms our limbs we'll lay,
While fragrant zephyrs round our temples play.
Retir'd from courts, and crowds, secure we'll set,
And freely feed upon our country treat.
No noisy faction here shall dare intrude,
Or once disturb our peaceful solitude.

No stately beds my humble roofs adorn
Of costly purple, by carv'd panthers borne.
Nor can I boast Arabia's rich perfumes,
Diffusing odors through our stately rooms.
For me no fair Egyptian plies the loam,
But my fine linen all is made at home.
Though I no down or tapestry can spread,
A clean soft pillow shall support your head,
Fill'd with the wool from off my tender sheep,

On which with ease and safety you may sleep.
The nightingale shall lull you to your rest,
And all be calm and still as is your breast.

On the Incomparable Mr. Waller

Hail chaste Urania! thy assistance bring,
And fire my breast while I attempt to sing,
In artless lays, Waller the poet's king.
Waller, the tuneful name my soul inspires,
And kindles in thy breast poetic fires.

Hail mighty genius! Favorite of the Nine!
Thy merits in four reigns distinguish'd shine.
Country and court, alternate, you enjoy,
One claims thy nobler thoughts, and one thy muse employ.

Chaste is thy muse, and lofty is her song,
Softer than Ovid and like Virgil strong.
Much thee thy country, more its language owe,
All that adorns it it receiv'd from you.
What weighty sense does in thy works abound!
And sterling lines are in thy poems found.
In sweetest numbers you your thoughts express,
The justest standard of our English verse.

A tender passion every bosom warms,
When e'er you sing of Sacharissa's charms,
O lovely maid! mild as the morning light,
When first its beams salute our longing sight.
As virgin fountains in their basins roll,
So calm, so bright is Sacharissa's soul.
As the fierce sun, by his meridian rays,
Exhales the moisture from this lower earth;
Again at night by dews the fields repays,
That nature labors with a double birth:
So you engross in your capacious soul
All that the world polite and learned call,

But in your works you do repay the whole,
With large additions of your own to all.
O happy isle that bare a son so bright,
Of whom the ages since have learnt to write.

[Lines On Childbirth]

Phoebus has thrice his yearly circuit run,
The winter's over, and the summer's done;
Since that bright day on which our hands were join'd,
And to Philander[11] I my all resign'd.

Thrice in my womb I've found the pleasing strife,
In the first struggles of my infant's life:
But O how soon by Heaven I'm call'd to mourn,
While from my womb a lifeless babe is torn?
Born to the grave ere it had seen the light,
Or with one smile had cheer'd my longing sight.

Again in travail pains my nerves are wreck'd,
My eye balls start, my heart strings almost crack'd;
Now I forget my pains, and now I press
Philander's image to my panting breast.
Ten days I hold him in my joyful arms,
And feast my eyes upon his infant charms.
But then the King of Terrors does advance
To pierce its bosom with his iron lance.
Its soul releas'd, upward it takes its flight,
Oh never more below to bless my sight!
Farewell sweet babes I hope to meet above,
And there with you sing the Redeemer's love.

And now O gracious Savior lend thine ear,
To this my earnest cry and humble prayer,
That when the hour arrives with painful throes,
Which shall my burden to the world disclose;
I may deliverance have, and joy to see
A living child, to dedicate to Thee.

[Lines On Her Mother's Death] [1] [2]

She's gone! she's gone! I saw her rise
And quickly gain the distant skies.
Sudden from Heaven a sacred mandate came,
Brought by a convoy of celestial flame.
She was prepar'd, the summons did obey,
And joyful left her tottering house of clay.
Her pains, her tears, her fears, are all now past
In joys unspeakable which ever last.
    Her soul in Jesus' arms remain,
    The grave her body does detain.
Parted a while, her joys will be complete,
When in the resurrection morn they'll meet.

Ah dearest, tenderest parent! must I mourn,
My heavy loss, and bathe with tears your urn!
Since now no more to me you must return.

O quickening spirit! now perform thy part,
Set up thy glorious kingdom in my heart;
That when those sands which in my glass do run
Are spent and all my work below is done,
I the dear saint may then in glory meet
Where sin and death lie vanquish'd at our feet:
    Where Jesus ever will improve
    Our souls with heavenly grace and love.

[Lines Regarding "Some Unhappy Affairs of Medford in the Years 1729 and 1730"]

Behold how good, how sweet, their joy does prove,
Where brethren dwell in unity and love!
When no contention, strife, or fatal jar
Disturb the peace, and raise the noisy war.
'Tis like the ointment, which of old was pour'd
On Aaron's head, and down his garments shower'd,
Through all the air perfuming odor spreads,

Diffusing sweetness to the neighboring meads.
Or like the dew on Hermon's lofty head
Which on the mounts of Sion moisture spread.
'Circled with peace, they shall within the land
As shining patterns and examples stand.
If sinners wrangle, let the saints agree;
The gospel breathes out nought but unity.
To such the blessing from the Lord is given,
Even life eternal, in the highest Heaven.

Hannah Griffitts

(1727-August 24, 1817)

For one who left so substantial a collection of manuscript poems, letters and essays, surprisingly little is known about the life of Hannah Griffitts of Philadelphia. She was born in 1727 to Thomas Griffitts, a local official in capacities that varied from mayor of Philadelphia to Judge of the Supreme Court, and Mary Norris, a member of one of colonial Pennsylvania's most respected families. Raised in this influential Quaker household, she indicates by the quality of her manuscripts that she received a sound basic education. Griffitts remained single all her life, presumably at least a partial explanation for the financial difficulty she experienced after the deaths of her parents: she mentioned in a letter to Susanna Wright in 1763 that she "keenly [felt] the confinement of [her] deprest circumstances."[1] But perhaps it was determination as well as poverty that led Griffitts to stay in Philadelphia during the British occupation of 1777-1778. Evidence regarding her political leanings during the Revolutionary War is contradictory, but she declared herself (despite her Quaker pacifism) in a letter to General Anthony Wayne:

> I am so good a whig that of consequence I must be a little of a politician. There was a time that I knew nor thought no more of politics than I did of grasping a sceptre but now the scene is changed and I believe every woman is desirous of being acquainted with what interests her country.[2]

Outliving the furor of the Revolution by nearly forty years, Hannah Griffitts died on August 24, 1817. She remained mentally alert throughout her long life, continuing to write poetry despite her gradually failing eyesight.

This much, and little else, is known about the external circumstances of Griffitts' life. Her voluminous correspondence, particularly that with other women poets in Pennsylvania, portrays a retiring woman with wide-ranging interests. Letters to Susanna Wright, Elizabeth Graeme Fergusson and Deborah Logan indicate a small network of friends among whom poems and letters were exchanged periodically. Adopting the pseudonym of "Fidelia," Griffitts circulated her poems among her close friends, charging them "to keep [the manuscripts] within the partial bounds of your family, where I am secure of that generous allowance I cannot expect out of it."[3] Her limited audience frequently urged Griffitts to publish her work, but she firmly resisted their suggestions.[4]

Though like Emily Dickinson she carefully guarded her work from publication, Hannah Griffitts nevertheless approached poetry with a seriousness that bordered on devotion. Even as a child of ten, she announced (in a piece reprinted here) the religious basis for her subsequent verse:

> The muse long banished and disused
> I now will consecrate to Thee.

More prolific than most of her contemporaries, Griffitts left over two hundred manuscript poems. Evidence of revision in those manuscripts indicates continued efforts to perfect her work. Using a variety of verse forms, she wrote elegies, religious meditations, satires and other occasional pieces. Political events, natural happenings, social occasions, tributes to friends, satiric attacks on prominent Patriots—all fall within the range of Hannah Griffitts' pen. But despite its variety, religious themes predominate in the poetry.

> O, my joy in heaven
> Will everlasting be—will feel no end,
> Nor know a period—safe in God I'll stand,
> Nor dread the storm that shakes a world to atoms.[5]

Though submission to God's will marked her work, submission to man's will suited her less well. Writing to Susanna Wright of a young boy then visiting her "as being of the sex superior," she hastened to add: "I borrow this word, it's not my own."[6] Yet she was quick to acknowledge her primary responsibilities among those traditionally assigned to women. Even for so prolific a woman poet, verse-making was "design'd but as amusement to [her] own melancholy hours."[7]

> ...Though these little affairs [her poems] sometimes divert a dull hour, I hope I have ... imitated my worthier friend [Susanna Wright] in my attachment to the riming humor, nor often visited the muses in a ragged petticoat binding, or been studying for verse when the stockin' ball was so much more necessary.[8]

Necessarily a secondary concern to her, Hannah Griffitts' verse was flawed and imperfect; but its variety and its wit offer a look at colonial Philadelphia that might make us wonder why it has remained so long unread.

Griffitts' extant manuscripts were collected and presented to the Library Company of Philadelphia by an anonymous donor, perhaps a member of the Logan family. Presently housed in the Historical Society of Pennsylvania, most of Griffitts' poems have never been published. Printed materials about Hannah Griffitts are few, but handwritten notes by John F. Watson in F. W. Leach's typescript "Genealogies of Old Philadelphia Families" in the Historical Society of Pennsylvania provide a sketchy (and occasionally contradictory) biographical outline. Briefer and more accessible references to Griffitts may be found in the *Pennsylvania Magazine of History and Biography*, 17 (1893), 28; 27 (1903), 109-111; 39 (1915), 286-287; and 75 (1951), 199. Samuel Hazard's *Register of Pennsylvania*, 8 (September 17, 1831), 178, gives an account of Griffitts by her cousin Deborah Logan. Three sources, in addition to the *Pennsylvania Magazine of History and Biography* listings above, reprint brief samples of Griffitts' poetry: Carl and Jessica Bridenbaugh, *Rebels and Gentlemen* (New York, 1962), p. 125; Linda DePauw and Conover Hunt, *Remember the Ladies: Women in America 1750-1815* (New York, 1976), p. 86; and Anne Wharton, *Through Colonial Doorways* (Philadelphia, 1893), pp. 54-55. A useful introductory account is available in M. Katherine Jackson's *Outlines of the Literary History of Colonial Pennsylvania* (Lancaster, 1906), pp. 153-154, and briefer comments are included in John F. Watson's *Annals of Philadelphia and Pennsylvania in the Olden Times* (Philadelphia, 1845), I, 559.

[Verses] [9]

To Thee, my life, my light, my love,
The Lord, my righteousness, I sing;
I feel thy quick'ning Spirit move,
To Thee I soar with ardorous wing.

What grateful praise elates my heart
When I thy wonderous love review;
With all my darlings then I'd part,
Could I but prove my service true.

The muse long banished and disused
I now will consecrate to Thee;
No trifling themes shall her abuse,
For Sion's song should all be free,

Free from the soiling spot of Earth
And all her base desires and fears,
From rousing carnal love or mirth,
And from the world's debasing cares.

*On the 13th February of 1765, A Day In Which I First Drank
Of the Cup of Sorrow In the Death of My Beloved Parent*

Lamented day, whose solemn hours shall roll,
And clothe in grief and tears my anxious soul,
My anxious soul shall trembling mark the day
That wrench'd my best and earthly all away,
Whorl'd in black clouds, the mortal vale of earth,
And wrap'd my darling in the arms of Death;
Oh Thou whose fiat gave the deadly stroke,
And ev'ry soft and strong engagement broke,
Loose, now I stand, from ev'ry mortal tie,
My only hope is immortality.
Thou knows my captive state, my clouded road,
That hides the prospect of thy smile, my God;
I feel thy chast'ning judgments o'er my soul,

The lightning flash, and Sinia's[10] thunders roll;
Oh, stretch thy arm, and screen a reptile worm,
Else I perish, 'midst the dreadful storm.
No friend on earth I have, that can revive
My fainting hope, and bid the mourner live;
Embitter'd deep, the awful cup I taste,
And all my hours, in [illegible] afflictive waste.
Oh speak a healing word, my Savior God,
Nor let me sink beneath my maker's rod;
Spare not, but sanctify thy chast'ning hand,
Till this vile rebel bows to thy command.
Thou know'st my wants and weakness, oh forbear,
Nor mark thy creature with an eye severe.
Oh speak a word of hope, or I am lost,
Upon the waves of furious tempests tost.
Oh, let thy tender eye of mercy view
A fainting mourner, and its strength renew;
In this, and all the future strokes from Thee,
Oh may I bow, in deep humility,
Nor know a thought, a wish, or hope or fear,
But what shall for thy sacred will appear,
Nor longer mourn, my darling is releast,
Nor doom'd with me, this bitter cup to taste;
But rather bless the tender Parent's hand,
That mov'd this flower to Canaan's promis'd land,
Where it shall flourish, in immortal bloom,
And smile, a favor'd victor o'er the tomb,
[illegible] dead, by ev'ry other meaner care,
Than joyful to rejoin my Parent here.
The dear and strongest union nature knew,
By death dissolv'd, these solemn hours renew,
And none, but such as weep their darling, gone,
Can feel the deep extensive stroke, I mourn,
As long as life and reason shall remain,
Thy dear lov'd image must revive my pain;
But though I thus lament the stroke to me,
I hail thy joy, in perfect liberty;
Thy tender bosom, and thy feeling mind,
To a weak nature of the flesh conjoin'd
But ill cou'd bear to [illegible] the outstretch'd rod,
And see thy offspring, thus chastis'd by God,
Whose gracious arm (to thee, a soul belov'd)

From the dark scene of future woes remov'd.
Oh, may I meet thee, on th' immortal shore,
Where sin shall wound, nor death shall part us more;
Here rest my hopes, my prospects, and my will,
As Heaven allots, my duty to fulfill,
To bow submiss to all the chast'ning rod,
Nor know a murm'ring thought against my God,
Till pitying love shall speak my soul release
And wing the prisoner, mind, to join the blest.

The Storm, 1765[11]

"Then He arose, and rebuked the winds and the sea, and there was a great calm." Matt[hew], 8th chapter, 26th verse

Let haughty man with fear adore
    That awful, sovereign Majesty,
Who governs Nature, by his power
    Supreme; nor asketh leave to be;

Happy for him, his God shall guide,
    Who can th' alternate change perform,
Bid Nature, in a calm subside,
    Or frown beneath the furious storm;

Whose highstretch'd arm, whene'er He please,
    Can swell the flood, beyond the shore,
Direct the vast machine with ease,
    And hold the reins of wild uproar.

Hark—now the awful charge is given,
    The winds rush forth, in fury rise,
Darken the blue serene of heaven,
    And dash their billows to the skies;

The boundless reservoirs, on high,
    United, join the floods below,

The deluge pours from earth and sky,
    A general, dreadful overflow;

The clash of elements combine,
    To swell the aggravated roar,
Till His almighty voice divine
    Bids the fierce tempest, rage no more;

Soon, as this "sovereign word" was spoke,
    Submissive Nature, calm appears,
The power of all its fury, broke,
    An infant's smiling softness wears;

The sun pours forth his beams of light,
    To bless the vegetative race;
And the rich canopy of night
    Expands, in full illustrious grace;

The amazing change, we see, "is thine,"
    Who gave to man th' reasoning soul;
But oh, how vast, "beyond our line,
    "Thou, that sustains the mighty whole."

Here fix our trust, though Nature shake,
    And frighted, feels her loosen'd tie;
The soul, amidst the general wreck,
    "Is safe, in God's immensity."

*To the Memory of Our Valued Friend, Samuel Fothergill,
Who Died the 6th Mo[nth] 1772*[12]

"I have fought a good fight, I have finish'd my course, I have kept the faith." 2 Tim[othy], 4th [chapter], 7th verse

Though cold the breast, where love of virtue glow'd,
And clos'd the lips, whence living language flow'd,
Though now, no more, thy bright example warm,
Thy precepts strike, or eloquence can charm,

Though now, no longer, lis'ning crowds attend
The powerful preacher, and the Christian friend,
Thy name, great man, shall o'er the grave survive,
Glow at our heart, and in our memory live.

Hail favor'd soul, now enter'd on thy rest,
Forever blessing, and forever blest,
"Who kept the faith, did to the end endure,
"Fought the good fight, and ran the race secure;"
Now share the fullness of the life divine,
And with the glorious Church Triumphant join,
Till we, from scenes of danger ever free,
Unite our chorus, in your harmony.

[two lines apparently omitted in manuscript copy]
With transport, close the warfare here below,
And smile like thee, a victor o'er the foe;
When men and angels, Heaven and earth shall join,
To swell the universal song divine,
Nor one discordant note of praise be found,
To break the concord of celestial sound.

Hail glorious period, whose illustrious ray
Sheds the glad dawn of everlasting day;
Where every conflict with the foe is o'er,
The tear shall drop, the sigh be heard no more;
Where conq'ring palms are by the victor won,
And endless rest insures the warfare done,
Where faith in perfect vision shall be found,
And Death, the tyrant, meet his final wound;

Where (through Messiah's mediating love)
Man shall possess th' immortal seats above,
Converse with angels, trace th' ethereal road,
And triumph, in the "Paradise of God;"
Warm'd with the prospect, let the pilgrim soar,
Press through the desert, to the promis'd shore,
That blest retreat, of full serene repose,
Where every grief shall cease, and every storm shall close.

                                              Fidelia

"Beware of the Ides of March," Said the Roman Augur To Julius Cesar[13]

Had Cesar took this useful hint,
    Ere to the senate house he enter'd,
Longer he might have liv'd to think,
    Nor 'midst his cruel murderers ventur'd.

Ladies, this wiser caution take,
    Trust not your tea to Marius Brutus;
Our draught he'll spoil, our china break,
    And raise a storm that will not suit us.

Then for the sake of Freedom's name,
    (Since British wisdom scorns repealing)
Come sacrifice to Patriot fame,
    And give up tea by way of healing.

This done, within ourselves retreat,
    Th' industrious arts of life to follow,
Let the proud Nabobs storm and fret,
    They cannot force our lips to swallow.

Though now the boist'rous surges roll,
    Of wicked North's[14] tempestuous ocean,
Leave him for Justice to control,
    And strive to calm our own commotion.

With us, each prudent caution meet,
    Against this blust'ring son of Thunder,
And let our firm resolve defeat
    His Lordship's ministerial blunder.

                                        Fidelia

*Inscription On A Curious Chamberstove In the Form of an Urn,
Contriv'd in Such A Manner as to Make the Flame Descend Instead
of Rising, Invented By The Celebrated B[enjamin] F[ranklin]* [15]

Like a Newton, sublimely he soar'd,
    To a summit before unattain'd,
New regions of science explor'd,
    And the palm of philosophy gain'd.

With a spark that he caught from the skies,
    He display'd an unparalleled wonder,
And we saw, with delight and surprise,
    His rod could defend[16] us from thunder.

O, had he been wise to pursue
    The track for his talent design'd,
What a tribute of praise had been due,
    To the teacher and friend of mankind.

But to covet political fame,
    In him was degrading ambition,
A spark, that from Lucifer came,
    And kindled the flame of sedition.

Let candor then write on his urn,
    "Here lies the reknowned inventor,
"Whose flame to the skies ought to burn,
    "But inverted, descends to the center."

On Reading Some Paragraphs in "The Crisis," April, '77

Pane—Though thy tongue may now run glibber,
    Warm'd with thy independent glow,
Thou art indeed the coldest fibber,
    I ever knew, or wish to know.

Here page and page, even num'rous pages,
    Are void of breeding, sense or truth;

I hope thou don't receive thy wages,
   As tutor to our rising youth.

Of female manners, never scribble,
   Nor with thy rudeness wound our ear;
Howe'er thy trimming pen may quibble,
   The delicate is "not thy sphere."

And now, to prove how false thy stories,
   By facts which won't admit a doubt,
Know there are "conscientious tories,"
   And one poor whig, at least, without.

Wilt thou permit the muse to mention
   A whisper, circulated round;
Let Howe increase the scribbler's pension,
   No more will Pane a whig be found;

For not from principle, but lucre,
   He gains his bread from out the fire;
Let Court and Congress both stand neuter,
   And the poor creature must expire.

                Fidelia

On the Death of John Roberts and Abraham Carlisle, Nov[embe]r 4th, 1778[17]

In the sad chambers of retir'd distress,
The scenes of speechless woe, where widows mourn
The tender husband lost, where orphans weep
The indulgent father, and sustaining friend,
The indulgent friend and father known no more,
Where the sad sister faints beneath the stroke
That rent th' associate brother from her heart;
Here, clad in solemn sympathy of woe,
My soul retires to share my neighbor's grief,
Give sigh for sigh, and mingle tears with tears;

Or deeper still, beyond the gentle power
Of words to heal, or tears to mitigate,
Deep, in the awful center of the soul,
(Hid from the view of an unfeeling world)
And wrap'd in fellow feeling of distress,
I will attend your melancholy steps,
And pay the tender tribute to your woes.

But words are vain, the powers of harmony
Are useless here, ev'n friendship's soothing voice
Has lost its balm, in woundings like to yours;
Ah then from Heaven, from gracious Heaven alone
Look for "the strength to stand," the healing power,
The balm of comfort, the sustaining friend;
May He supply those soft cementing bands,
Which brutal laws rent from your bleeding hearts,
Direct your trembling footsteps, and be found,
The husband, father, and the brother lost.

And you, the guiltless victims of the day
(Who to a timid city's late reproach
And blush of its inhabitants) have fallen,
A prey to laws, disgraceful to the man,
Fallen—on the cruel shores that gave you birth,
Fallen—on th' ungrateful shores your fathers plan'd
"On the firm basis of true liberty,
"The laws of justice, and the rights of man";
Long shall your names survive the brutal deed,
And fair, transmitted down to better times,
Stand the reproach of ours, when lawless power
And wealth, by rapine gain'd, shall shroud its head
In infamous oblivion, or be held
The warning, not example, of mankind.

And you, whose mad ambition, lawless grasp
Of proud dominion, and oppressive power
Have spread the flames of war around the shores
Where peace once smil'd, and social union dwelt,
How will you stand the retributive hour,
Or bear the close of dread decision's voice,
When, as you mingled deep the cup of woe
For suffering souls, so will your souls partake

The deeply mingled cup of woe again?
You have dissolv'd the tender ties of nature,
And torn asunder (by the barbarous hand
Of cruel laws) the dear, the soft connections
Which Heaven had join'd and blest, till you arose
The scourge of desolation on their peace;
To you the widow and the orphan look
With heartfelt anguish, as their source of woe,
And in the silent pang, from you demand
The tender husband and the father lost.

Though here the voice of nature breath'd in vain
To tigers fierce, and adamantine rocks,
Or hearts unfeeling, and as hard as theirs,
The day will come, and wing'd with swift approach
When piercing deep, arm'd in tremendous power,
The voice of God and conscience shall be heard;
Oh, in "this day of pleading," if His hand
Mark you severe, as you have others mark'd,
How will your souls sustain His dread decision,
Whose laws are justice, and whose words are truth?[18]

                                        Fidelia

To the Memory of My Late Valuable Friend Susannah Wright, who Died Dec[embe]r 1st, 1784 (In the 88th Year of Her Age)

Shall thou, whose gentle muse in softest strain
    Wept others' sorrow with a feeling breast,
Ah shall Veneria close her lot of pain,
    Nor leave a muse, her virtues to attest.

Not so; the muse once favor'd and belov'd
    Shall trace her mild benignity of heart,
The soul that wish'd each human ill remov'd,
    The hand that every comfort would impart.

And though with innate powers superior blest,
    The striking sense and energy of mind,

How veil'd their luster, while her form express'd
    The humble, courteous, diffident, and kind.

While o'er the "tomb of friendship" sorrow flow'd
    In feeling grief, and deep reflection strong,
How with the theme her gentle bosom glow'd,
    How sweet her powerful harmony of song.

For genius, thus distinguish'd and admir'd,
    Above ambition's low contrasted care,
She walk'd with wisdom, in the "vale retir'd,"
    And left the world its tinsel and its glare.

Warm to the ties of nature and of love,
    She own'd their influence and cementing power,
(And in this sphere of duty, fond to move)
    From them, the pleasing and the painful hour.

Did suffering wound, or death remove the friend,
    She felt the anguish of its keenest dart;
Did brighter fancy, the social-hour attend,
    She shared the pleasure, with a grateful heart.

Nor to this narrow spot alone confin'd,
    (Virtue, more wide, will all its powers expand)
She pour'd the balm, compassionately kind,
    On human sufferings, with a healing hand.

Thus through each period of a lengthen'd day,
    (Fulfill'd the tender claim, the social tie)
"She kept the noiseless tenor of her way,"[19]
    Yet sigh'd for good the world could not supply,

Till nature droop'd beneath the waste of years,
    Panted for life, and long'd to be undress'd:
A life beyond these sublunary spheres,
    A life distinguish'd by eternal rest.

Perfected thus, may thou, departed friend,
    The full fruition of thy bliss enjoy,
A bliss that fears no change, decrease or end,
    A portion time nor death can e'er destroy.

And while this bosom, once to friendship dear,
   In artless verse embalms its kindred clay,
Center'd in God, releas'd from sorrowing care,
   "Thy mortal shall surpass thy natal day."[20]

Mercy Otis Warren

(September 14, 1728 O.S.—October 19, 1814)

Historian, dramatist and poet, Mercy Otis Warren left a prolific record of America's revolutionary years. Third child born to
the established Barnstable, Massachusetts, family of merchant-
lawyer-farmer James Otis and Mary Allyne, she received no formal
education. She was allowed, however, to share many of her brothers'
lessons with the Reverend Jonathan Russell. Forming a particularly
close relationship with her oldest brother James (an active patriot
until his periods of insanity disabled him), Mercy Otis frequently
pursued her studies with him even after he had entered Harvard
College. Access to Russell's library and a penchant for solitude and
reading combined to acquaint her with the poetry of Pope, Dryden,
Milton and Shakespeare and with Raleigh's *History of the World*.
Additionally, her interest in politics was sharpened by the frequent
political discussions to which she was exposed because of her father's
positions as judge of the county court of common pleas and as
colonel of the militia.

In November, 1754, Mercy Otis married James Warren, a
Plymouth merchant who encouraged his wife's studies and her
growing literary activity. After their marriage, except for an eight
year residence at Milton Hill near Boston, Mercy and James Warren
lived in Plymouth, maintaining a house in town and another rural
residence which Mercy called "Clifford Farm." Although Mercy
Warren's physical world never extended beyond a thin strip of the
Atlantic coast from Boston to Providence, her circle of friends
came to include many of the most influential figures in revolutionary and early national America. Her extensive correspondence
records her relationships with John and Abigail Adams, Sam and
Elizabeth ("Betsey") Adams, John and Hannah Winthrop, Thomas
Jefferson, Alexander Hamilton, Elbridge Gerry, George and Martha
Washington, and Catherine Macaulay-Graham, an English supporter

of the Revolution.

Burdened with the social obligations necessary to her husband's growing political activity and with the raising of five sons,
Mercy Warren was careful that she "not neglect the smallest part/Of
social duty"[1] for her writing and her political and historical studies.
But despite these restrictions, she began writing poetry as a young
woman. Circulating her early work only among close friends, she
wrote philosophical and religious verse, poems on friendship and
nature, eulogies and other occasional pieces. Conventional themes
from nature and religion mark early pieces such as "On Winter"
(January, 1759) or "An Address to the Supreme Being" (undated).
But gradually these materials gave way to more political motifs. By
1774, Warren had turned to revolutionary themes: "The Squabble
of the Sea Nymphs," for example, recounted the Boston Tea Party,
and "A Political Reverie" foretold an independent America. Writing
to her husband, who was away working for "the great public cause,
which agitated all America, in 1776," she even resigned herself to
family separation by noting that it had become a political necessity:

> The times demand exertions of the kind,
> A patriot zeal must warm the female mind.

A devoted patriot, Mercy Warren reflected the political turmoil of revolutionary America in her verse. As her own contribution
to "the public cause," Warren wrote (for her first publication) a
satiric verse drama, *The Adulateur*, which appeared serially in the
Massachusetts Spy beginning March 26, 1772. Ridiculing the apparently self-serving motives of Massachusetts' Tory leadership,
The Adulateur introduced such characters as Rapatio (Governor
Thomas Hutchinson), Meagre (Foster Hutchinson, brother to Thomas) and Brutus (the patriot voice of James Otis, Jr.). A pamphlet
edition appeared in 1773, expanded into five acts with a new focus
on the Boston Massacre as a result of plagiary by an unknown
author. After the success of *The Adulateur*, Warren's other satiric
dramas appeared regularly: *The Defeat* (1773), *The Group* (1775),
The Blockheads (1776), and *The Motley Assembly* (1779).

But Warren seemed not entirely comfortable with her role as

satirist despite the popular success of her dramas. Though her plays and verses were published anonymously, she questioned the propriety of a woman venting the sharp political sentiments of her plays. In a letter to John Adams, dated January 30, 1775, after the favorable reception of *The Group*, she speculated that

> though from the particular circumstance of our unhappy time, a little personal acrimony might be justifiable in your sex, must not the female character suffer. (And will she not be suspected as deficient in the most amiable part thereof, that candor and charity which ensures her both affection and esteem,) if she indulges her pen to paint in the darkest shades, even those whose vice and venality have rendered contemptible.[2]

Warren feared for her reputation, but Adams was quick to reassure her that "the faithful historian delineates characters truly, let the censure fall where it will."[3] Apparently such reinforcements were sufficient; Mercy Warren continued to draw her characters as she saw them, apparently growing in self-confidence as she worked.

Concerned with national rather than explicitly feminist liberties, Warren's developing confidence in her writing did not prevent her from recognizing "the appointed subordination [of women] (perhaps for the sake of order in families)" in an undated letter to "Betsey" (otherwise unidentified). Nevertheless she cautioned "dear Betsey" in the same letter that she should "by no means acknowledge such an inferiority as would check the ardor of our endeavors to equal in all mental accomplishments the most masculine heights. . . ."[4] Unwilling to accept culturally imposed limitations, Warren attributed women's intellectual inferiority to a deficient education. In a published letter to her son Winslow, she explained that she had "ever considered human nature as the same in both sexes. . . . The foibles, the passions, the vices, and the virtues appear to spring from the same source and, under similar advantages, frequently reach the same degree of perfection, or sink to those stages of depravity disgraceful to the human form. . . ."[5] Despite occasional concern that she might overstep womanly bounds, Mercy Warren offers no apologies for her work or for her sex.

In 1790, Warren's *Poems, Dramatic and Miscellaneous* was

published in Boston. Apparently quite proud of her collection, she signed her name to her work for the first time. Her will bequeathed the copyright to her favorite son Winslow as "the only thing she could properly call her own."[6] *Poems, Dramatic and Miscellaneous* contains *The Ladies of Castille* and *The Sack of Rome*, two late verse dramas very different from her early satires, and a selection of eighteen "miscellaneous" poems. Dedicated to George Washington, the volume has a list of subscribers that reads like a roll call of prominent citizens of the early United States. Despite a growing rift with John Adams over their opposing views of the new constitution (Mercy Warren was an active anti-Federalist), Adams thanked her warmly for the work she presented him:

> The poems are not all of them new to me, by whom some of them have been read and esteemed some years ago. However foolishly some European writers may have sported with American reputation for genius, literature and science: I know not where they will find a female poet of their own to prefer to the ingenious author of these compositions.[7]

His admiration was echoed by others, including a favorable review by "Q" in the *Massachusetts Magazine* for April, 1790. Perhaps most welcome of all was the praise she received from her husband in a letter written while she was in Boston seeing her book through the press:

> I suppose you are busily engaged in the business of an author of great abilities, discernment, and judgment, yet diffident and therefore hunting for criticism and advice, and correcting the proof with a trembling heart. If you had half the good opinion of yourself that I have of you, you certainly would not feel half the anxiety you do now.[8]

Twentieth-century readers may react less favorably to Warren's *Poems*. The conventional imagery and diction and the moralizing tone that mark her earlier verse also characterize the 1790 volume, parts of which were written as early as 1774. But her ode "To Mrs. Montague" (reprinted here) suggests that

> A sister's hand may wrest a female pen,
> From the bold outrage of imperious men,

perhaps for the purpose of presenting another viewpoint. A few of the poems convey a genuine sense of the human cost of the Revolution, others of its humor, or of Warren's grief at the loss of a son to tuberculosis. While most of the *Poems, Dramatic and Miscellaneous* are conventional, sometimes polemical, Mercy Warren's volume occasionally provides a fresh look at revolutionary and early national themes.

Warren seldom wrote verse after the publication of her *Poems*, burying her "little talent for poetry . . . in the grave of [her] dear children,"9 three of whom died in 1785, 1791 and 1800 respectively. But some of her lessened commitment to poetry may have resulted from her greater attentions to constitutional politics and history. Warren's anti-Federalist contribution to the heated discussions of the proposed constitution is contained in her anonymous *Observations on the New Constitution, and on the Federal Conventions* (1788), originally attributed to Elbridge Gerry. Her three-volume *History of the Rise, Progress and Termination of the American Revolution*, still an important resource for students of early American history, appeared in 1805. Maintaining an active correspondence despite a growing blindness, Warren employed her disabled son James as her amanuensis in her last years. Increasingly isolated from her earlier friends by her anti-Federalist positions, she retained her constant attention to politics to the end. Rufus Griswold, a nineteenth-century anthologist of women's poetry, has said of her that "she was intelligent and honest enough to be always a partisan."10

Mercy Warren's manuscript poems and letters are in the collection of the Massachusetts Historical Society. Manuscript copies of the same poems are located in the Houghton Library at Harvard University, though these copies are not in Mercy Warren's hand; probably they were copied by James Warren, Jr. Except for several scattered periodical publications, Warren's major works have already been listed. Some of her correspondence is reproduced in the *Warren-Adams Letters*, part of the Massachusetts Historical Society *Collections*, 72 (1917); 73 (1925).

Two full-length biographical studies, neither of which is completely satisfactory, are available in Alice Brown's *Mercy Warren* (New York, 1896), and in Katharine Anthony's *The First Lady of the Revolution: . . . . Mercy Warren* (Garden City, N. Y., 1958). Maud Hutcheson's "Mercy Warren: A Study of Her Life and Works" (diss., The American University, 1951) provides a more reliable account. Useful brief sketches have been supplied by Maud Hutcheson's "Mercy Warren, 1728-1814," *William and Mary Quarterly*, third series, 10 (1953), 378-402, and by Robert A. Feer's "Mercy Warren," *Notable American Women*, eds. Edward James, Janet Wilson James and Paul Boyer (Cambridge, Mass., 1971), III, 545-546. Elizabeth Ellet's *The Women of the American Revolution* (New York, 1848; rpt. New York, 1969), I, 76-106, furnishes a mid-nineteenth century perspective while a detailed account of Mercy Warren as historian is contained in William R. Smith's *History as Argument: Three Patriot Historians of the American Revolution* (The Hague, 1966), pp. 73-119.

A Thought On the Inestimable Blessing of Reason, Occasioned By Its Privation To A Friend Of Very Superior Talents and Virtues, 1770[11]

What is it moves within my soul,
And as the needle to the pole,
Directs me to the final cause,
The central point of nature's laws?
'Tis reason, Lord, which thou hast given,
A ray divine, let down from Heaven,
A spark struck from effulgent light,
Transcendent, clear, divinely bright,
Thou hast bestow'd lest man should grope
In endless darkness, void of hope.
Creative being! who reason gave,
And by whose aid the powers we have
To think, to judge, to will, to know,
From whom these reasoning powers flow,
Thy name be ever magnified
That thus to angels we're allied,
Distinguish'd thus in the great chain,
Nor left the least in thy domain.
Yet should'st thou but a moment frown,
Or wink this boasted reason down,
'Twould level proud imperious man
With the least worm in nature's plan.
Then humbly will I Thee implore,
Whom worlds of rationals adore,
That thou this taper should preserve,
From reason's laws let me ne'er swerve,
But calmly, mistress of my mind,
A friend to virtue and mankind,
Oh! gently lead me on to peace,
May years the heavenly gleam increase,
Nor waste beneath the frown of age
As I tread down time's narrow stage,
But brighter burn as life decays,
More fit to join the heavenly lays.
And when the tenement shall fall,
When broken down this feeble wall,
Then may the glad enlighten'd soul

Freed from these clogs, this dull control,
Expand her wings, shake off her load,
And rise to glorify her God

To Mr. Adams[1][2]

Though short! Far short my pen of the sublime
That urges on and bids me write in rhyme,
And hope my friend the effort will excuse,
Nor blame the heart, but check the niggard muse.
    Is it a wild enthupostick[13] flame,
That swells the bosom panting after fame,
Dilates the mind: with every sail's unfurl'd,
To catch the plaudit of a gazing world?
    Is there no permanent, no steady pole,
To point us on, and guide the wand'ring soul?
Does prejudice and passion rule mankind?
Are there no springs that actuate the mind
Whose deep meanders have some nobler source
Than vain self love, to guide their winding course?
    That gen'rous ardor styled benevolence,
Is it an art to gratify the sense
Or give imagination further scope?
That airy queen, who guides the helm of hope
Holds a false mirror to the dazzled sight,
A dim perspective, a delusive light,
That swells the bubbles of life's short'ned span,
While wisdom smiles at the deluded man,
Wrap'd in extaticks,[14] by imagin'd fame,
When the next moment will blot out his name.

    Can't the wise precepts of a Plato's school
(Or shall I name a still more perfect rule)
Rouse up the soul, to that exalted height,
To walk by reason, and reject the cheat:
Or are the fetters that enslave the mind
Of that firm base, that adamantine kind,
So firmly lock'd, and so securely reve'd,[15]

The more we search, the more are we deceived?
Are truth, and friendship, no where to be found,
And patriot virtue nothing but a sound?
    Then may a Cesar equal honor claim
With noble Brutus, celebrated name,
For the poor tribute of a short applause.
One stabs a tyrant trampling on the laws,
While the proud despot marks his baneful way
With virtue's tears, and triumphs o'er his prey.
Self the sole point in which they're both agreed.
By this Rome's shackled, or by this she's freed.
    Self love, that stimulus to noblest aims,
Bids Nero light the capitol in flames,
Or bids H—^{16} sell his native land
And his vile brother lend his perjur'd hand,
While freedom weeps and Heav'n delays to shed
Its awful vengeance on the guilty head.

    If such is life, and fancy throw the bowl,
If appetite and caprice rule the whole,
If virtuous friendship has no solid base,
But false deception holds the sacred place,
Then from thy mem'ry race out every line,
Nor recollect one sentiment of mine
But dark oblivion, sable veil draw o'er
And I'll forbear to interrupt the more.
    For if vice boasts her origin the same,
With social joy and patriotic flame,
Then I must wish to bid the world farewell,
Turn anchorite and choose some lonely cell
Beneath some peaceful hermitage reclin'd
To weep the misery of all mankind,
Till days and years, till time shall cease to roll
And truth eternal strike the wond'ring soul.

Plimouth, October 11, 1773

To the Hon[ora]ble James Warren, Esq., President of the Congress of Massachusetts, on the Death of His Friend Major-General Warren,[17] Who Fell in the Battle of Bunker Hill, June 17th, 1775

When proud Brittannia stretch'd her hostile hand,
And purple currents stain'd this injur'd land,
When despotism shook her servile chains
And thundering cannon rattled o'er the plains,
When faithless Gage each sacred sanction broke
And wrap'd the neighboring villages in smoke,
The curling flames in mounting columns rose,[18]
And show'd the world the rancor of our foes.
    A gen'rous ardor fir'd each manly mind
And all the patriot in the hero shin'd:
Valor and virtue lighted from the skies
And let down freedom as the glorious prize;
While justice held the golden scales on high
And fierce Bellona shook the trembling sky,
The steady beam in equilibria held
Till martial worth should win it in the field.
    Among the foremost ranks have WARREN press'd
Till his great soul rush'd from his bleeding breast;
He greatly fell, pierc'd by a thousand wounds,
That seal his fame beyond time's narrow bounds;
As his last sigh breath'd blessings to this land,
The sword fell guilty from each miscreant hand
That pierc'd this early victim to the cause
Of justice, truth, of liberty, and laws.
    Heaven who its gifts bestows with hand benign
Had form'd his genius for the bold design,
Early to tread the independent field,
And plant the palm on fair Columbia's shield.
Soft were his manners, gentle and serene,
A manly courage mark'd his modest mein.
True friendship warm'd and generous worth combin'd
To dignify and raise his humane mind.
    Such was thy friend, such was the man you mourn
While blooming laurels spring to dress his urn;
The moss grown tomb supports the deathless bays,
And virtue's hand his monument shall raise.
Let no rash foot disturb the sacred shade,

But softly tread where your lov'd WARREN'S laid,
From the rich turf, more lasting glory springs
Than crowns confer, or scepters lend to kings.
    Thus Charles's minions say good Hambden die
And mount from Chalgrove to his native sky;
But o'er his grave what multitudes arose
Who fought for freedom, and subdued her foes;
"To sleep the brave" while every bosom sighs,
Yet round his tomb ten thousand heroes rise
Who snatch the lance, and bind the target on
And bid defiance to Brittannia's throne.
They dare to die, and mark the field of fame
As WARREN died, and leave a deathless name.

To Fidelio,[19] Long Absent On the Great Public Cause, Which Agitated All America, In 1776

The hill tops smile o'er all the blooming mead,
As I alone, on Clifford's summit tread;
Traverse the rural walks, the gurgling rills,
Survey the beauties of th' adjacent hills;
Taste the delights of competence and health,
Each sober pleasure reason lends to wealth:
Yet o'er the lawn a whisp'ring echo sighs,
Thy friend is absent—my fond heart replies—
Say—do not friendship's joys outweigh the whole?
'Tis social converse, animates the soul.
Thought interchang'd, the heavenly spark improves,
And reason brightens by the heart it loves;
While solitude sits brooding o'er her cares,
She oft accelerates the ills she fears;
And though fond hope with silken hand displays,
The distant images of halcyon days,
Her sable brow contracts a solemn air,
That treads too near the threshold of despair;
'Till heav'n benign the choicest blessings lend,
The balm of life, a kind and faithful friend:
This highest gift, by heav'n indulg'd, I claim;

Ask, what is happiness?—My friend, I name:
Yet while the state, by fierce internal war,
Shook to the center, asks his zealous care,
I must submit, and smile in solitude,
My fond affection, my self love subdu'd:
The times demand exertions of the kind,
A patriot zeal must warm the female mind.

   Yet, gentle hope!—come, spread thy silken wing,
And waft me forward to revolving spring;
Or ere the vernal equinox returns,
At worst, before the summer solstice burns,
May peace again erect her cheerful stand,
Disperse the ills which hover o'er the land;
May every virtuous noble minded pair,
Be far remov'd from the dread din of war;
Then each warm breast where gen'rous friendships glow,
Where all the virtues of the patriot flow,
Shall taste each joy domestic life can yield,
Nor enter more the martial bloody field.

   But hark!—alas! the brave Montgomery[20] dies,
Oh, heaven forbid that such a sacrifice,
My country or my sex should yield again,
Or such rich blood pour o'er the purpled plain:
May guilty traitors satiate the grave,
But let the sword forever—spare the brave;
I weep his fall—I weep the hero slain,
And mingle sighs with his Janetta's[21] pain:
Yet while I weep, and lend the pitying sigh,
I bow the knee, and lift my soul on high,
That virtue, struggling with assiduous pains,
May free this country from despotic chains.
Long life I ask, and blessings to descend,
And crown the efforts of my constant friend;
My early wish, and evening prayer the same,
That virtue, health, and peace, and honest fame,
May hover o'er thee, till time's latest hour,
Commissionate the dread resistless power;
Then gently lay thee by thy Marcia's[22] clay,
'Till both shall rise, and on a tide of day,
Be wafted on, and skim the ambient plains
Through lucid air, and see the God who reigns.

Where cherubims in borrow'd luster shine,
We'll hand in hand our grateful homage join;
Beneath his throne, where list'ning angels stand,
With raptur'd seraphs wait his least command.

Clifford Farm, 1776

[Prologue For Lines] To A Patriotic Gentleman, Who Presented A Small Book of Bark, Requesting A Poem Might Be Written Therein, On Primitive Simplicity

On the smooth papyrus of ancient times,
Nature's bright charms, I'd paint in simple rhymes;
The bliss superior of those happy days,
When on the bark the bard inscrib'd his lays;
But, when immers'd amidst ten thousand cares,
Domestic duties, and some foreign fears;
When avocations of the social kind,
Engross the heart, and fill the busy mind,
Pegasus often does his aid refuse,
And sentiment will not assist the muse.
    Thus circumstanc'd, I'll not indulge the pride,
To pick one flower from Parnassus' side;
Much less attempt its summit to explore,
Though much I love Scamander's rippling shore;
I'll check my wish, and drop my humble wing,
Pleas'd with the laurels that for others spring:
Yet snatch a moment, when my friends command,
And point the period with a willing hand;
And if the lagging numbers slowly move,
I'll hope a pardon from the voice of love.
Critics may censure, but if candor frowns,
I'll quit the pen, and keep within the bounds,
The narrow bounds, prescrib'd to female life,
The gentle mistress, and the prudent wife:
Maternal precepts, drawn from sacred truth,
Shall warm the bosom of the list'ning youth;
While the kind mother acts her little part,

And stamps the tablet on the infant heart,
Each fervent wish, I to my country lend,
And thus subscribe, the patriot's faithful friend.

Plymouth, October, 1779

*Lines, Written On the Anniversary Of the Death of Mr. C[harles]
W[arren],[23] an Amiable and Accomplished Young Gentleman, Who
Died in St. Lucar, 1785.*

His resignation, fortitude, and piety, witnessed the excellence of that religion
which supported him with dignity and calmness, and through many months of
languid illness, reason justified to him the hope of the Christian.

Oh! lend a moment to a parent's grief,
As wounded nature asks this kind relief!—

Long have I trod o'er life's most brilliant stage,
Read its deceptive, visionary page,
Its richest hope in rapture lifted high,
I now survey with retrospective eye.

Its brightest boon, oft my transported heart
In fancy hug'd—but time's insidious dart
Check'd each fond wish—relentless swept away
As tender foliage in a frosty day,
Youth, vigor, friendship; and the ripening bloom
Of early genius, shrouds in C—s's tomb.

A youth just form'd, as if by heav'n design'd
To show the virtues in a youthful mind;
His manners gentle, and his heart sincere,
Mild his deportment—but to vice severe;
He aim'd alone at life's sublimest end,
Rose to the saint, and soften'd to the friend.
With manly grace, and piety serene,
Met the last foe with an unclouded mein.

A burning hectic's secret fire betray'd,
'Till yielding nature bow'd his languid head;
When strangers' tears were sprinkled o'er his grave,
From which no tears, nor virtue's self could save.
Kind foreign hands have dress'd his sacred urn,
While weeping friends in distant climates mourn;
No brother's foot the solemn dirge attends,
Yet innate worth commanded many friends;
The father mourns with many a heartfelt sigh,
While to the grave bends the maternal eye;
Her busy mind, too curious, would inquire,
Why was he lent—or why so soon expire?

Is it from life's best joys my heart to wean?
Or are severer pangs behind the scene?—
Let me not ask—but humbly bow my will,
And own my God, the God of mercy still;
Adore and tremble at Jehovah's name,
Whose hand, omnific, still supports my frame;
Obey each precept of his laws divine,
Nor at the darkest providence repine;
Though strip'd of all earth calls its choicest store,
Yet if upheld by all supporting power,
I'll calmly walk on to life's utmost verge,
And, undismay'd, approach the boundless marge,
Of that broad space where mighty systems roll,
And radiant glories strike the wondering soul.

Then may the youth whose soul benign on earth,
Breath'd truth and sweetness from his early birth,
Descend a moment from the realms above,
Deputed thence a messenger of love,
To aid my faith, and catch the parting breath,
And waft my soul from the cold bed of death;
Lead the glad spirit through th' ethereal sea,
And ope the gates to an eternal day.

To Mrs. Montague,[24] *Author of "Observations On the Genius and Writings of Shakespeare"*

Will Montague, whose critic pen adds praise,
Ev'n to a Shakespeare's bold exalted lays;
Who points the faults in sweet Corneille's page,
Sees all the errors of the Gallic stage—
Corrects Voltaire with a superior hand,
Or traces genius in each distant land?
Will she across the Atlantic stretch her eye,
Look o'er the main, and view the western sky;
And there Columbia's infant drama see—
Reflect that Britain taught us to be free;
Survey with candor what she can't approve;
Let local fondness yield to gen'rous love;
And, if fair truth forbids her to commend,
Then let the critic soften to the friend.

The bard of Avon justly bears the meed
Of fond applause, from Tyber to the Tweed;
Each humbler muse at distance may admire,
But none to Shakespeare's fame e'er dare aspire.
And if your isle, where he so long has charm'd,
If Britain's sons, when by his mantle warm'd,
Have soar'd in vain to reach his lofty quill,
Nature to paint with true Shakespearean skill—
A sister's hand may wrest a female pen,
From the bold outrage of imperious men.

If gentle Montague my chaplet raise,
Critics may frown, or mild good nature praise;
Secure I'll walk, and placid move along,
And heed alike their censure or their song;
I'll take my stand by fam'd Parnassus' side,
And for a moment feel a poet's pride.

Plymouth, July 10, 1790

Annis Boudinot Stockton

(July 1, 1736-February 6, 1801)

Born in Darby, Pennsylvania, to tradesman Elias Boudinot of French Huguenot descent and Catherine Williams, Annis Boudinot Stockton left few records of her childhood. Her extant manuscripts and correspondence indicate that her education, especially in the popular literature of the day, had not been neglected, but of her training or formal schooling (if she had any), nothing is known. Her first literary efforts began before her marriage to Richard Stockton, prominent New Jersey lawyer, landowner and Signer of the Declaration of Independence; some of her earliest surviving poems celebrate their courtship. Although no record has survived, the Stocktons were probably married in 1755, perhaps in spite of familial disapproval (if we give credence to Annis Stockton's aside in "The Dream. An Ode"):

> I found thee all my own in spite of those
> Whose cold unfeeling minds would bid us part.[1]

Sometime after she had moved with her new husband to the Stockton estate near Princeton, she named her home "Morven," after the imaginary land of Ossian's (James Macpherson's) Fingal. The romance of that title and the elaborately stylish gardens she cultivated at Morven share their origins with her verse: pastoral, sentimental, imitative of popular British modes.

Despite the burdens of raising six children and managing a sizeable household, Annis Stockton continued her writing throughout her lifetime, often using the pseudonym "Emelia" (sometimes spelled "Amelia"). Perhaps encouraged by her husband's admiration for her work, she occasionally published individual poems in colonial periodicals. Her first known publication, "To the Honorable Col. Peter Schuyler" (reprinted here), appeared in the *New York Mercury* for January 9, 1758, and was quickly reissued by the *New American Magazine* for January, 1758. Primarily though, Stockton restricted her audience to her friends and acquaintances. Her correspondence with poet Elizabeth Graeme Fergusson, the "Laura" of the poems included here, resulted in frequent exchanges of verse; one of Fergusson's poetic commonplace books, apparently written in 1787, was addressed to Annis Stockton.[2] A friend and fellow resident of Princeton, Esther Burr copied two of Stockton's poems into her journal in 1757.[3] George Washington, an acquaintance greatly admired by Stockton, was the frequent recipient of her odes, many of which he warmly acknowledged.

But Stockton's quiet world of family, friends and poetry was shattered by the turmoil of the Revolution. Committed patriots, the Stocktons found themselves on the military as well as the political battlefront. Morven was occupied by the British under Cornwallis during the Battle of Princeton in December, 1776. Annis Stockton had carefully secreted many state papers and the records of the American Whig Society at Princeton before the British arrived, a service for which she was later named an honorary member of the Society. No such foresight could have preserved Morven: the estate was sacked; plate and papers (including some of Stockton's early poems) were stolen. Although the family had been evacuated, Richard Stockton was taken prisoner soon after their escape. Washington's quick recapture of Princeton enabled Annis Stockton and her children to return to their ruined home. Although Richard Stockton was released in 1777, ill treatment in prison probably hastened his death in 1781. Annis Stockton remained at Morven until the marriage of her eldest son, when she left the estate to him and moved to the home of her youngest daughter, Abigail Field of Burlington County, where she died on February 6, 1801.

A prolific poet, imitative of the couplets and alternately rhymed quatrains of Pope, Young, Thomson and Gray, Annis Stockton embraced the artificial conventions and sentimentality of much contemporary English poetry, developing in her work themes of courtship, marriage, nature, friendship, patriotism, old age and grief. Uncertain about the propriety of publication for women, she hedged her apparent desire to publish her work with careful rationalization.

In a letter to her brother, Elias Boudinot, dated May 1, 1789, about one of her several odes to Washington, she explained that "if you think it will only add one sprig to the wreath the country twines to bind the brows of my hero, I will run the risk of being sneered at by those who criticize female productions of all kinds."[4] Careful to protect her reputation, yet desiring recognition for her work, Stockton may reflect her ambivalence in her rewriting practices. Her manuscripts indicate few revisions except for those poems that were subsequently published. A comparison of the manuscript "To Mr. Stockton in England, An Epistle, 1769" with "By a Lady in America to her Husband in England" (reprinted here) from the *Pennsylvania Magazine*, for example, reveals the addition of four lines and the reworking or omission of several others. Comparisons between other manuscript poems and published versions indicate similar reworking, perhaps a signal that her attention to poetry was more than the necessity to "jingle" when "the fit is on [her] ,"[5] as she had indicated to Elias Boudinot in 1781.

Because Stockton circulated her verse freely among her friends, her extant manuscripts are widely scattered. The largest collection of her verse, a commonplace book and several loose sheets, is housed in the Princeton University Library. Other manuscripts are distributed among the Historical Society of Pennsylvania, the Washington Papers at the Library of Congress, and the Esther Burr journal in Yale University's Beinecke Library. Published poems are inserted anonymously in several colonial periodicals, among them the *New-York Mercury,* the *New American Magazine*, the *Pennsylvania Magazine*, the *Columbian Magazine* and the *New Jersey Gazette*. Additionally, two of her poems are appended to the Reverend Samuel Stanhope Smith's *Funeral Sermon on the Death of the Hon. Richard Stockton . . .* (Trenton, N. J., 1781).

Stockton's role in the American Revolution has interested a variety of nineteenth and early twentieth century historians. Biographical sketches are available in Elizabeth Ellet's *The Women of the American Revolution* (New York, 1850; rpt. New York, 1969), I, 13-34, in Thomas Glenn's *Some Colonial Mansions and Those Who Lived in Them* (Philadelphia, 1899), pp. 61-93, and in Harry C. Green and Mary W. Green's *Pioneer Mothers in America*

(New York, 1912), I, 133-139. Family histories, including John Stockton's *A History of the Stockton Family* (Philadelphia, 1881), and Thomas C. Stockton's *The Stocktons of New Jersey and Other Stocktons* (Washington, D. C. 1911), pp. 40-45 (with information on Annis Stockton drawn largely from John Stockton's earlier account), provide biographical anecdotes. (Both histories cite Annis Stockton as the author of a drama, *The Triumph of Mildness*, but no manuscript or other reference to the play has surfaced in my research.) More recent discussions of Stockton, including excerpts from her verse, are available in Lyman H. Butterfield's "Morven: A Colonial Outpost of Sensibility. With Some Hitherto Unpublished Poems by Annis Boudinot Stockton," *Princeton University Library Chronicle,* 6 (November, 1944), 1-16, in his "Annis and the General: Mrs. Stockton's Poetic Eulogies of George Washington," *Princeton University Library Chronicle,* 7 (November, 1945), 19-39, and in Alfred Bill's *A House Called Morven* (Princeton, N. J., 1954), pp. 18-33.

Epistle to Mr. S[tockton] [6]

When lions in the deserts quit their prey,
And tuneful birds forsake the leafy spray;
When fish for land shall leave the wat'ry main,
And rivers to their fountains flow again;
When spring shall cease the flow'ry bud to shoot,
And autumn mild refuse the blushing fruit;
Then and then only could my heart refrain
To vent to thee its pleasures and its pain.
But even then, thou dearest of thy kind,
Thy lov'd idea would engross my mind.
Oh, could my anxious heart but once believe
What my vain thought would tempt me to receive,
When with the voice of eloquence and grace
You would persuade me I have power to please.
But, ah, so conscious of my own demerit
In contemplating thee, I lose my spirit.
Like Sheba's queen I shrink and die away
When I the treasures of thy mind survey.
But if the powers of genius ever heard
A votary's prayer, and e'er that prayer prefer'd,
On me may wit and elegance bestow
Some emanation bright, some softer glow,
Some sweet attractive that thy heart may twine,
Stronger than beauty, with each nerve of mine.
For, oh! I find on earth no charms for me
But what's connected with the thought of thee!

To the Honorable Col. Peter Schuyler [7]

Dear to each muse, and to thy country dear,
Welcome once more to breathe thy native air:
Not half so cheering is the solar ray,
To the harsh rigor of a winter's day;
Nor half so grateful fanning breezes rise,
When the hot dog star burns the summer skies,
Caesaraes' shore with acclamation rings,

And, welcome Schuyler, every shepherd sings.
See for thy brows, the laurel is prepar'd,
And justly deem'd, a patriot, thy reward;
Ev'n future ages shall enroll thy name,
In sacred annals of immortal fame.

By A Lady in America to Her Husband in England[8]

To thee whom Albion's distant shore detains,
And mirth and song accost in various strains,
I send all health—Oh hear my humble lay,
And with one smile my anxious love repay.

For me—not whispers of the rising gale,
Breath'd from the south to cheer the frozen vale;
Nor gently sloping shores where maids lave,
And shells are polish'd by the lashing wave;
Nor rivers gliding by the flow'ry meads,
Whose silver currents sparkle through the reeds;
Nor sprightly spring, nor autumn fill'd with stores;
Nor summer's coverts in sequester'd bow'rs,
Can yield a pleasure, while the dear lov'd youth,
For whom my soul preserves eternal truth,
Is absent from Cesaria's fertile plain,
And gentle echo bears my sighs in vain.

The goat shall cease the mountain's top to graze,
The fish for land shall leave their native seas,
The bees no more the flow'ry thyme shall taste,
Nor thirsty harts to limpid streams shall haste,
When I forget the sacred vow to bind,
Or put thy dear idea from my mind;
My mind—so late the seat of joy sincere,
Thy absence makes a prey to gloomy care.

My flowers—in vain they court my friendly hand,
Left in their beds the wint'ry blasts to stand;
For thee—the lily bloom'd, the garden's pride,

And blushing hyacinths with roses vied;
For thee—I tortur'd every fruit that grew,
To make the season ever smile anew:
But now untouch'd upon the boughs they die,
And lose their flavor ere they tempt my eye;
While pensive in each silent shade I mourn,
And count the tedious hours till thou return.

Emelia

On Hearing That General Warren[9] Was Killed on Bunker Hill, the 17th Of June, 1775

Ill-fated hand that sent the cruel dart
That pierc'd brave Warren's generous human heart—
That heart which, studious of his country's good,
Held up her rights and seal'd them with his blood!
Witness those fam'd resolves at Suffolk made,
Drawn by his pen, and by his counsel led.[10]
But boast not, Gage, though he unburied lies;
Thousands of heroes from his dust shall rise,
Who still shall freedom's injur'd cause maintain,
And shew to lawless kings the rights of men!
For thee, blest shade, who offer'd up thy life,
A willing victim in the glorious strife,
Thy country's tears shed o'er thy sacred urn,
Sweeter than dewdrops in a vernal morn,
In rich libations to thy memory pour,
And waft their odors to the heavenly shore.
Nature herself fresh floweret wreaths shall weave
To scatter daily on thy honor'd grave,
While all the brave and all the good shall come
To heap unfading laurels on thy tomb.

Addressed to General Washington in the Year 1777 After the Battles of Trenton and Princeton[11]

The muse affrighted at the clash of arms,
And all the dire calamities of war,
From Morven's peaceful shades has long retir'd,
And left her faithful votary to mourn
In sighs, not numbers, o'er her native land.
Dear native land, whom George's hostile slaves
Have drenched with blood, and spread destruction round.
But thou, my country's better genius come,
Heroic Washington, and aid my song!
While I the wonders of thy deeds relate,
Thy martial ardor, and thy temp'rate zeal—
Describe the fortitude, the saint like patience,
With which thou hast sustain'd the greatest load,
That ever guardian of his country bore.
What muse can sing the hardships thou endur'd;
Unarm'd, uncloth'd, undisciplin'd thy men;
In winter's cold unhospitable reign;
And press'd by numerous hosts of veteran troops,
All well appointed for the hardy fight:
When quite deserted by the tatter'd bands
Which form'd thy camp—(all but a chosen few,
Of spirits like thy own) was forced to fly
From Hudson's side before the victor foe.
Ah! who can paint the horrors of that morn,
When fame, with brazen trumpet, sounded loud
That Washington retreats! Caesarea's maids,
Old men and matrons, children at the breast,
With hair dishevell'd, and with streaming eyes,
Implore the God of battles to protect
Thee, their best hope, and now their only care.
—Oh, greatly favor'd by the God of hosts!
He gave to thee to turn the battle's fate,
And shew his power to potentates below:
While lines of Hessian captive slaves announce
Thy triumph, and their haughty lord's disgrace.
—Not good Aeneas who his father bore,
And all his household gods from ruin'd Troy,
Was more the founder of the Latian realm,
Than thou the basis of this mighty fabric,

Now rising to my view, of arms, of arts,
The seat of glory in the western world.
—For thee awaits the patriot's shining crown;
The laurel blooms in blest elysian groves,
That twin'd by angel hands shall grace thy brow.
A vacant seat among the ancient heroes,
Of purple, amaranth and fragrant myrtle
Awaits for thee—high rais'd above the rest,
By Cato, Sydney, and the sacred shades
Of bright illustrious line, from Greece and Rome,
Gallic, American or British shores,
And long to hail thee welcome to the bower.
—Late may they lead thee to the blest abode,
And may'st thou meet the plaudit of thy God;
While future ages shall enroll thy name
In sacred annals of immortal fame.

                                        Emelia

To Laura[1][2]

Permit a sister muse to soar
To heights she never tried before,
And then look up to thee;

For sure each female virtue join'd,
Conspire to make thy lovely mind
The seat of harmony.

Thy fame has reach'd the calm retreat,
Where I secluded from the great,
Have leisure for my lays;

It rais'd ambition in my breast,
Not such as envious souls possess,
Who hate another's praise.

But that which makes me strive to gain,
And ever grateful to retain,
    Thy friendship as a prize;

For friendship soars above low rules,
The formal fetters of the schools
    She wisely can despise;

So may fair Laura kindly condescend,
And to her bosom take another friend.

To the Same

And does my Laura kindly condescend,
And will she deign to be Emelia's friend?
Will she accept the humble wreath I twine,
Nor be dishonor'd by such praise as mine?

Transcendent goodness, what can I repay,
The favor far exceeds my highest lay:
On you Appolo shines with brightest beam,
Which makes your praise alone an equal theme
For numbers such as yours inspir'd by him.

An Extempore Ode in a Sleepless Night by a Lady Attending on Her Husband in a Long and Painful Illness[13]

I
Sleep, balmy sleep, has clos'd the eyes of all
But me! ah me! no respite can I gain;
Though darkness reigns o'er the terrestrial ball,
Not one soft slumber cheats this vital pain.

II
All day in secret sighs I've pour'd my soul,
My downy pillow, us'd to scenes of grief,

Beholds me now in floods of sorrow roll,
Without the power to yield his pains relief:

III

While through the silence of this gloomy night,
My aching heart reverb'rates every groan;
And watching by that glimmering taper's light,
I make each sigh, each mortal pang my own.

IV

But why should I implore sleep's friendly aid?
O'er me, her poppies shed, no ease impart;
But dreams of dear departing joys invade,
And rack with fears my sad prophetic heart.

V

But vain is prophecy when death's approach,
Through years of pain, has sap'd a dearer life,
And makes me, coward like, myself reproach,
That e'er I knew the tender name of wife.

VI

Oh! could I take the fate to him assign'd!
And leave the helpless family their head!
How pleas'd, how peaceful, to my lot resign'd,
I'd quit the nurse's station for the bed.

VII

O death! thou canker-worm of human joy!
Thou cruel foe to sweet domestic peace!
He soon shall come, who shall thy shafts destroy;
And cause thy dreadful ravages to cease.

VIII

Yes, the Redeemer comes to wipe the tears,
The briny tears, from every weeping eye.
And death and sin, and doubts, and gloomy fears,
Shall all be lost in endless victory.

Morven, December 3rd, 1780

An Elegy Sacred to the Memory of Richard Stockton, Esqr.[14]

Why does the sun in usual splendor rise
To pain, with hated light, my aching eyes?
Let sable clouds enshroud his shining face,
And murmuring winds re-echo my distress;
Be Nature's beauty with sad glooms o'er spread,
To mourn my Lucius[15] number'd with the dead.
   Mute is that tongue which listening senates charm'd.
Cold is that breast which every virtue warm'd.
Drop fast my tears, and mitigate my woe:
Unlock your springs, and never cease to flow:
For worth like his demands this heart-felt grief,
And drops like these can only yield relief.
   O! greatly honor'd in the lists of fame!
He dignified the judge's, statesman's name!
How ably he discharg'd each public trust,
In counsel firm, in executing just,
Can best be utter'd by his country's voice,
Whose approbation justified their choice.
And now their grateful tears shed round his hearse,
A nobler tribute yield, than loftiest verse.
   But ah! lamented shade! thy private life
(Thy weeping children, thy afflicted wife
Can testify) was mark'd with every grace
That e'er illumin'd or adorn'd the place
Of husband, father, brother, master, friend,
And swell those sorrows now which ne'er shall end.
   Can we forget how patiently he bore
The various conflicts of the trying hour;
While meekness, faith, and piety refin'd,
And steadfast hope rais'd his exalted mind
Above the sufferings of this mortal state,
And help'd his soul in smiles to meet her fate?
   O fatal hour! severely felt by me—
The last of earthly joy my eyes shall see!
The friend, the lover, every tender name
Torn from my heart, the deepest anguish claim.
Drop fast my tears, and mitigate my woe;
Unlock your springs, and never cease to flow:
For worth like his demands this heart-felt grief,
And drops like these can only yield relief.

To me in vain shall cheerful spring return,
And tuneful birds salute the purple morn.
Autumn in vain present me all her stores;
Or summer court me with her fragrant bowers—
Those fragrant bowers were planted by his hand!
And now neglected and unprun'd must stand.

Ye stately elms and lofty cedars mourn!
Slow through your avenues you saw him borne,
The friend who rear'd you, never to return.

Ye muses! whom he lov'd and cherish'd too,
Bring from your groves the cypress and the yew,
Deck, with unfading wreaths, his sacred tomb,
And scatter roses of immortal bloom.

Goddess of sorrow! tune each mournful air;
Let all things pay the tributary tear;
For worth like his demands this heart-felt grief,
And tears alone can yield a sad relief.

Morven, March 9th, 1781

Elegy on the Destruction of the Trees By the Icicles, Sunday and Monday of February the 17th and 18th, 1788

Ah! see them weep! The guardians of the trees,
Dryads and hamadryads, flock around;
Their deep-toned sighs increase the hollow breeze,
And their green hair lies scatter'd on the ground.

Ah! what avails to them this sight sublime!
Though Nature deck'd in crystal looks more gay
Than genial Spring in her soft verdant prime,
Each sprig more dazzling than the new-born day!

Though Iris paints the fields in tints which glow
More variegated than the diamond mine,
Where the bright Queen of Ocean weaves her bow,
And on the clouds suspends the seal divine!

While squadrons of hoar frost from Zembla's cave,
Encrusting all their tender bodies o'er,
Tearing their limbs, their helpless trunks they leave
Expos'd and naked to the tempest's roar!

"Come, Flora, weep with us," the dryads cry,
"For you must too this awful fate deplore;
"Entomb'd in ice our trees in ruins lie,
"Nor their hack'd forms can gentle Spring restore.

"Say, what will shade you when fierce Leo reigns?
"Or where can Pan and Silvius safe retire
"When thirsty Sirius drinks the dewy plains,
"And Phoebus' fiery steeds proclaim his ire?

"Then did our cool recess asylum yield,
"To all the rural powers a sweet retreat;
"And when the ploughman drove his team afield,
"We gave him shelter from the raging heat."

                                        Emelia

Elizabeth Graeme Fergusson

(February 3, 1737-February 23, 1801)

Prolific poet, translator, diarist and correspondent, Elizabeth Graeme Fergusson became a well-known figure in pre-Revolutionary Pennsylvania's literary coterie. Born in 1737 in Philadelphia to Ann Diggs and Dr. Thomas Graeme, prominent local physician, member of the Provincial Council and justice of the supreme court of Pennsylvania, she was carefully educated at home. Two years after her birth, the Graemes moved to a country estate, later named Graeme Park, near Philadelphia, where she spent much of the rest of her life. As a young woman, perhaps in 1757, Elizabeth Graeme became engaged to William Franklin, son of Benjamin Franklin, a relationship that was abruptly terminated by William two years later during a prolonged visit to England. Never in robust health, Fergusson apparently went into a depression which she relieved by translating the twenty-four books of Fénelon's *Télémaque* into English heroic verse (a translation that she reworked some twenty years later, hoping for publication which never came). Sent to England for her health in 1764, she kept a journal that brought her a local reputation as a writer on her return to Pennsylvania after her mother's death in 1765. Assuming Ann Graeme's role as mistress of Graeme Park, Fergussen raised two of her dead sister's children, John and Anna Young (herself a poet) and established a weekly literary salon frequented by many of Philadelphia's most prominent citizens, among them William Smith, provost of the College of Philadelphia, and Benjamin Rush.

On April 21, 1772, Elizabeth Graeme married Henry Hugh Fergusson (also Ferguson), ten years her junior. Apparently the wedding was held secretly, but the Fergussons moved into Graeme Park after the death of Thomas Graeme that same year. The marriage seems to have been an unfortunate one. Writing to a Mrs. Campbell (otherwise unidentified) on May 9, 1779, Fergusson noted that "of the seven years that I have been married, my husband has lived but two years and a few months with me."[1] Part of their estrangement almost certainly resulted from the clash of their politics: while moderately whiggish Elizabeth Fergusson hoped for a compromise to end the Revolution, her husband became an ardent Tory, proscribed by the colonies in 1778, with all his property (including Graeme Park) subject to confiscation. Elizabeth Fergusson's sympathies were also called into question as a result of her involvement (through her husband) as a go-between for offers from the British to prominent patriot leaders. In October, 1777, she carried a message urging colonial surrender from the Rev. Jacob Duché of Philadelphia to George Washington, who reported the incident to the Continental Congress. Then in June, 1778, she brought an offer for a bribe from George Johnstone, a member of the British peace commission, to Joseph Reed, delegate to the Continental Congress and aid to Washington; that proposal also became public. Though never herself accused of treason, only lengthy litigation and the intervention of prominent friends prevented the confiscation of Graeme Park; Fergusson's subsequent financial difficulties forced the sale of her estate in 1791. She died at a friend's house near Graeme Park in 1801, attended by Benjamin Rush.

At the center of Philadelphia's literary world for a time, Fergusson counted among her friends and correspondents such poets as Nathaniel Evans, Hannah Griffitts (see pages 55-69), Francis Hopkinson, Annis Stockton (see pages 87-100), and niece Anna Young Smith (see pages 169-178). She circulated her manuscripts among these friends (and others) and occasionally published her work in local periodicals, usually under the pseudonym "Laura." Composing Biblical paraphrases, especially of the Psalms, satires, odes, translations and a variety of occasional verse, Fergusson treated themes of religion, grief, marriage, friendship, education and politics. Strongly influenced by English heroic verse, she seldom strayed from conventional structures, diction or images, but despite those self-imposed restrictions, much of her personal experience found its way into her verse. Conflicting loyalties and the difficulties of marriage, for example, are explored in her verse of the Revolutionary period. Such descriptive titles as "An Advertisement Written One Evening When Mr. F[ergusso]n Went to Stay a Day in the City and Passed a

Week and the Writer Did Not Know Where He Was, November, 1774" and "Il Pensoroso: or the Deserted Wife," written from 1780 to 1782 (both too lengthy for inclusion here), mark poems that must have been intended only for herself. A more public treatment of the same theme is available in her lines "On a Beautiful Damask Rose; Emblematical of Love and Wedlock," which provides a cryptic comment on marriage:

> A transient, rich, and balmy sweet
> Is in thy fragrance found;
> But soon the flow'r and scent retreat—
> Thorns left alone to wound.

Although this poem was published by "Laura" in the *Columbian Magazine* for May, 1789, most of her verse remains in manuscript.

An indefatigable writer, Elizabeth Graeme Fergusson left several handwritten volumes of material from which her biography can be reconstructed. Most of her manuscripts, including extant segments of *Telemachus*, paraphrases of the Psalms, other poetry and her correspondence, are located in the Historical Society of Pennsylvania. The Princeton University Library has two manuscript poems, the University of Pennsylvania a single poem; the Dickinson College Library has a Fergusson commonplace book of verse on deposit, and at least one other commonplace book is still in private hands. Fergusson's publications include a verse dialogue with Nathaniel Evans, part of his *Poems on Several Occasions* (Philadelphia, 1772), pp. 145-160, and individual pieces appearing sporadically in the *Pennsylvania Magazine* and the *Columbian Magazine*. (Mary Maples Dunn notes that some Fergusson poems were printed in the *American Magazine and Monthly Chronicle* but I have been unable to locate them.) Several nineteenth-century anthologists printed selections from her works, among them Rufus W. Griswold, ed., *The Female Poets of America* (Philadelphia, 1849), pp. 24-27, and Evert A. Duyckinck and George L. Duyckinck, eds., *The Cyclopaedia of American Literature* (New York, 1855), I, 233-237. Early biographical sketches are available in the anonymous "Account of the Life and Character of Mrs. Elizabeth Ferguson," *Port Folio*, new series, 1 (June, 1809), 520-527, Samuel Knapp's *Female Biography*

(Philadelphia, 1836), pp. 215-222, and Elizabeth Ellet's *The Women of the American Revolution* (New York, 1848), I, 219-232. Brief sketches of Fergusson's literary activities are developed in Anne Wharton's *Salons Colonial and Republican* (Philadelphia, 1900), pp. 13-24, Katherine Jackson's *Outlines of the Literary History of Colonial Pennsylvania* (Lancaster, Pa., 1906), pp. 96-101, and Ellis P. Oberholtzer's *The Literary History of Philadelphia* (Philadelphia, 1906), pp. 76-83. Some of Fergusson's correspondence and other papers relating to those incidents for which she was suspected of treason during the Revolution are printed in William Reed's *Life and Correspondence of Joseph Reed* (Philadelphia, 1847), I, 381-398. Simon Gratz's "Material for a Biography of Mrs. Elizabeth Fergusson née Graeme," *Pennsylvania Magazine of History and Biography*, 39 (1915), 257-321, 385-409; 41 (1917), 385-398, provides a generous sampling of other manuscript correspondence. The most useful recent accounts are those of Carl and Jessica Bridenbaugh, *Rebels and Gentlemen* (New York, 1942), pp. 111-113, and Mary Maples Dunn, "Elizabeth Graeme Ferguson," *Notable American Women*, eds. Edward T. James, Janet Wilson James and Paul S. Boyer (Cambridge, Mass., 1971), I, 610-611.

A Parody on the Foregoing Lines [Out of Mr. Pope's Eloise to Abelard] [2]

> How happy is the country parson's lot?
> Forgetting bishops, as by them forgot;
> Tranquil of spirit, with an easy mind,
> To all his vestry's votes he sits resign'd:
> Of manners gentle, and of temper even,
> He jogs his flocks, with easy pace, to heaven.
> In Greek and Latin, pious books he keeps;
> And, while his clerk sings psalms, he—soundly sleeps.
> His garden fronts the sun's sweet orient beams,
> And fat church-wardens prompt his golden dreams;
> The earliest fruit, in his fair orchard, blooms;
> And cleanly pipes pour out tobacco's fumes.
> From rustic bridegroom oft he takes the ring;
> And hears the milk-maid plaintive ballads sing.
> Back-gammon cheats whole winter nights away,
> And Pilgrim's Progress helps a rainy day.

An Ode Written on the Birthday of Mr. H[enry] F[e]r[gusson] By His Wife When They Had Been Married Two Years, He Aged 26 Years, March 12, 1774

> Birth day odes to lords and kings,
> Oft are strain'd and stupid things!
> Poet laureate's golden lays,
> Fulsome hireling's hackney'd praise!
>
> Yet that heart which glows sincere,
> Sure may hail the passing year,
> Which reminds of the birth
> Of a friend of genuine worth,
>
> A friend, that is too cool a name
> For the tender ardent flame
> Which I feel for Henry's bliss,
> All that woman's heart can wish.

What shall I say: the pen is dull
And languid though the heart is full?
Expression is in feeling lost,
For shallow strains oft babble most.

And selfish too I find is all
My love I would to Henry call;
For sure I rise but in the scale,
One prosperous wind expands each sail.

With him I sink, with him ascend,
My little bark doth his attend!
As through the sham of life we glide,
Upon one ebb or flowing tide.

Then as below we share one fate,
May death at once our souls translate,
Descend one moment to the tomb,
And fall at once near mercy's throne;

Be veil'd at once our [illegible] there,
That thought shall shield us from despair,
And blunt the sting which death prepares
For man and all his short liv'd heirs.

But till that serious hour is come near,
Let us dispell each gloomy fear;
Support and comfort each shall prove,
Till earthly yield to Heavenly love.

Gr[aeme] Park

Upon the Discovery of the Planet By Mr. Herschel of Bath and By Him Nam'd the Georgium Sidus in Honor of his Britannic Majesty[3]

Whether the optics piercing eyes
Have introduc'd to view,
A distant planet of the skies,
Bright, wonderful, and new?

Or whether we are nearer thrown[4]
To the grand fount of light,
And from that source each mist is flown
That wrapt the star in night?

Too deep this point, a female pen
Dare not such heights explore;
The subject's left to learned men,
Of philosophic lore!

A star is found, that's clear, and hail'd
With Britain's monarch's name:
If his terrestrial glory's fail'd,
The Heavens enroll his fame.

On the Death of Leopold, Hereditary Prince of Brunswick, Who was Drowned in the Oder, April 17, 1785, in Attempting to Save Some Children Whose Mother had Left Them on the Banks of that River[5]

When Caesar's bark by furious storms was driven,
The world's fam'd hero seem'd the care of heaven;
A crown allur'd, or death appear'd in view,
No track but one he dauntless could pursue:
But Brunswick, eager, stem'd the boist'rous wave
One feeble, helpless cottage-race to save;
A little brood a mother left behind,
Did in his breast maternal feelings find.
"I am but man as they," he nobly cried,
Then launch'd advent'rous in the rushing tide:
Thus angel-like he spake, and God-like died.[6]

Montgomery County, July 5, 1785   Laura

Nathan's Parable, Paraphrased From the 12th Chapter of the 2d Samuel[7]

From Sion's God a sacred mission went;
To Israel's king was holy Nathan sent:
The pious seer, the solemn mandate heard,
Obey'd the summons, and the word rever'd:
Swift to Jerusalem the prophet flew,
And stood before the chosen monarch's view.

"I come," he cries, "strict justice to demand,
And ask decision at thy royal hand:
Within one city's small enclosed round,
Two men wide differing in estates were found.
Rich was the one in every kind of good
Which life can boast of elegance and food:
Poor was the other, but with all content,
As through life's vale with cheerful steps he went:

Much flocks and herds adorn'd the great man's lot,
His grazing cattle low'd on ev'ry spot:
One little ewe lamb was the poor man's joy,
He let no ill the harmless thing annoy;
Before his hearth, the favor'd pet was rear'd,
And as his children to his sight endear'd:
With him she fed; and drank from out his cup,
And with his infants did each evening sup;
Within his bosom laid her snowy fleece,
And calmly slept in innocence and peace;
As his young daughter to his soul was dear,
Like his own Rachel was this ewe-lamb near.

"A weary traveller came along that way,
And with the rich man sought a night to stay;
Of his fat flocks and numerous herds none died,
No social supper did the host provide:
Churlish he grudg'd the traveller his meat,
Nor from his stalls the hungry guest would treat:
With haste he did the poor man's favorite slay;
By force he dragg'd the bleating ewe away;
Reeking he tore it with remorseless breast,
And for their supper the fond darling drest."

Then Judah's monarch glow'd with vengeful ire,
And from his glance flash'd keen resentment's fire.
To holy Nathan he the word return'd,
(While his rais'd bosom with emotion burn'd)
"As the Lord lives and rules supreme on high,
Who did this deed I swear shall surely die!
There shall the choicest of his herds be sent,
In four-fold number to the poor man's tent;
Because no pity in his soul was found,
Be his name level'd with the lowly ground."

The prophet then in solemn tone began:
"David," he says, " 'Tis thou that art the man.
All Israel's wealth before its monarch lay,
When the fair Bathsheba thou stol'st away;
She was the ewe lamb of Uriah's heart,
And thou fulfil'st the rich man's cruel part."

Laura

On a Beautiful Damask Rose, Emblematical of Love and Wedlock[8]

Queen of the garden! O how oft
    Thy praises have been sung!
In numbers eloquent and soft,
    To please the fair and young.

O! sure thou wast the first form'd flow'r
    Which hail'd young Eden's grove,
The darling of the nuptial bow'r,
    And emblem fit for love.

A transient, rich, and balmy sweet
    Is in thy fragrance found;
But soon the flow'r and scent retreat—
    Thorns left alone to wound.

Laura

On the Mind's Being Engrossed By One Subject[9]

When one fond object occupies the mind,
In nature's scenes we still that object find;
And trees, and meads, and sweetly purling rill,
By us made mirrors with ingenious skill,
Reflect the constant subject of our thought;
We view that image in their substance wrought.
The common peasant treads the fresh turn'd soil,
And hopes of future crops his steps beguiles.
The nat'ralist observes each simple's use,
Where lodg'd the healthy, where the baneful juice.
The lover sees his mistress all around
And her sweet voice in vocal birds is found;
He views the brilliant glories of the skies,
But to remind him of her sparkling eyes.
Th' alchemist still anxious seeks the gold,
For this he pierces every cavern's fold:
Trembling to try the magic hazel's pow'r,
Which points attractive to the darling show'r.
While pious Hervey in each plant and tree
Can nought but God and his redeemer see.
When zephyrs play, or when fierce Boreas roars,
The merchant only for his bark implores.
The beau and belle attentive dread the sky,
Lest angry clouds the sprightly scene deny.
But if a coach's procur'd, torrents may pour,
And winds, and tempests, shattered fleets devour.
Thus over all, self-love presides supreme,
It cheers the morn, and gives the ev'ning dream.
Though oft we change through life's swift gliding stage,
And seek fresh objects at each varying age,
Here we are constant, faithful to one cause,
Our own indulgence as a center draws.
That faithful inmate makes our breast its home,
From the soft cradle, to the silent tomb.

Montgomery

*Lines Written on Reading Dr. More's Journal in France, and the
Massacre of the Priests in Prison Previous to their Trial at Orleans*[10]

> Down with the Bastile, 'tis too small a place,
> For we'll imprison half the Gallic race:
> For since the people sovereign rule the land,
> And deal forth justice with unerring hand,
> Be these first slaughter'd that's most fit to die,
> Belov'd and loving the pure Deity;
> Let fett'red priests immediate vengeance feel,
> And in their hallow'd bosoms sheath our steel.

July 4, 1794   Laura

Martha Brewster

(fl. 1741-1757)

All we know of Martha Wadsworth Brewster of Lebanon, Connecticut, is what she included in her *Poems on Divers Subjects* (1757). Her acrostic verses name her family, husband Oliver and children Ruby and Wadsworth, but tell little else about them than her concern for their spiritual development and good conduct. Brewster's *Poems* (as the full title suggests) encompass a broad range of themes and forms: her more than 1100 lines include letters, farewells to friends who are moving, epithalamiums, eulogies, scriptural paraphrases, a love poem, a quaternion, a dream (in prose), meditations, and other occasional pieces, although religious and family themes predominate. Among colonial women poets, only Anne Bradstreet (whose work Brewster may have known) attempted a similarly broad range of materials in her verse.

Apparently some of Brewster's readers were sufficiently impressed by her work to doubt its authenticity. The heading to her paraphrase of II Chronicles 6:16-18 notes that "it being falsely reported that the author borrowed her poetry from Watts and others, the following scripture was presented to her to translate into verse in a few minutes extempore as a vindication from that aspersion, which was accordingly performed. . . ."[1] Such skepticism indicates the anomaly of a woman poet in rural Connecticut. Though she was probably able to establish herself as a poet to the satisfaction of her neighbors, Brewster approached publication cautiously. Like many other colonial women writers, she prefaced her *Poems* with an appeal to the reader that marks her consciousness of herself as a woman poet, a "novelty":

> But since some have a gust for novelty,
> I here presume upon your clemency,
> For rare it is to see a female bard,

Or that my sex in print have e'er appear'd:
Let me improve my talent though but small,
And thus it humbly wait upon you shall.[2]

No recorded response to Brewster's slim volume attests to its reception, but the poems did appear in two editions, in New London, Connecticut (1757) and in Boston (1758), perhaps evidence of at least a local audience. Secondary references are brief and few: Kenneth Silverman's *Colonial American Poetry* (New York, 1968), p. 42, notes in passing that Brewster "consciously recaptured" Bradstreet's tone; Emily Stipes Watts' *The Poetry of American Women from 1632 to 1945* (Austin, Texas, 1977), pp. 25-27, provides an introductory survey.

From *An Essay on the Four Ages of Man, Resembling the Four
Seasons of the Year*

> The winter season shall an emblem be,
> The leaves are shed, the fruits all housed be;
> The vivid blood is chil'd in ev'ry vein,
> But still the root doth life and growth retain;
> A snowy robe adorns instead of hairs,
> And underneath a wither'd face appears;
> And thus she lies benumb'd nor strives to rise,
> 'Till the benign influence of the skies
> Destroys her foe, and gently calls her forth
> In brighter beauty and with larger growth:
> So may the Sun of Righteousness arise,
> And the Celestial Dove descend the skies,
> And quicken ev'ry age of mortal dust,
> And make this state more glorious than the first,
> Nor let the aged sinner die accurs'd;
> Makes us to grow 'till we advance so far,
> To raise our feet up high beyond the stars;
> There wholesome fruit and living water flows,
> There we may bathe, and take a sweet repose.

*A Farewell to Some of My Christian Friends at Goshen, in Lebanon.
April 5th, 1745*

> Dear friends, through grace we've died and liv'd,
> 　Mourn'd and rejoic'd together,
> Hence may we live alone to God,
> 　And reign with Him for ever.
>
> Come view that pure electing love,
> 　Which never did begin;
> Which in a way of justice wrought,
> 　And triumphs over sin.
>
> His holy, pure and piercing eyes,
> 　In one eternal view,

Sees all past, present, and to come,
    Which unto us are new.

There is a wheel within a wheel,
    Beyond what we descry;
He'll make us feel sin's deadly wound,
    And then His blood apply.

He makes His glories shine around,
    The world doth disappear;
Anon the veil doth interpose,
    And then we mourners are.

He fitteth instruments for use,
    By which He feeds us rare,
We feast with joy at length adore,
    Those that the citterns are.

He shews 'tis not in them, but Him,
    Alone our refuge lies;
We own with praise, at length we turn,
    And do the means despise.

His tender mercies still pursues,
    And bids us have our eye
On Him through them, and use them still,
    Which through him yield supply.

The operations of His hand,
    O! may we much regard,
Though what He doth we know not now,
    We shall know afterward.

Then let us not with Jonah fret,
    Although our gourds decay:
And may we not with Jacob grieve,
    When Joseph's sent away;

God meant it all for good; and thus
    To us He often shows
A Sampson's riddle; so our thorns
    May bear the sweetest rose.

'Till Heaven be poor they shall have store,
    Whom God hath made his choice,
They on Him rest, are in Him blest,
    And ever shall rejoice.

O! Sojourn not in Mesheck then,
    A land of toil and woe,
Nor in the tents of Kedar dwell,
    'Tis dark and dang'rous too.

Dear friends, the life is more than meat,
    The soul excels the clay;
O labor then for gospel food,
    Which never shall decay.

Don't hoard up treasure for your babes,
    That moth and rust defile,
But plant them where the gospel dews
    Doth most enrich the soil.

And finally my dearest friends,
    Let's pray for Zion's peace,
Although her walls are broken down,
    The Lord will her increase.

Jehovah as a wall of fire
    Shall be to her also;
Salvation shall for bulwarks be,
    Her [cup?] shall over flow.

Lord humble each of us that we
    At thy dear feet may lie,
O Jesus! strengthen what remains,
    That ready is to die.

And guide us safely by thine eye,
    That we may never slide,
For thou thy self, unto thy self,
    Must be our only guide.

A Funeral Poem, on the Death of the Reverend Isaac Watts, D. D.

O help! Eternal instant help invoke,
Ye Churches, least this heavy awful stroke
Prove insupportable to us indeed,
Which makes our souls in tenderest passions bleed.
Great Watts is set, that bright and glorious star,
Which oft conducted strangers from a-far
To come by faith and view their sav'or's se[at] ,
And pay their humble tribute at his feet.
Ye Heaven born souls, whom his seraphic lays
Has oft inspir'd to shout your Maker's praise.
Those sacred relics still your minds engage,
They shall survive, to bless from age to age.
No celebrated mortal knew thy worth.
No skill but such as thine, can set it forth:
And where can that be found but where thou art,
And Gabriel now must act that friendly part.
And all the golden harps have full employ,
To sing him welcome, and to magnify,
Wisdom and grace that caus'd a lump of clay
T' enclose a star of so divine array.
To write his character I never can,
It so exceeds my Muse's narrow plan.
Nor will the noblest bard's [hyperboles?]
Speak but his due, and that shall well suffice.
But since in mourning all do claim a right,
Permit my feeble Muse to bring her mite.
A humble tribute at the doctor's hearse,
Who was the Phoenix of the universe.
For why his absence gives so keen a wound,
Absent for ever, O that dreadful sound!
Out of his spicy ashes let one rise
To bless our church, our nation and allies.
But could his righteous soul no more endure?
Our foolish vanities are so impure.
Spend no more precious time to do us good?
Stay froward Muse, instruction was his food:
Nay, but his sublime soul, that oft did rise,
On wings of faith, above the upper skies;
Did burst at length the brittle cords of life
For life immortal, free from sin and strife.

The pearly gates flew open to receive
The Heavenly kinsman; but did we conceive
The hallalujahs he doth instant raise,
And rivals seraphs in ascribing praise,
Our hearts would melt in flames of sacred fire,
And Christ, and Grace would be our whole desire.
The nimble cherubs that patrol the sky
Oft met him soaring to the realms on high,
Waiting his exit from earth's mean employ,
No sooner's sign'd but with ecstatic joy
They clap their wings, and set each harp to sound,
Making the vast of Heav'n to echo round;
O Watts's vacant mansion will be fill'd,
What praise to God will this great songster yield?
His music while below, all ears did wound,
How will it then in these bright orbs resound?
Then swift as light'ning they his soul convoy,
Like lackeys waiting 'til with perfect joy
His now enlarg'd capacity is crown'd,
The least conceit of which, our senses drown.
Nor will I mention painted glories here,
Elysian fields have no resemblance there.
But here the Summum-Bonum of his bliss,
He's like his Lord, and sees him as he is.
When he expir'd might I have been his heir,
I would have beg'd Urania for my share.
But all in vain, his Music's out of reach,
But still his works, yea e'en his ashes preach.

> His Anagram
> Isaac Watts
> Was is at act.

Say who below has acted better?
Or who above a greater debtor?

A Letter to My Daughter Ruby Bliss

My only daughter dear, my heart's delight,
Since cruel distance keeps thee from my sight
I breathe forth sighs into the empty air,
My best desires pursue thee ev'ry where.
My ardent love can reach thee where thou art,
And mingle with thy sympathizing heart.
My breast a magazine of tend'rest passions,
Pregnant with grief, seeks vent in sev'ral fashions:
Sometimes the optic fountains up do break,
And liquid salts do deluge o'er my cheek:
Each filial due performance strikes my heart,
And mournful pleasure shoots through ev'ry p[art?] ;
[Illegible] fancies o'er the mind still float,
Sometimes your joys, and prosp'rous state I dote,
But grim distrust soon rifles my repose,
Presents you sick, bereav'd and full of woes:
O absence! absence! sharper than a thorn,
The tender scion from the stock is torn:
But sure my fond affections wildly rove,
My nobler pow'rs in higher orbs should move.
O glorious Landlord! Thou hast pruned me,
Then grant me grace, to bear much fruit to Thee.
My pleasant branch, which thou hast grafted, Lord,
Make her the charge of angels, and afford
Thy special benediction while alive,
Then to some glorious mansion her receive:
But while she's station'd here, let her obtain
Such precious fruit as shall embalm her name:
Let bud, and branch, and tree securely stand,
Drest by the culture of thy gracious hand:
Planted by purling streams, and crystal founts,
In gospel soil, and circle-ed about,
With a bright rainbow of the promises,
A sure defence and costly purchas'd peace.
Cheer up my drooping heart, shake off thy woes,
Though cruel distance means to interpose.
There is a place where we may daily meet,
With joint request, before the Mercy Seat;
In hopes of which your tender mother rests,
Until your countenance her eyes shall bless.

An Acrostic For My Husband

Oh! may propitious Heaven still extend
Lasting delights, to solace thee my friend:
Injoying ev'ry lawful sweet below,
Viewing by faith, the fountain whence they flow,
Erected be his throne, within thy heart,
Rule and replenish there, thy ev'ry part.

Blest with a vine, whose love and loyalty,
Richer than choicest wine her progeny,
Each like an olive branch adorn thy house,
With the fair transcript of thy loving spouse:
Soft are the charms inviolable bands
Twine round the lover's heart, raptur'd he stands:
Eternal King that hast these powers giv'n,
Renew our love to Thee, and love us up to Heaven.

Judith Sargent Murray

(May 1, 1751-July 6, 1820)

An early feminist, publicly arguing for equitable legal and educational opportunities for women, Judith Sargent Murray was born in 1751 in Gloucester, Massachusetts, to Winthrop and Judith (Saunders) Sargent, a prominent shipowning merchant family. She obtained an unusually extensive education by studying with her brother Winthrop as he prepared for Harvard College. After marrying sea captain and trader John Stevens on October 3, 1769, she moved with him to a mansion now known as the Sargent-Murray-Gilman-Hough House, probably built for the young couple by Winthrop Sargent. The exact beginnings of Judith Sargent's writing career are unknown, but the family records mention her poetry as a young woman with some satisfaction. The earliest dated piece still extant is her prose "Reflections in the manner of Hervey—occasioned by the death of an Infant Sister," written in October, 1775, though it wasn't published until 1794.[1] It was during this period in her first marriage that Judith Sargent Stevens and the rest of the Sargent family were converted to the liberal theology of Universalism by the itinerant minister John Murray, who so welcomed their support that he elected to use Gloucester as his permanent base.

Financial reverses forced John Stevens to flee the country in 1786 to avoid debtor's prison; he died shortly thereafter in the West Indies. Continuing her involvement with the Universalist movement, Judith Sargent Stevens apparently accepted the preacher with the doctrine: she married John Murray in October, 1788. Encouraged by her husband to continue the writing she began long before their marriage, Murray combined authorship with the raising of their daughter, Julia Maria, born in 1791 (a son George, born in 1789, died shortly after birth).

By 1793, the Murrays had moved to Boston in support of Universalist activities there. Financial difficulties and John Murray's failing health, culminating in a paralyzing stroke in 1809, meant years of struggle for Murray as she attempted to supplement their income with her writing. Their daughter married Adam Louis Binga-mon, heir to a wealthy Mississippi Territory planter, in 1812. Thus relieved of economic hardship, Murray was able to devote much of her time as she attended her husband to preparing his *Letters and Sketches of Sermons* (3 volumes, 1812-1813) and to finishing his autobiography, *Records of the Life of the Rev. John Murray* (1816). After John Murray's death in 1815 and the posthumous publication of his autobiography, Judith Murray moved to Natchez, Mississippi, to live with her daughter; she died there in 1820, leaving many of the manuscripts by which she had hoped to "descend with celebrity to posterity" at the mercy of mildew.

Even as a young woman, Murray had been (in the words of a persona) "seized with a violent desire to become a writer."

> I would be Cesar, or I would be nothing. The smoothness of Addison's page, the purity, strength and correctness of Swift, the magic numbers of Pope—these must all veil to me. The Homers and Vergils of antiquity, I would rival; and, audacious as I am, from the Philenias[2] of the present age, I would arrogantly snatch the bays.[3]

Admitting that she had "pretentions originating perhaps in arro-gance,"[4] she nevertheless addressed her readers with an uncommon candor: "I would be distinguished and respected by my contempor-aries; I would be continued in grateful remembrance when I make my exit; and I would descend with celebrity to posterity."[5] Such grand ambitions led Judith Sargent Murray through a writing career remarkable for its eclecticism of theme and genre.

While Murray's earliest work was largely poetry, the lively issues of the Revolution soon encouraged her to branch into prose, most of her essays prefaced by a poem on a related theme. Even her early prose revealed her unorthodox applications of revolutionary rhetoric. The patriot battle cries of liberty and equality, for example, were adapted to feminist ends in her "Equality of the Sexes," written in 1779 but not printed until 1790. Appearing in the *Gentleman and Lady's Town and Country Magazine* for October, 1784, "Desultory Thoughts upon the Utility of Encouraging a Degree of Self-Complacency, Especially in Female Bosoms" explored her theories regarding women's education: not only should women be educated as companions for men and instructors of young children, but they should also be prepared for economic self-sufficiency. Noting that American women "only contend for the capability for the female mind to become possessed of any attainment within the reach of masculine exertion,"[6] Murray was finally convinced that the United States was working toward "improving on the opinions of a Wollstonecraft."[7] "I may be accused of enthusiasm," she wrote in 1798, "but such is my confidence in the sex, that I expect to see our young women forming a new era in female history."[8]

Ambitious, optimistic, forceful, Judith Sargent Murray turned the energy of her pen to other issues as well. Though her devout Universalism, for example, occasionally led to controversy, she firmly held to the legitimacy of her religious themes:

> Say, who is authoriz'd to probe my breast,
> Of whatsoever latent faith possess'd;
>
> . . . .
>
> Religion is 'twixt God and my own soul,
> Nor saint, nor sage, can boundless thought control.

Publishing individual poems and essays under the pseudonym "Constantia" (later as Honora-Martesia or simply Honora) in Boston and Philadelphia periodicals and finding over five hundred subscribers for a three-volume collection of essays, poems and plays called *The Gleaner* (1798), Murray ranged among religious, moral, political, social and literary materials. Having observed "the indifference, not to say contempt, with which female productions are regarded,"[9] she boldly appropriated a male persona for her "Gleaner" series, much of which first appeared in the *Massachusetts Magazine*. Juxtaposing a fictionalized narrative series with a plea for literary nationalism, a favorable review of Mercy Warren's plays or a discussion of the separation of spirit and matter, Murray's variety found wide appeal. Complementing her prose with the Popean couplets that she favored throughout her life, she developed such pre-romantic themes as the immanence of God in the natural world,

Through nature tracing—Nature's God.[10]

Other less public themes appear in individual poems: the death of her infant son, the birth of a nephew, the uncertainties of war. Much of Murray's poetry, with its artificial diction and imagery, lacks the forcefulness that characterizes her prose; nevertheless, the variety and unconventionality of her themes found a ready audience.

Few of Judith Sargent Murray's manuscripts have survived, but numerous publications, many of them already mentioned, are extant. The fullest bibliography of her works is provided by Vena Field in her monograph *Constantia: A Study of the Life and Works of Judith Sargent Murray 1751-1820* (Orono, Me., 1931), pp. 106-108. Although the bibliography omits *Some Deductions from the System Promulgated in the Page of Divine Revelation* (1782) and eight letters in the collections of the Massachusetts Historical Society, Field's *Constantia* provides a reliable (if uncritical) survey of Murray's biography and works. Letters of Murray to Mercy Warren are included in *Warren-Adams Letters,* II, Massachusetts Historical Society *Collections,* 73 (1925), 328-329, 346. Chester E. Jorgenson's "Gleanings from Judith Sargent Murray," *American Literature,* 12 (March, 1940), 73-78, reconstructs Murray's neoclassical aesthetic and her concept of liberty. A useful brief biography is available in Janet Wilson James's "Judith Sargent Murray," *Notable American Women,* eds. Edward T. James, Janet Wilson James, and Paul S. Boyer (Cambridge, Mass., 1971), II, 603-605.

Verses, Wrote at a Period of the American Contest, Replete With Uncertainty [11]

Now expectation reigns in every breast,
Suspense, corroding, chases balmy rest;
Trembling inquietude all pale appears,
And every loyal breast for Britain fears.

Columbia's sons, at this important hour,
Echo their loud huzzas for Gallic pow'r;
While Moderation, rising from her throne,
Her wonted calmness now no more her own,
Girts with solicitude her peaceful brow,
And offers tremulous the ardent vow;
Dark apprehension broods along the plain,
Extending o'er the soul its sad domain.

The theme, portentous, every bosom swells,
To one grand subject every thought impels;
Each moment now, more interesting grows,
For see—the gathering nations interpose—
Bourbon equips the fleet ordain'd to guard,
Expected ills from Albion's race to ward!

English America—with France combin'd,
Discordant pow'rs in leagues of friendship join'd;
While British squadrons hostile legions bear,
Rush to the field, and for the fight prepare.
Deep hid the great event—involv'd in fate—
While worlds impatient for the issue wait:
For ample realms our warring chiefs contend,
And countless wilds their glowing wishes blend;
Vast is the theatre—augustly spread—
And the broad circle clustering heroes tread.
An auditory universe attends,
And wrapt in silence expectation bends;
A thousand pens uplifted wait to catch,
From dark oblivion's gulf events to snatch,
With laurel bays to crown the Gallic name,
Or for Britannia blow the trump of fame.

Mean time, great Heaven, permit a suppliant's pray'r,
Who, humbly prostrate, seeks thy guardian care;

Beyond myself, one blooming youth I prize,
From my torn breast, for him my wishes rise;
O save a brother, mid the deathful field,
Spread o'er his sacred life the immortal shield;
Give him the path of honor to pursue,
To keep the radiant eminence in view:
And if his manly steps no more I meet,
My early friend no more with rapture greet,
If on this ball, amid this cloud wrapt sphere,
No more my youthful warrior shall appear,
Oh, sing a requiem to his parting soul,
Descending angels every pang control;
To realms of light refulgent be his path,
In his right hand the radiant torch of faith.

Constantia

Lines, Occasioned by the Death of an Infant[1][2]

Soft—tread with care, my darling baby sleeps,
And innocence its spotless vigils keeps.
Around my cradled boy the loves attend,
And, clad in smiles, the dimpling graces bend:
While his fair angel's task, so late assign'd,
Assumes the charge of the immortal mind.
Hail guardian spirit! watch with tender care,
And for each opening scene my child prepare;
Shield him from vice—to virtue stimulate,
Around his every step assiduous wait:
Not one weak moment thou thy post resign,
Implant the gen'rous wish—the glow divine;
Warn if thou canst—or, 'gainst the bursting storm,
His little frame with growing firmness arm;
Teach him to suffer—teach him to enjoy,
And all thy heavenly influence employ.
Attendant spirits, hear my ardent prayer,
In paths of rectitude my infant rear;

Trust me, his mother shall her efforts join,
To shield, and guide, her utmost powers combine.
    'Twas thus I plann'd my future hours to spend,
With my soft hopes maternal joys to blend;
But agonized nature trembling sighs!
And my young sufferer in the struggle dies:
As the green bud though hid from outward view,
On its own stem invigorated grew,
Yet ere its opening leaves could look abroad,
The howling blast its latent life destroy'd:
So shrieking terror all destructive rose,
Each moment fruitful of increasing woes,
And ere my tongue could mark his natal day,
(With eager haste great nature's dues to pay)
Its native skies the gentle spirit sought,
And clos'd a life with early evil fraught.
For me, the clay cold tenement I press'd,
And sorrow's keenest shafts transfix'd my breast;
Dear pledge of love—all tremulous I cried—
Fair hope, full many a week thou hast supplied;
To give thee life, I would endure again—
And every pang without regret sustain!
But icy death thy pretty features molds,
And to no mortal gaze thy worth unfolds.
    Thy funeral knell with melancholy sound,
Borne on the heavy gale—diffusing round
A dirgeful gloom—proclaims I must obey,
And bears thy beauteous image far away:
To the absorbing grave I must resign,
All of my first born child that e'er was mine!
And though no solemn train of mourners bend,
Or on thy hearse with tearful woe attend,
Too insignificant thy being view'd,
To be but by a father's steps pursu'd,
Yet thy pale corse the hand of Beauty grac'd,
When on thy urn the new pluck'd flow'rs she plac'd,
The purple blow when her soft hand enwreath'd,
And o'er my dead the sigh of pity breath'd.
    And still to shade and deck th' yearly tomb,
Fancy's rich foliage shall forever bloom,
Embowering trees in stately order rise,
While fragrant sweets the damask rose supplies;

The drooping lily too shall lowly bend,
And none but genial showers shall e'er descend.
    Say white rob'd cherub—whither dost thou stray,
Mid what celestial walk pusue thy way;
To some sequester'd bower hast thou repair'd,
Where thy young hopes may be to knowledge rear'd;
Where the untutor'd, the infantile mind,
With sacred joy the path of truth may find;
Where guardian angels wait the glad employ,
The latent seeds of evil to destroy;
Where wisdom blending, innocence entwines
With infant sweetness; where improvement shines;
Where all thy little powers thou may'st expand;
Where unassuming, thou may'st understand
Those laws, by which the Great First Cause directs,
And from eventual ruin man protects.
    Go on my son—thy radiant path pursue,
In paradise I trust thy face to view,
To mark the progress my Celestial makes,
That virtue, which my soul to transport wakes;
And, my sweet boy, prepare the flowery wreath,
For yet a little, and thy air I breathe;
Misfortunes frequent will reduce this clay,
Will bear the animating spark away:
And sure thy gentle spirit will descend,
With some blest choir my parting soul attend,
My dying requiem studious to compose,
To lead me where each sacred pleasure flows.
While here—alas—thou mock'd my ardent grasp,
For in my arms a lifeless form I clasp'd:
But there, I shall enjoy the dear embrace,
Amid the infant host my cherub trace.
    Nor smile ye censurers that I thus lament
A being scarce into existence sent;
What said the rock of ages—while he wore
This mortal coil—and all our sorrows bore:
"Regard those innocents—their worth revere,
"Their angels in the court of God appear;
"Immortal denizens of Heav'n they are,
"And in that kingdom radiant honors share."
August decision—and my heart believes,
With humble joy this soothing truth receives;

Nor fears to err, when in the Just One's path,
Howe'er mysterious may be its faith,
For God himself descends, with light divine,
And an eternal day shall yet be mine.

Constantia

Valedictory Epilogue to "Who's the Dupe," A Farce Which is the Production of the Elegant Pen of Mrs. Cowley ... Written by Constantia, in the Spring of 1790, and Spoken by Mr. Allen.[13]

At length these mirthful haunts we must resign,
These haunts where candor, wit and beauty shine.
Deputed by my friends to bid adieu,
To own for them their obligations too,
Regretting I pronounce the season o'er,
That the sweet comic muse will charm no more,
Till gathering winter shall majestic rise,
And live long night sit regent in the skies.
    The social months have spread their fleeting wing,
And on swift pinions hastes the rosy spring;
Young breathing zephyr passeth o'er the lee,
And jocund nature owns the new born glee;
Business, and pleasure, summon us away,
Our humbler parts in real life to play.
And as we circling tread the checker'd round,
Where many an ill, and many a good is found,
These gladsome hours will frequent rise to view,
While mem'ry will the fleecy joys pursue,
At Farquar's humor o'er and o'er will laugh,
Wit's sparkling bowl with thirst insatiate quaff,
The whims of good Sir Timothy inhaling,
Chuckling to hear the knight confess his failing,
Honest old Broadside with delight retracing,
And all his virtues in due order placing,
Open, and frank, yet tender as sincere,
In any character burn to appear,
If fair integrity but point the way,
The Commodore will cheerfully obey.

Frankley shall teach us elegance and ease,
While we like Morley will the blessing seize,
Dup'd by no musty, metaphysic rules,
The plague of reason, and the craft of schools.
    Gradus exhibits a most precious sample,
Take him, sweet audience, as an example;
So did Dan Pope in dulcet numbers sing,
"Drink deep, or taste not the Pierian spring;"
But that a female note should dare to swell,
To point at pedants, and our follies tell,
Must surely startle male prerogative,
And the alarm to sovereign man must give;
By Jove I fancy that these pretty railers,
Will soar beyond our tribe of "larned fellows!"
Gods 'twere enough to turn a lordly brain,
To see these women o'er our empire gain;
The burnish'd shafts of wit intrepid seizing,
Aiming at every art, and always pleasing.
    But seriously, I envy not their flights,
Nor care, though they ascend the loftiest heights;
This heart, devoted to the virtuous fair,
In their improvements takes a tender share,
With them in mild equality would dwell,
Rejoicing when their opening minds excel.
    And were it otherwise, the sex would rise,
O'er yielding reason steal with sweet surprise;
E'en now, a Cowley's decent form inspires,
Wraps my glad soul, and all my fancy fires;
In Briton's isle the lovely authoress lives,
And just applause from kindred bards receives;
Full many a quip, and crack, compose her train,
Vast and prolific is her magic reign;
Pit, box, and gallery have all combin'd,
The grateful public too its voice hath join'd,
Laugh'd, and applauded, hasting to bestow,
The well earn'd meed, the fruits on worth which grow.
    Nor to the comic muse is she confin'd,
Extensive plans employ her glowing mind;
Her skillful hand the cypress bud enwreaths,
The tragic air her muse submissive breathes;
Ranting Melpom—is by her art supported,
Though with the giggling slut she is conforted.

Forth from a field so ample, we have chose,
To our attempts to form the richest close,
Her little Doiley, and his strange conceit,
Smiling to see the gudgeon catch the bait.
   But at so wild a rate if I go on,
Regardless of the place, or time, or ton,
You'll wish perhaps old Doiley's fate were mine,
When mid his comrades he assay'd to shine.
   And I protest your powers are wonderous great,
For while for your decision here I wait,
Just like our hero's, my unfaithful tongue,
Nay all my trembling nerves are near unstrung,
Pray tell me then, since words are grown so scarce,
In your own language, how you like the farce;
If you approve, and if you wish to show it,
Clap loud your hands, and all the house will know it.

[Lines Prefacing Essay No. XIX. A Sketch of the Gleaner's Religious Sentiments] [14]

Say, who is authoriz'd to probe my breast,
Of whatsoever latent faith possess'd;
If in my life no crimson stains appear,
Nor badge schismatic I am known to wear;
If I obedient to the laws am found,
By the same bands my brethren own, am bound,
What is the mode of my belief to you,
While I the track of rectitude pursue?
Religion is 'twixt God and my own soul,
Nor saint, nor sage, can boundless thought control.

[Lines Prefacing Essay No. LXIX. Probable Utility of an Amicable Combination Among the Sons and Daughters of Literature]

If the soft bands of amity entwin'd,
And kindred motives sway'd each letter'd mind,
The scatter'd rays of genius to collect,
And all its broad diverging pow'rs connect—
With hues more vivid, science then would glow,
And arts expansive, to perfection grow:
But arm'd against themselves, their efforts die,
No kindling heat the sep'rate sparks supply;
Corrosive mildews sick'ning envy spreads,
And desolation marks the path she treads!
Her fatal progress worth innate impedes,
Hope fades appall'd, and prostrate science bleeds!

[Lines Prefacing Essay No. LXXXIX. Observations on Female Abilities, Cont'd]

The historic page with many a proof abounds,
And fame's loud trump the sex's worth resounds;
The patriot's zeal, the laurell'd warrior's claim,
The scepter'd virtues, wisdom's sacred name,
Creative poesy, the ethic page,
Design'd to form and meliorate the age,
With heroism, with perseverance fraught,
By honor, truth, and constancy enwrought,
And those blest deeds which elevate the mind,
With female genius these are all combin'd:
Recording story hands their virtues down,
And mellowing time awards their fair renown.

[Lines Prefacing Essay No. XCVI. A Spirit of National Independence Recommended]

Were I at liberty my plans to choose,
My politics, my fashions, and my muse
Should be American—Columbia's fame
Hath to Columbia's meed a righteous claim:
Her laws, her magistrates I would revere,
Holding this younger world supremely dear.

*Lines to Philenia*15

Ah lovely mourner! why should you refuse
To lend effulgence to a humbler muse?
The orb of day with sovereign splendor crown'd,
Who spreads diffusive light and pleasure round;
In whose fair train the white rob'd hours are led,
Beneath whose beam the floweret lifts its head;
Whose native fire and native heat sustains,
And o'er the natural world unrival'd reigns:
This genial orb with bounteous hand bequeaths,
Round the fair moon a silver radiance breathes;
While Luna from the orient source receives
The softer luster which she mildly gives;
With steps unequal o'er the welkin bends,
Through the blue vault with decent pride attends
The lucid path of that all potent ray,
Which yields, upholds, and paints the rosy day.
Mean time the unletter'd swain with grateful tongue,
Full many a carol to her praise hath sung;
Unconscious whence she consequence derives,
The homage of a gladsome heart he gives:
    Thus sweet Philenia I suppos'd thy worth
Would shield and cultivate my feebler growth;
Rich in reflected excellence, I thought
My growing name would be with music fraught;
That at the sound, genius would clap its wing,
And science would unnumber'd trophies bring;

That on the boldest pinions it would soar,
New paths disclose, and ampler fields explore;
While up th' eventful steep, as it ascended,
Fan'd by the breeze, my little skiff attended;
For there is fascination in a name,
Which oft bestows the glittering wreath of fame;
So, late posterity, deem they inherit,
Through a long line, the meed once paid to merit;
The kindred blood which swells their purple veins,
They fondly fancy, ancient worth sustains:
And few there are who that observance pay,
Which truth in honest colors can display.
Thus said my beating heart, and much elated,
In blithsome mood the plenteous harvest waited;
Or, if officious thought the glass presented,
And from my hopes integrity dissented,
By reason proving that it must be wrong
To wear what could not to myself belong,
My ready tongue the answer still supplied;
As thus by rectitude the cause was tried:
To taste and genius she will stand confest;
The muses will the flowing line attest;
Rich in her native strength, she stands secure,
To her the garland of applause is sure;
And while around the splendid orb I move,
My lowly verse its genial rays may prove.
Thus slyly arguing, while I sought for fame,
The two Constantias might be thought the same,
For 'tis not every reader can decide,
The multitude but on the surface glide;
At least the regent of the peaceful night,
More beauteous shows when clad in full orb'd light.
  But ah, alas! the transient beam is fled,
Its cheering influence no more is spread;
The animating fair ceases to guide,
Alone I venture on the impetuous tide;
Groping my opaque way, and wandering far,
Without the disk of my sweet polar star.

       Constantia

Ann Eliza Bleecker

(October, 1752-November 23, 1783)

Ann   Eliza Bleecker was born in New York City, the daughter
of Brandt Schuyler (a prosperous merchant who died before she was
born) and Margareta Van Wyck. An avid reader of contemporary
British poetry even as a child, she apparently began writing verses
at an early age, in the process building a local reputation as an author. It was not until she married John J. Bleecker, in 1769, however, that she was encouraged to save her work. According to her
daughter, Margaretta V. Faugeres (also a poet), even that later work
was carefully winnowed, for in Ann Bleecker's frequent attacks of
despondency, she destroyed "all the pieces which were not as melancholy as herself."

After their marriage, the Bleeckers moved to Poughkeepsie
for two years and then to Tomhanick, eighteen miles north of
Albany, where John Bleecker had inherited land. Accustomed to
city life among the best society of the Hudson Valley, Ann Bleecker
may have had mixed feelings about her rural surroundings. "Return
to Tomhanick" and the second of her poems "To Mr. L—" reveal
her attraction to the pastoral setting; yet a clear sense of the loneliness of frontier living is present in the first "To Mr. L—" and in
her later letters.

The quiet resolution of that inner conflict was not an option
for Ann Bleecker. Caught up in the turmoil of the Revolutionary
War, she was forced to flee her home in the summer of 1777. General Burgoyne's sudden invasion while her husband was away in
Albany forced her to leave Tomhanick on foot with her two small
daughters. Rejoining her husband after a day's journey, Ann Bleecker
and her family fled south. The youngest child, Abella, died of
dysentery during that hard retreat. The next few months witnessed
the deaths of Bleecker's mother and sister and of many friends, but

the family returned to Tomhanick after Burgoyne's defeat. Threats from roving bands of Tories forced another flight to Albany in 1779, and in 1781 John Bleecker was captured by Loyalists. Although he was rescued before being taken into Canada, the six days of uncertainty as to his fate brought on a nervous collapse for Ann Bleecker. The stillbirth of the fetus she was carrying at the time of her husband's capture only increased the melancholy that dominates her later poems and letters. A letter of April 8, 1780, succinctly reveals her state of mind: "But think not I dislike my situation here; on the contrary, I am charmed with the lovely scene the spring opens around me. Alas! the wilderness is within: I muse so long on the dead until I am unfit for the company of the living."[1] She died at Tomhanick in 1783 at the age of 31 and was buried in Albany.

Though lacking in subtlety and unquestionably derivative, Bleecker's poetry is unique in its combination of romantic and pastoral scenes with more realistic vignettes. In very personal terms, she records the effects of the American Revolution on a rural woman. She makes her poems occasions for narrating her fears of "the cruel savage" or Tory raiders, and in quieter times, for inviting friends to Tomhanick, for teasing, for complaining, for mourning. Shakespeare, Homer, Pope, Dryden and Gray provide temporary escapes from the surrounding dangers of the war. But comparing the lighter tone of her early poems with the melancholy of the later pieces reveals the psychological toll of Ann Bleecker's vulnerable situation.

Written without thought of publication, many of Bleecker's poems are letters in verse. Her love of nature, her loneliness, her condescension to her rustic neighbors, her melancholy and her patriotism all find their way into poetry. Occasionally viewing her plight in grand terms, she compares her situation to that of Orpheus "surrounded . . . by brutes" or of Aeneas in mourning. At other times she sketches a simpler environment of garden flowers and native forests. But for all the variety in theme and tone, Bleecker notes one constant in her poetic life. Like so many women poets in colonial America, she records the difficulty with which she continues to write:

> . . . amidst domestic cares to rhyme
> I find no pleasure, and I find no time.

Ann Bleecker's manuscripts have apparently been lost, but the efforts of her daughter Margaretta resulted in the publication of thirty-six of her poems, two prose pieces and several of her letters in *The Posthumous Works of Ann Eliza Bleecker . . .* (New York, 1793). The texts for all of the following poems have been taken from this volume. Fourteen of the poems had previously appeared in the *New-York Magazine* between February, 1790, and December, 1791. (Caroline May's *The American Female Poets,* published in Philadelphia in 1848, anthologizes "Hymn Written in Despondency" as Bleecker's although it does not appear in *The Posthumous Works.)*

The Posthumous Works includes Faugeres own essays and poems, as well as a detailed memoir of her mother. That memoir and Bleecker's letters form the major sources for later biographical articles. A number of nineteenth-century **anthologists** (Griswold, Kettell, Duyckinck, May) include biographical notes and selections from Bleecker's work in their volumes, but the most useful, concise biographical article is Lewis Leary's "Ann Eliza Bleecker" in *Notable American Women* (Cambridge, 1971), I, 179-178. James C. Hendrickson's *Ann Eliza Bleecker: Her Life and Works* (Columbia thesis, 1935) is useful for its biography and bibliography, but weaker in its discussion of the poetry. Elizabeth Ellet's *Women of the American Revolution* (New York, 1850), II, 243-246, also contains an accurate biographical sketch, as does George W. Schuyler's *Colonial New York: Philip Schuyler and his Family* (New York, 1885), II, 173-179. Emily Ford's "Early Poetry of the State of New York," in *Early Prose and Verse,* eds. Alice Earle and Emily Ford (New York, 1893), pp. 111-114, contains much the same biographical material but gives direct attention to the poetry as well as the poet. Emily Stipes Watts' *The Poetry of American Women from 1632 to 1945* (Austin, Texas, 1977), pp. 45-51, discusses Bleecker as "the best lyric poet of her day."

To Mr. L******2

The sun that gilds the western sky
    And makes the orient red,
Whose gladsome rays delight the eye
    And cheer the lonely shade;

Withdraws his vegetative heat,
    To southern climes retires;
While absent, we supply his seat
    With gross material fires.

'Tis new-year's morn; each rustic swain
    Ambrosial cordials take;
And round the fire the festive train
    A semi-circle make:

While clouds ascend, of sable smoke,
    From pipes of ebon hue,
With inharmonic song and joke
    They pass the morning through.

You tell me this is solitude,
    This Contemplation's seat;
Ah no! the most impervious wood
    Affords me no retreat.

But let me recollect: 'tis said,
    When Orpheus tun'd his lyre
The fauns and satyrs left the shade,
    Warrm'd by celestial fire.

His vocal lays and lyra[3] made
    Inanimated marble weep;
Swift-footed Time then paus'd, 'tis said,
    And sea-born monsters left the deep:

Impatient trees, to hear his strain
    Rent from the ground their root:—
Such is my fate, as his was then,
    Surrounded here—by brutes.

To the Same

Dear brother, to these happy shades repair,
And leave, Oh leave the city's noxious air:
I'll try description, friend—methinks I see
'Twill influence your curiosity.
    Before our door a meadow flies the eye,
Circled by hills, whose summits crowd the sky;
The silver lily there exalts her head,
And op'ning roses balmy odors spread,
While golden tulips flame beneath the shade.
In short, not Iris with her painted bow,
Nor varied tints an evening sun can show,
Can the gay colors of the flow'rs exceed,
Whose glowing leaves diversify this mead:
And when the blooms of Flora disappear,
The weighty fruits adorn the satiate year;
Here vivid cherries bloom in scarlet pride,
And purple plums blush by the cherries' side;
The sable berries bend the pliant vines,
And smiling apples glow in crimson rinds;
Ceres well pleas'd, beholds the furrow'd plain,
And show'rs her blessings on th' industrious swain;
Plenty sits laughing in each humble cot;
None wish for that which heaven gives them not.
But sweet Contentment still with sober charms,
Encircles us within her blissful arms;
Birds unmolested chaunt their early notes,
And on the dewy spray expand their throats;
Before the eastern skies are streak'd with light,
Or from the arch of Heaven retreats the night,
The musical inhabitants of air,
To praise their Maker, tuneful lays prepare.
Here by a spring, whose glassy surface moves
At ev'ry kiss from Zephyr of the groves,
While passing clouds look brighter in the stream,
Your poet sits and paints the rural scene.

On the Immensity of Creation[4]

Oh! could I borrow some celestial plume,
This narrow globe should not confine me long
In its contracted sphere—the vast expanse,
Beyond where thought can reach, or eye can glance,
My curious spirit, charm'd should traverse o'er,
New worlds to find, new systems to explore:
When these appear'd, again I'd urge my flight
Till all creation open'd to my sight.
    Ah! unavailing wish, absurd and vain,
Fancy return and drop thy wing again;
Could'st thou more swift than light move steady on,
Thy sight as broad, and piercing as the sun,
And Gabriel's years too added to thy own;
Nor Gabriel's sight, nor thought, nor rapid wing,
Can pass the immense domains of th' eternal King;
The greatest seraph in his bright abode
Can't comprehend the labors of a God.
Proud reason fails, and is confounded here;
—Man how contemptible thou dost appear!
What art thou in this scene?—Alas! no more
Than a small atom to the sandy shore,
A drop of water to a boundless sea,
A single moment to eternity.

Tomhanick, 1773

Written in the Retreat From Burgoyne[5]

Was it for this, with thee a pleasing load,
I sadly wander'd through the hostile wood;
When I thought fortune's spite could do no more,
To see thee perish on a foreign shore?
    Oh my lov'd babe! my treasures left behind
Ne'er sunk a cloud of grief upon my mind;
Rich in my children—on my arms I bore
My living treasures from the scalper's pow'r:

When I sat down to rest beneath some shade,
On the soft grass how innocent she play'd,
While her sweet sister, from the fragrant wild,
Collects the flow'rs to please my precious child;
Unconscious of her danger, laughing roves,
Nor dreads the painted savage in the groves.
   Soon as the spires of Albany appear'd,
With fallacies my rising grief I cheer'd;
"Resign'd I bear," said I, "heaven's just reproof,
"Content to dwell beneath a stranger's roof;
"Content my babes should eat dependent bread,
"Or by the labor of my hands be fed:
"What though my houses, lands, and goods are gone,
"My babes remain—these I can call my own."
But soon my lov'd Abella hung her head,
From her soft cheek the bright carnation fled;
Her smooth transparent skin too plainly shew'd
How fierce through every vein the fever glow'd.
—In bitter anguish o'er her limbs I hung,
I wept and sigh'd, but sorrow chain'd my tongue;
At length her languid eyes clos'd from the day,
The idol of my soul was torn away;
Her spirit fled and left me ghastly clay!
   Then—then my soul rejected all relief,
Comfort I wish'd not for, I lov'd my grief:
"Hear, my Abella!" cried I, "hear me mourn,
"For one short moment, oh! my child return;
"Let my complaint detain thee from the skies,
"Though troops of angels urge thee on to rise."
All night I mourn'd—and when the rising day
Gilt her sad chest with his benignest ray,
My friends press round me with officious care,
Bid me suppress my sighs, nor drop a tear;
Of resignation talk'd—passions subdu'd,
Of souls serene and christian fortitude;
Bade me be calm, nor murmur at my loss,
But unrepining bear each heavy cross.
   "Go!" cried I raging, "stoic bosoms go!
"Whose hearts vibrate not to the sound of woe;
"Go from the sweet society of men,
"Seek some unfeeling tiger's savage den,
"There calm—alone—of resignation preach,

My Christ's examples better precepts teach."
Where the cold limbs of gentle Laz'rus lay
I find him weeping o'er the humid clay;
His spirit groan'd, while the beholders said
(With gushing eyes) "see how he lov'd the dead!"
And when his thoughts on great Jerus'lem turn'd,
Oh! how pathetic o'er her fall he mourn'd!
And sad Gethsemene's nocturnal shade
The anguish of my weeping Lord survey'd:
Yes, 'tis my boast to harbor in my breast
The sensibilities by God exprest;
Nor shall the mollifying hand of time,
Which wipes off common sorrows, cancel mine.

October 29, 1777

To Miss Catharine Ten Eyck[6]

Come and see our habitation,
    Condescend to be our guest;
Though the veins of warring nations
    Bleed, yet here secure we rest.

By the light of Cynthia's crescent,
    Playing through the waving trees;
When we walk, we wish you present
    To participate our bliss.

Late indeed, the cruel savage
    Here with looks ferocious stood;
Here the rustic's cot did ravage,
    Stain'd the grass with human blood.

Late their hands sent conflagration
    Rolling through the blooming wild,
Seiz'd with death, the brute creation
    Mourn'd, while desolation smil'd.

Spiral flames from tallest cedar
Struck to heav'n a heat intense;
They cancell'd thus with impious labor,
Wonders of Omnipotence.

But when Conquest rear'd her standard,
And th' aborigines were fled,
Peace, who long an exile wander'd,
Now return'd to bless the shade.

Now Aeolus blows the ashes
From sad Terra's black'ned brow,
While the whist'ling swain with rushes
Roofs his cot, late levell'd low.

From the teeming womb of Nature
Bursting flow'rs exhale perfume;
Shady oaks, of ample stature,
Cast again a cooling gloom.

Waves from each reflecting fountain,
Roll again unmix'd with gore,
And verging from the lofty mountain,
Fall beneath with solemn roar.

Here, embosom'd in this Eden,
Cheerful all our hours are spent;
Here no pleasures are forbidden,
Sylvan joys are innocent.

Elegy on the Death of Gen. Montgomery[7]

Melpomene, now strike a mournful string,
Montgomery's fate assisting me to sing!
Thou saw him fall upon the hostile plain
Yet ting'd with blood that gush'd from Moncalm's veins,
Where gallant Wolfe for conquest gave his breath,
Where num'rous heroes met the angel Death.

Ah! while the loud reiterated roar
Of cannon echoed on from shore to shore,
Benigner Peace, retiring to the shade,
Had gather'd laurel to adorn his head:
The laurel yet shall grace his bust; but , oh!
America must wear sad cypress now.
Dauntless he led her armies to the war,
Invulnerable was his soul to fear:
When they explor'd their way o'er trackless snows,
Where Life's warm tide through every channel froze,
His eloquence made the chill'd bosom glow,
And animated them to meet the foe;
Nor flam'd this bright conspicuous grace alone,
The softer virtues in his bosom shone;
It bled with every soldier's recent wound;
He rais'd the fallen vet'ran from the ground;
He wip'd the eye of grief, it ceas'd to flow;
His heart vibrated to each sound of woe:
His heart too good his country to betray
For splendid posts or mercenary pay,
Too great to see a virtuous land opp'rest,
Nor strive to have her injuries redress'd.
Oh had but Carleton suffer'd in his stead!
Had half idolatrous Canadia bled!

      'Tis not for him but for ourselves we grieve,
Like him to die is better than to live,
His urn by a whole nation's tears bedew'd,
His mem'ry blest by all the great and good:
O'er his pale corse the marble soon shall rise,
And the tall column shoot into the skies;
There long his praise by freemen shall be read,
As softly o'er the hero's dust they tread.

Recollection[8]

Soon as the gilded clouds of evening fly,
And Luna lights her taper in the sky,
The silent throught-inspiring solemn scene

Awakes my soul to all that it has been.
I was the parent of the softest fair
Who e'er respir'd in wide Columbia's air;
A transient glance of her love-beaming eyes
Convey'd into the soul a paradise.
How has my cheek with rapture been suffus'd,
When sunk upon my bosom she repos'd?
I envied not the ermin'd prince of earth,
Nor the gay spirit of aeriel birth;
Nor the bright angel circumfus'd with light,
While the sweet charmer liv'd to bless my sight.
    What art thou now, my love!—a few dry bones,
Unconscious of my unavailing moans:
Oh! my Abella! oh! my bursting heart
Shall never from thy dear idea part!
Through Death's cold gates thine image will I bear,
And mount to Heav'n, and ever love thee there.

Tomhanick, February 10, 1778

On Reading Dryden's Virgil[9]

Now cease these tears, lay gentle Virgil by,
Let recent sorrows dim the pausing eye:
Shall Aeneas for lost Creusa mourn,
And tears be wanting on Abella's urn?
Like him I lost my fair one in my flight
From cruel foes—and in the dead of night.
Shall he lament the fall of Illion's tow'rs,
And we not mourn the sudden ruin of ours?
See York on fire—while borne by winds each flame
Projects its glowing sheet o'er half the main:
Th' affrighted savage, yelling with amaze,
From Allegany sees the rolling blaze.
Far from these scenes of horror, in the shade
I saw my aged parent safe convey'd;
Then sadly follow'd to the friendly land,
With my surviving infant by the hand.

No cumb'rous household gods had I indeed
To load my shoulders, and my flight impede;
The hero's idols sav'd by him remain;
My gods took care of me—not I of them!
The Trojan saw Anchises breathe his last,
When all domestic dangers he had pass'd:
So my lov'd parent, after she had fled,
Lamented, perish'd on a stranger's bed.
—He held his way o'er the Cerulian Main,
But I return'd to hostile fields again.

1778

To Miss M. V. W.[10]

Peggy, amidst domestic cares to rhyme
I find no pleasure, and I find no time;
But then, a Poetess, you may suppose,
Can better tell her mind in verse than prose:
True—when serenely all our moments roll,
Then numbers flow spontaneous from the soul:
Not when the mind is harassed by cares,
Or stunn'd with thunders of intestine wars,
Or circled by a noisy, vulgar throng,
(Noise ever was an enemy to song.)
    What though the spiral pines around us rise,
And airy mountains intercept the skies.
Faction has chas'd away the warbling Muse,
And Echo only learns to tattle news;
Each clown commences politician here,
And calculates th' expenses of the year;
He quits his plow, and throws aside his spade,
To talk with squire about decrease of trade:
His tedious spouse detains me in her turn,
Condemns our measures and neglects her churn.
Scarce can I steal a moment from the wars
To read my Bible, or to say my pray'rs:
Oh! how I long to see those halcyon days

When Peace again extends to us her rays,
When each, beneath his vine, and far from fear,
Shall beat his sword into a lab'ring share.
    Then shall the rural arts again revive,
Ceres shall bid the famish'd rustic live:
Where now the yells of painted sons of blood
With long vibrations shake the lonely wood,
All desolate, Pomona shall behold
The branches shoot with vegetable gold:
Beyond the peasant's sight the springing grain
Shall wave around him o'er the ample plain;
No engines then shall bellow o'er the waves,
And fright blue Thetis in her coral caves,
But commerce gliding o'er the curling seas,
Shall bind the sever'd shores in ties of peace.
    Then Washington, reclining on his spear,
Shall take a respite from laborious war,
While Glory on his brows with awful grace
Binds a tiara of resplendent rays.
How faint the luster of imperial gems
To this immortal wreath his merit claims!
See from the north, where icy mountains rise,
Down to the placid climes of southern skies,
All hail the day that bids stern discord cease,
All hail the day which gives the warrior peace:
Hark! the glad nations make a joyful noise!
And the loud shouts are answer'd from the skies;
Fame swells the sound wrapt in her hero's praise,
And darts his splendors down to latest days.

Tomhanick, January, 1780

Return to Tomhanick

Hail, happy shades! though clad with heavy snows,
At sight of you with joy my bosom glows;
Ye arching pines, that bow with every breeze,
Ye poplars, elms, all hail my well-known trees!

And now my peaceful mansion strikes my eye,
And now the tinkling rivulet I spy;
My little garden Flora hast thou kept,
And watch'd my pinks and lilies while I wept?
Or has the grubbing swine, by furies led,
Th' inclosure broke, and on my flowrets fed?
    Ah me! that spot with blooms so lately grac'd,
With storms and driving snows is now defac'd;
Sharp icicles from ev'ry bush depend,
And frosts all dazzling o'er the beds extend:
Yet soon fair Spring shall give another scene,
And yellow cowslips gild the level green;
My little orchard sprouting at each bough,
Fragrant with clust'ring blossoms deep shall glow.
Ah! then 'tis sweet the tufted grass to tread,
But sweeter slumb'ring in the balmy shade;
The rapid humming bird, with ruby breast,
Seeks the parterre with early blue bells drest,
Drinks deep the honeysuckle dew, or drives
The lab'ring bee to her domestic hives:
Then shines the lupin bright with morning gems,
And sleepy poppies nod upon their stems;
The humble violet and the dulcet rose,
The stately lily then, and tulip blows.
    Farewell my Plutarch! farewell pen and Muse!
Nature exults—shall I her call refuse?
Apollo fervid glitters in my face,
And threatens with his beam each feeble grace:
Yet still around the lovely plants I toil,
And draw obnoxious herbage from the soil;
Or with the lime-twigs little birds surprise,
Or angle for the trout of many dyes.
    But when the vernal breezes pass away,
And loftier Phoebus darts a fiercer ray,
The spiky corn then rattles all around,
And dashing cascades give a pleasing sound;
Shrill sings the locust with prolonged note,
The cricket chirps familiar in each cot,
The village children, rambling o'er yon hill,
With berries all their painted baskets fill,
They rob the squirrels' little walnut store,
And climb the half exhausted tree for more;

Or else to fields of maize nocturnal hie,
Where hid, th' elusive water-melons lie;
Sportive, they make incisions in the rind,
The riper from the immature to find;
Then load their tender shoulders with the prey,
And laughing bear the bulky fruit away.

Phillis Wheatley

(1753?-December 5, 1784)

Modern readers have given the slight collection of poems and letters by Phillis Wheatley a heavy burden to carry. Produced by a black slave woman in pre-Revolutionary Boston, *Poems on Various Subjects, Religious and Moral* (1773) and Wheatley's other miscellaneous pieces have engendered a continuing controversy: does Phillis Wheatley express the injustice of her slavery in subtly duplicious lines designed to fool a white press, or does she simply accept her lot as slave, rejoicing in her new-found Christianity? It should not be necessary to take part in the controversy (which may reveal more about Wheatley's readers than about her poetry) to discover sufficient reason for investigating this "sooty prodigy," as Rufus Griswold called her in *Female Poets of America* (1849).

Phillis Wheatley had an unpromising beginning in the American colonies. Arriving as a child of seven or eight in a slave ship (perhaps from Senegal?) in 1761, she was purchased by John and Susanna Wheatley, prominent Boston residents. Endearing herself to the Wheatleys and revealing a talent for language and literary study, she was accorded treatment unique among slaves and among women. Treated (almost) as a family member, the child learned to read and write and was relieved of most of her household duties to pursue her studies. Within sixteen months of her arrival, she had "attained the English language . . . to such a degree as to read any, the most difficult part of the Sacred Writings."[1] Assiduous missionary activity in the Wheatley home no doubt influenced her decision to become a communicant in Boston's Old South Church in 1771. Not surprisingly, Christianity and the "Sacred Writings" became dominant shapers of her attitudes.

Following "an intrinsic ardor [that] prompts to write," Wheatley began her poetry as a child. Her first published verse appeared in the *Newport Mercury* for December 21, 1767: "On Messrs. Hussey and Coffin," an occasional piece that memorialized their narrow escape from death at sea. Most of Wheatley's subsequent verse was in a similar vein, occasional pieces, usually elegies, written at the request of particular individuals and for particular events. (Fourteen of her thirty-eight poems in *Poems on Various Subjects* are elegies.) The education she received from her owners' twin children, Mary and Nathaniel, introduced her to the classics and to the English literature of the day. Steeped in Alexander Pope and his contemporaries, Wheatley's verse seldom varied from neoclassical forms and themes. Conventionally abstract ideas of death, freedom, salvation, learning and imagination permeated the vague images of her poems.

It will come as no surprise that a black woman poet conversant with the poetic mode of the day excited a good deal of attention in colonial Boston. And Phillis Wheatley began to collect an even wider audience for her work when she published in broadside "An Elegiac Poem, on the Death of the Celebrated Divine . . . George Whitefield" in 1770. Encouraged by the favorable attention, she later made arrangements for a volume of her work to be published in London. Always in fragile health, she was sent to England on a therapeutic voyage in 1773. During her brief stay, she corresponded with the Countess of Huntingdon (to whom she dedicated her book) and saw her *Poems on Various Subjects, Religious and Moral* well on its way to completion.

Wheatley's book was a success, but the protected environment to which she was accustomed began to dissolve. Mary Wheatley married the Reverend John Lathrop in 1771 and moved away, dying in 1778. Susanna Wheatley died in 1774, and her husband in 1778; Nathaniel elected to remain in England. Facing the turmoil of the Revolutionary War and her loss of protection (she had been freed by John Wheatley three months before his wife died), she was left to her own meagre resources. She married John Peters in April, 1778, a union that resulted in three children who died in infancy. Descriptions of John Peters are scanty and contradictory. He was free and black in difficult times; he may have been proud and indolent, shiftless and prone to debt. Wheatley's marriage was an unhappy one; she spent her last years in miserable poverty, dying on December 5, 1784.

Her poetry, some letters and a proposal for a second book are all that survive her, meagre evidence for what was a remarkable achievement in its day.[2] Firmly grounded in a neoclassical aesthetic, Wheatley's verse shows little development from early pieces such as "America" to the later "Liberty and Peace," published just before she died. Nevertheless, the poetry is of interest today for more than the circumstances of its author. Phillis Wheatley's blackness may inform but should not preoccupy our view of her work.

> —Ethiopians speak
> Sometimes by simile, a victory's won.

Perhaps the "simile" needs attention as well as the "Ethiopian."

Wheatley's verse, in its rare personal moments, conveys a sense of the human that breaks through her typically abstract formulas. The poetry, for example, contains evidence of the author's concern with the suffering of the Revolution (in which she shared, being forced to flee Boston with her husband):

> Now sheathe the sword that bade the brave atone
> With guiltless blood for madness not their own.

Her patriotic sentiments (and perhaps her desire for personal freedom) are apparent in her verse throughout her lifetime, but nowhere more clear than in a letter dated February 11, 1774, to the Reverend Samson Occom, an itinerant Indian clergyman. She discusses the relationship between

> civil and religious liberty, which are so inseparably united, that there is little or no enjoyment of one without the other: . . . in every human breast, God has implanted a principle, which we call love of freedom; it is impatient of oppression and pants for deliverance. . . . How well the cry for liberty, and the reverse disposition, for the exercise of oppressive power over others agree—I humbly think it does not require the penetration of a philosopher to determine.[3]

Abolition and women's rights were not Wheatley's preoccupations, but her political attitudes provide an example of the human touch missing from some of her poems. They allow us to sense one dimension of the women behind the poetic mask.

Recent discoveries of manuscript poems and letters reveal that Wheatley materials are somewhat scattered. The most comprehensive edition of her poems and letters is Julian D. Mason, Jr.'s *The Poems of Phillis Wheatley* (Chapel Hill, N.C., 1966), but it should be supplemented by the poetry in Robert C. Kuncio's "Some Unpublished Poems of Phillis Wheatley," *New England Quarterly*, 43 (1970), 287-297, Carl Bridenbaugh's "The Earliest-Published Poem of Phillis Wheatley," *New England Quarterly*, 42 (1969), 583-584, and Phil Lapansky's "Deism: An Unpublished Poem by Phillis Wheatley," *New England Quarterly*, 50 (1977), 517-520. William H. Robinson prints one newly discovered piece and three previously known poems from manuscripts in the Massachusetts Historical Society as an appendix to *Phillis Wheatley in the Black American Beginnings* (Detroit, 1975), pp. 75-80. He includes two other Wheatley poems in his *Early Black American Poets* (Debuque, Iowa, 1969), pp. 97-112. An earlier volume of *Poems and Letters by Phillis Wheatley*, ed. Charles F. Heartman (New York, 1915), was reprinted by Mnemosyne Publishing Company in 1969. James A. Rawley is preparing a new edition of the Wheatley canon.

Hundreds of secondary materials regarding Phillis Wheatley are available to interested readers, most of them more concerned with her remarkable (if scanty) biography than with her poetry. The principal source for biographical sketches is a memoir by Margaretta Matilda Odell, "a collateral descendent of Mrs. Wheatley" who had been "familiar with the name and fame of Phillis from her childhood,"[4] published in *Memoir and Poems of Phillis Wheatley* (Boston, 1834; new editions in 1835 and 1838); the 1838 edition was reprinted by Mnemosyne in 1969. Nathaniel B. Shurtleff's "Phillis Wheatley, the Negro-Slave Poet," in the *Boston Daily Advertiser* for December 21, 1863, is brief but valuable. Charles Heartman's *Phillis Wheatley (Phillis Peters): A Critical Attempt and a Bibliography of Her Writings* (New York, 1915) is useful but difficult to obtain; Dorothy Porter's entries for Wheatley in "Early

American Negro Writings: A Bibliographical Study," *Publications of the Bibliographical Society of America*, 39 (1945), 261-266, are more accessible. Mukhtar Ali Isani's "The First Proposed Edition of *Poems on Various Subjects* and the Phillis Wheatley Canon," *American Literature*, 49 (March, 1977), 97-103, provides new evidence for dating Wheatley's early work. Other important twentieth century studies include Benjamin Brawley's *The Negro in Literature and Art in the United States* (New York, 1930; rpt. 1971), pp. 15-37; Vernon Loggins' *The Negro Author* (New York, 1931), pp. 16-29; Sidney Kaplan's *The Black Presence in the Era of the American Revolution* (New York, 1973), pp. 150-170; Gregory Rigsby's "Form and Content in Phillis Wheatley's Elegies," *College Language Association Journal*, 19 (1975), 248-257; Terence Collins' "Phillis Wheatley: The Dark Side of Her Poetry," *Phylon*, 36 (1975), 78-88; Bernard Bell's "African-American Writers," in *American Literature, 1764-1789: The Revolutionary Years*, ed. Everett Emerson (Madison, Wisc., 1977), pp. 171-193; and James A. Rawley's "The World of Phillis Wheatley," *New England Quarterly*, 50 (December, 1977), 666-677. Saunders Redding's "Phillis Wheatley," *Notable American Women*, eds. Edward James, Janet Wilson James and Paul Boyer (Cambridge, Mass., 1971), III, 573-574, furnishes a reliable introductory survey.

America[5]

New England first a wilderness was found,
Till for a continent 'twas destin'd round;
From field to field the savage monsters run
E'er yet Brittania had her work begun.
Thy power, O Liberty, makes strong the weak,
And (wond'rous instinct) Ethiopians speak
Sometimes by simile, a victory's won.
A certain lady had an only son;
He grew up daily, virtuous as he grew.
Fearing his strength which she undoubted knew,
She laid some taxes on her darling son,
And would have laid another act there on.
"Amend your manners, I'll the task remove,"
Was said with seeming sympathy and love.
By many scourges she his goodness tried
Until at length the best of infants cried;
He wept, Brittania turn'd a senseless ear.
At last awaken'd by maternal fear:
"Why weeps Americus, why weeps my child?"
Thus spake Brittania, thus benign and mild.
"My dear mama," said he, "shall I repeat—"
Then prostrate fell, at her maternal feet.
"What ails the rebel?" great Brittania cried.
"Indeed," said he, "you have no cause to chide:
"You see each day my fluent tears, my food,[6]
"Without regard, what no more English blood?
"Was length of time drove from our English veins
"The kindred he to Great Brittania deigns?"
Tis thus with thee, O Brittain, keeping down
New English force, thou fear'st his tyranny and thou didst frown.
He weeps afresh to feel this iron chain;
Turn, O Brittania, claim thy child again,
Riecho[7] Love, drive by thy powerful charms
Indolence slumbering in forgetful arms.
See Agenoria diligent employs
Her sons, and thus with rapture she replies,
"Arise my sons, with one consent arise,"
Lest distant continents with vult'ring eyes
Should charge America with negligence;
They praise industry but no pride commence
To raise their own profusion, O Brittain see,
By this New England will increase like thee.

A Poem on the Death of Charles Eliot, Aged 12 Mo[nths]. To Mr. S[amuel] Eliot[8]

Through airy realms, he wings his instant flight
To purer regions of celestial light.
Unmov'd he sees unnumber'd systems roll
Beneath his feet, the universal whole
In just succession run their destin'd round
And circling wonders spread the dread profound,
Th' ethereal now, and now the starry skies,
With glowing splendors, strike his wond'ring eyes.
    The heav'nly legions view, with joy unknown,
Press his soft hand, and seat him on the throne,
And smiling, thus: "To this divine abode,
"The seat of saints, of angels and of God:
"Thrice welcome thou."—The raptur'd babe replies,
"Thanks to my God, who snatch'd me to the skies
"E'er vice triumphant had possess'd my heart;
"E'er yet the tempter claim'd my better part;
"E'er yet on sins' most deadly actions bent;
"E'er yet I knew temptation's dread intent;
"E'er yet the rod for horrid crimes I knew,
"Not rais'd with vanity or 'press'd with woe;
"But soon arriv'd to heaven's bright port assign'd,
"New glories rush on my expanding mind!
"A noble ardor now, my bosom fires,
"To utter what the heav'nly muse inspires!"
    Joyful he spoke—exulting cherubs round
Clap loud their pinions, and the plains resound.
Say, parents! why this unavailing moan?
Why heave your bosoms with the rising groan?
To Charles, the happy subject of my song,
A happier world, and nobler strains belong.
Say, would you tear him from the realms above?
Or make less happy, frantic in your love?
Doth his beatitude increase your pain?
Or could you welcome to this earth again
The son of bliss?—no, with superior air,
Methinks he answers with a smile severe,
"Thrones and dominions cannot tempt me there!"
    But still you cry. "O Charles! thy manly mind,
"Enwrap our souls, and all thy actions bind,

"Our only hope, more dear than vital breath,
"Twelve moons revolv'd, and sunk in shades of death.
"Engaging infant! nightly visions give
"Thee to our arms, and we with joy receive;
"We fain would clasp the phantom to our breast;
"The phantom flies, and leaves the soul unblest!"
Prepare to meet your dearest infant friend,
Where joys are pure, and glory with out end.

Boston, Sept[embe]r 1st, 1772

To the University of Cambridge, in New-England[9]

   While an intrinsic ardor prompts to write,
The muses promise to assist my pen;
'Twas not long since I left my native shore,
The land of errors, and Egyptian gloom:
Father of mercy, 'twas thy gracious hand
Brought me in safety from those dark abodes.

   Students, to you 'tis giv'n to scan the heights
Above, to traverse the ethereal space,
And mark the systems of revolving worlds.
Still more, ye sons of science, ye receive
The blissful news by messengers from heav'n,
How Jesus' blood for your redemption flows.
See him with hands out-stretcht upon the cross;
Immense compassion in his bosom glows;
He hears revilers, nor resents their scorn:
What matchless mercy in the Son of God!
When the whole human race by sin had fall'n,
He deign'd to die that they might rise again,
And share with him in the sublimest skies,
Life without death, and glory without end.

   Improve your privileges while they stay,
Ye pupils, and each hour redeem, that bears
Or good or bad report of you to heav'n.

Let sin, that baneful evil to the soul,
By you be shunn'd, nor once remit your guard;
Suppress the deadly serpent in its egg.
Ye blooming plants of human race divine,
An Ethiop tells you 'tis your greatest foe;
Its transient sweetness turns to endless pain,
And in immense perdition sinks the soul.

On Being Brought From Africa to America

'Twas mercy brought me from my pagan land,
Taught my benighted soul to understand
That there's a God, that there's a Savior too:
Once I redemption neither sought nor knew.
Some view our sable race with scornful eye,
"Their color is a diabolic dye."
Remember, Christians, Negroes, black as Cain,
May be refin'd, and join th' angelic train.

An Hymn to the Morning

Attend my lays, ye ever honor'd nine,
Assist my labors, and my strains refine;
In smoothest numbers pour the notes along,
For bright Aurora now demands my song.

Aurora hail, and all the thousand dyes,
Which deck thy progress through the vaulted skies:
The morn awakes, and wide extends her rays,
On ev'ry leaf the gentle zephyr plays;
Harmonious lays the feather'd race resume,
Dart the bright eye, and shake the painted plume.

Ye shady groves, your verdant gloom display
To shield your poet from the burning day:
Calliope awake the sacred lyre,
While thy fair sisters fan the pleasing fire:
The bow'rs, the gales, the variegated skies
In all their pleasures in my bosom rise.

See in the east th' illustrious king of day!
His rising radiance drives the shades away—
But Oh! I feel his fervid beams too strong,
And scarce begun, concludes th' abortive song.

An Hymn to the Evening

Soon as the sun forsook the eastern main
The pealing thunder shook the heav'nly plain;
Majestic grandeur! From the zephyr's wing,
Exhales the incense of the blooming spring.
Soft purl the streams, the birds renew their notes,
And through the air their mingled music floats.

Through all the heav'ns what beauteous dyes are spread!
But the west glories in the deepest red:
So may our breasts with ev'ry virtue glow,
The living temples of our God below!

Fill'd with the praise of him who gives the light,
And draws the sable curtains of the night,
Let placid slumbers soothe each weary mind,
At morn to wake more heav'nly, more refin'd;
So shall the labors of the day begin
More pure, more guarded from the snares of sin.

Night's leaden sceptre seals my drowsy eyes,
Then cease, my song, till fair Aurora rise.

On Imagination

Thy various works, imperial queen, we see,
How bright their forms! how deck'd with pomp by thee!
Thy wond'rous acts in beauteous order stand,
And all attest how potent is thine hand.

From Helicon's refulgent heights attend,
Ye sacred choir, and my attempts befriend:
To tell her glories with a faithful tongue,
Ye blooming graces, triumph in my song.

Now here, now there, the roving Fancy flies,
Till some lov'd object strikes her wand'ring eyes,
Whose silken fetters all the senses bind,
And soft captivity involves the mind.

Imagination! who can sing thy force?
Or who describe the swiftness of thy course?
Soaring through air to find the bright abode,
Th' empyreal palace of the thund'ring God,
We on thy pinions can surpass the wind,
And leave the rolling universe behind:
From star to star the mental optics rove,
Measure the skies, and range the realms above.
There in one view we grasp the mighty whole,
Or with new worlds amaze th' unbounded soul.

Through Winter frowns to Fancy's raptur'd eyes
The fields may flourish, and gay scenes arise;
The frozen deeps may break their iron bands,
And bid their waters murmur o'er the sands.
Fair Flora may resume her fragrant reign,
And with her flow'ry riches deck the plain;
Sylvanus may diffuse his honors round,
And all the forest may with leaves be crown'd:
Show'rs may descend, and dews their gems disclose,
And nectar sparkle on the blooming rose.

Such is thy pow'r, nor are thine orders vain,
O thou the leader of the mental train:
In full perfection all thy works are wrought,

And thine the sceptre o'er the realms of thought.
Before thy throne the subject-passions bow,
Of subject-passions sov'reign ruler Thou,
At thy command joy rushes on the heart,
And through the glowing veins the spirits dart.

  Fancy might now her silken pinions try
To rise from earth, and sweep th' expanse on high;
From Tithon's bed now might Aurora rise,
Her cheeks all glowing with celestial dyes,
While a pure stream of light o'erflows the skies.
The monarch of the day I might behold,
And all the mountains tipt with radiant gold,
But I reluctant leave the pleasing views,
Which Fancy dresses to delight the Muse;
Winter austere forbids me to aspire,
And northern tempests damp the rising fire;
They chill the tides of Fancy's flowing sea,
Cease then, my song, cease the unequal lay.

To the Right Honorable William, Earl of Dartmouth, His Majesty's Principal Secretary of State for North-America, & C.[10]

        Hail, happy day, when, smiling like the morn,
Fair Freedom rose New-England to adorn:
The northern clime beneath her genial ray,
Dartmouth, congratulates thy blissful sway:
Elate with hope her race no longer mourns,
Each soul expands, each grateful bosom burns,
While in thine hand with pleasure we behold
The silken reins, and Freedom's charms unfold.
Long lost to realms beneath the northern skies
She shines supreme, while hated faction dies:
Soon as appear'd the Goddess long desir'd,
Sick at the view, she languish'd and expir'd;
Thus from the splendors of the morning light
The owl in sadness seeks the caves of night.

No more, America, in mournful strain
Of wrongs, and grievance unredress'd complain,
No longer shalt thou dread the iron chain,
Which wanton Tyranny with lawless hand
Had made, and with it meant t' enslave the land.

Should you, my lord, while you peruse my song,
Wonder from whence my love of Freedom sprung,
Whence flow these wishes for the common good,
By feeling hearts alone best understood,
I, young in life, by seeming cruel fate
Was snatch'd from Afric's fancy'd happy seat:
What pangs excruciating must molest,
What sorrows labor in my parent's breast?
Steel'd was that soul and by no misery mov'd
That from a father seiz'd his babe belov'd:
Such, such my case. And can I then but pray
Others may never feel tyrannic sway?

For favors past, great Sir, our thanks are due,
And thee we ask thy favors to renew,
Since in thy pow'r, as in thy will before,
To soothe the griefs, which thou did'st once deplore.
May heav'nly grace the sacred sanction give
To all thy works, and thou for ever live
Not only on the wings of fleeting Fame,
Though praise immortal crowns the patriot's name,
But to conduct to heav'ns refulgent fane,[11]
May fiery coursers sweep th' ethereal plain,
And bear thee upwards to that blest abode,
Where, like the prophet, thou shalt find thy God.

Liberty and Peace, a Poem[12]

Lo! Freedom comes. Th' prescient Muse foretold,
All eyes th' accomplish'd prophecy behold:
Her port describ'd, "She moves divinely fair,
"Olive and laurel bind her golden hair."

She, the bright progeny of Heaven, descends,
And every grace her sovereign step attends;
For now kind Heaven, indulgent to our prayer,
In smiling Peace resolves the din of war.
Fix'd in Columbia her illustrious line,
And bids in thee her future councils shine.
To every realm her portals open'd wide,
Receives from each the full commercial tide.
Each art and science now with rising charms
Th' expanding heart with emulation warms.
E'en great Britannia sees with dread surprise,
And from the dazzling splendor turns her eyes!
Britain, whose navies swept th' Atlantic o'er,
And thunder sent to every distant shore:
E'en thou, in manners cruel as thou art,
The sword resign'd, resume the friendly part!
For Galia's power espous'd Columbia's cause,
And new-born Rome shall give Britannia law,
Nor unremember'd in the grateful strain,
Shall princely Louis' friendly deeds remain;
The generous prince th' impending vengeance eyes,
Sees the fierce wrong, and to the rescue flies.
Perish that thirst of boundless power, that drew
On Albion's head the curse to tyrants due.
But thou appeas'd submit to Heaven's decree,
That bids this realm of Freedom rival thee!
Now sheathe the sword that bade the brave atone
With guiltless blood for madness not their own.
Sent from th' enjoyment of their native shore
Ill-fated—never to behold her more!
From every kingdom on Europa's coast
Throng'd various troops, their glory, strength and boast.
With heart-felt pity fair Hibernia saw
Columbia menac'd by the tyrant's law:
On hostile fields fraternal arms engage,
And mutual deaths, all dealt with mutual rage;
The Muse's ear hears mother Earth deplore
Her ample surface smoke with kindred gore:
The hostile field destroys the social ties,
And ever-lasting slumber seals their eyes.
Columbia mourns, the haughty foes deride,
Her treasures plunder'd and her towns destroy'd:

Witness how Charlestown's curling smokes arise,
In sable columns to the clouded skies!
The ample Dome, high-wrought with curious toil,
In one sad hour the savage troops despoil.
Descending Peace and power of War confounds;
From every tongue celestial Peace resounds:
As for the east th' illustrious king of day,
With rising radiance drives the shades away,
So Freedom comes array'd with charms divine,
And in her train Commerce and Plenty shine.
Britannia owns her independent reign,
Hibernia, Scotia, and the realms of Spain;
And great Germania's ample coast admires
The generous spirit that Columbia fires.
Auspicious Heaven shall fill with fav'ring gales,
Where e'er Columbia spreads her swelling sails:
To every realm shall Peace her charms display,
And Heavenly Freedom spread her golden ray.

Anna Young Smith

(November 5, 1756-April 3, 1780?)

Children of John and Jane Graeme Young, Anna and her brother John were raised by their aunt Elizabeth Fergusson (see pages 101-111) at Graeme Park near Philadelphia after the death of their mother. Anna Young's poetry and correspondence suggest a close relationship with her aunt which may have encouraged Young to emulate Fergusson in choosing a literary avocation. Most of her extant poems were written before her marriage to Dr. William Smith of Philadelphia on November 30, 1775,[1] a marriage to which her father had not consented. She died as a young woman, on April 3, 1780, apparently as a result of the birth of her third child.[2]

Few biographical records of Anna Young Smith remain, but much can be inferred from her poems and from Elizabeth Fergusson's annotations of them. Smith characteristically treated political and feminist themes as well as the more conventional subjects of love and courtship, gratitude, sensibility and grief. Fergusson noted, for example, that her niece was "a warm Whig"[3] (unlike her brother John who became an active Tory), an assessment borne out in Smith's verse:

> Where e'er the barb'rous story shall be told,
> The British cheek shall glow with conscious shame.

Seldom given to equivocation, Smith also declared her sentiments "On Reading Swift's Works" about women:

> But thy harsh satire, rude, severe, unjust,
> Awakes too oft our anger or disgust.
>
> . . . .
>
> E'en while we laugh, we mourn thy wit's abuse,
> And while we praise thy talents, scorn their use.

Other more traditional lyrics, some of them printed here, contribute a fuller sense of Smith's range as a poet.

Many of Smith's verses have been preserved in Elizabeth Fergusson's commonplace book, written for Annis Stockton (see pages 87-100) probably in 1787. Several of the poems were published under Smith's pseudonym "Sylvia": "An Elegy to the Memory of the American Volunteers . . ." appeared in the *Pennsylvania Magazine* during her lifetime and eight other pieces were printed in the *Universal Asylum and Columbian Magazine* after her death. *Memoirs of the Historical Society of Pennsylvania*, ed. Edward Armstrong (Philadelphia, 1864), I, 461-463, reprinted "An Elegy to the Memory of the American Volunteers . . ." with a brief biographical note.

*An Ode to Gratitude, Inscribed to Miss Eliza[beth] Graeme by her
Niece, Anna Young, Philadelphia, 1770*[4]

1

Oh gratitude thou power benign,
Who does such warmth impart!
Teach my unskillful mind to sing
The feelings of my heart.

2

Teach me to thank the gracious maid,
Who rear'd my infant years;
That gives me every useful aid,
And mourns my faults with tears.

3

Nor tenderness I can't repay,
Nor half her love recount;
Each rising morn and setting day
Still adds to the amount.

4

All gracious God who rules on high,
Eliza's love regard.
Oh recompense her piety!
Her tender care reward!

5

Bless her with life, with health, with joy,
With happiness and peace,
Content that sweetens each employ,
And makes each station please.

6

That this be fair Eliza's lot,
My constant prayer shall be;
An orphan's prayers are ne'er forgot
By Him who all can see.

Occasional Verses on the Anniversary of the Death of my Grand-father, Dr. Thomas Graeme[5]

> In vain, sweet sleep, I seek thy gentle aid,
> And court thy pleasures in this silent shade;
> Still in remembrance wakes the painful sigh,
> And fond affection fills my streaming eye;
> Not these long years have blotted from my mind
> The friend I on this mournful day resign'd;
> Ye honored shade, while heaven extends my days,
> My grateful heart thy generous worth shall praise;
> Thy virtues still shall in my bosom glow;
> At thy good name the ready tear shall flow:
> Thy kind instruction guide my erring youth,
> Thy blest example point the path of truth.
> And on each circling year on this sad day,
> To this my breast in votive tribute pay.
> And oh, coy sleep, since now you fly my head,
> On Damon's[6] pillow thy kind balsam shed;
> Around his bed your peaceful wings extend;
> And pour your soothing blessings on my friend:
> Oh hear my sighs, ye bright angelic powers,
> And shield from every ill his slumb'ring hours:
> May health's blest bloom this much lov'd face adorn,
> And wake with sprightly cheer each coming morn.
> So shall his Sylvia's heart again rejoice,
> And beat responsive to his well known voice;
> For oh without him life no joy can give,
> Bereft of him it is but death to live!
> His tender love can pain, dread terror disarm,
> And health from him must gain its power to charm.
> Oh then in pity to this anxious breast,
> Ye gentle spirits guard his [illegible] rest;
> Bring him again to bless this waking heart
> With all the joys that love can e'er impart.

On Reading Swift's Works[7]

Ungenerous bard, whom not e'en Stella's charms
Thy vengeful satire of its sting disarms!
Say when thou dipp'st thy keenest pen in gall,
Why must it still on helpless woman fall?
Why must our "dirt and dullness" fill each line,
Our love of "follies, our desire to shine?"
Why are we drawn as a whole race of fools,
Unsway'd alike by sense or virtue's rules?
Oh! had thy heart with generous candor glowed,
Hadst thou alone on vice thy lash bestow'd,
Had there fair Purity her form imprest,
And had the milder virtues fill'd thy breast;
Thy sprightly page had been by all approv'd,
And what we now admire, we then had loved.
But thy harsh satire, rude, severe, unjust,
Awakes too oft our anger or disgust.
Such are the scenes which still thy pen engage,
That modesty disdains the shameless page.
'Tis true, we own thy wit almost divine,
And view the diamond 'midst the dunghill shine:
Oh, had it sparkled on the breast of youth,
To charm the sage, and to instruct with truth,
To chase the gloom of ignorance away,
And teach mankind with wisdom to be gay;
Thy perfect style, thy wit serenely bright,
Would shed through distant climes their pleasing light;
Mankind would grateful to thy muse attend,
And after ages hail thee as their friend!
But now, so oft filth chokes thy sprightly fire,
We loathe one instant, and the next admire—
Even while we laugh, we mourn thy wit's abuse,
And while we praise thy talents, scorn their use.

Philadelphia, 1774   Sylvia

Ode to Sensibility

1

Oh Sensibility divine!
Who only joys bestows,
An humble votary at thy shrine;
Receive thy suppliant's vows!

2

Celestial maid, thy nameless charms
To Beauty's self adds grace.
Tis thou can oft the brave disarm,
Beyond the perfect face.

3

Thine is the brightly glittering tear!
In Pity's [illegible] eye.
Tis thine to prompt the sigh sincere
Of generous sympathy.

4

Tis thine the sweetly mantling blush
O'er Virtue's cheek to spread;
Tis thine at [illegible] enticing touch
The cherub's smile to shed.

5

Without thee Beauty's lifeless form
But coldly we approve;
Tis thou alone on earth can warm,
And ev'ry passion move.

6

Thine is the fever's decent joy,
Thine friendship's softest scenes,
Thine are those sweets which cannot cloy,
Thine pleasure's brightest dreams.

7

Then come thou friend of bliss sincere!
Within my bosom dwell,
With all these keen sensations near,
We feel but cannot tell.

8

Still may I feelingly alive
To thy loved influence be.
Oh may I ne'er thy power survive,
Ne'er live bereft of thee.

Philadelphia, 1774   Sylvia

A Song[8]

1

When first I heard my Damon's sighs,
When first I read his sparkling eyes,
Against their power I idly strove:
And proudly thought I ne'er could love.

2

His virtues oft I warmly prais'd,
I thought alone esteem they rais'd,
That worth like his I should approve;
But still I thought not it was love.

3

When e'er I heard his angel tongue,
On all his words I fondly hung;
With ev'ry sound my heart would move,
But yet I knew not it was love.

4

Though soft compassion I betray'd,
With joy the anxious youth survey'd:
His artless sighs my bosom mov'd,
I pity felt and own'd I lov'd.

5

Since that blest day no doubts molest,
No jealous fears disturb my breast,
Convinc'd my Damon ne'er will rove,
But still deserve his Sylvia's love.

6

I feel no wish my bosom swell,
But still in Damon's heart to dwell:
This tender wish may Heaven approve,
And kindly bless our mutual love.

Sylvia

Philadelphia, Nov[embe]r 25, 1774

An Elegy to the Memory of the American Volunteers, who Fell in the Engagement Between the Massachusetts-Bay Militia, and the British Troops. April 19, 1775.[9]

Let joy be dumb, let mirth's gay carol cease,
See plaintive sorrow comes bedew'd with tears;
With mournful steps retires the cherub peace,
And horrid war with all his train appears.

He comes, and crimson slaughter marks his way,
Stern famine follows in his vengeful tread;
Before him pleasure, hope, and love decay,
And meek-eye'd mercy hangs the drooping head.

Fled like a dream are those delightful hours,
When here with innocence and peace we rov'd
Secure and happy in our native bowers,
Blest in the presence of the youths we lov'd.

The blow is struck, which through each future age
Shall call from pity's eye the frequent tear;
Which gives the brother to the brother's rage,
And dyes with British blood, the British spear.

Where e'er the barb'rous story shall be told,
The British cheek shall glow with conscious shame;
This deed in bloody characters enroll'd,
Shall stain the luster of their former name.

But you, ye brave defenders of our cause,
The first in this dire contest call'd to bleed,
Your names hereafter crown'd with just applause,
Each manly breast with joy-mixt woe shall read;

Your memories, dear to every free-born mind,
Shall need no monument your fame to raise,
Forever in our grateful hearts enshrin'd,
And blest by your united country's praise.

But O permit the muse with grief sincere,
The widow's heart-felt anguish to bemoan,
To join the sisters, and the orphans tear,
Whom this sad day from all they lov'd has torn:

Blest be this humble strain if it imparts
The dawn of peace to but one pensive breast,
If it can hush one sigh that rends your hearts,
Or lull your sorrows to a short liv'd rest.

But vain the hope, too well this bosom knows
How faint is glory's voice to nature's calls:
How weak the balm the laurel wreath bestows,
To heal our breasts, when love or friendship falls.

Yet think, they in their country's cause expir'd,
While guardian angels watch'd their parting sighs,
Their dying breasts with constancy inspir'd,
And bade them welcome to their native skies.

Our future fate is wrapt in darkest gloom
And threat'ning clouds, from which their souls are freed;
Ere the big tempest burst they press the tomb,
Not doom'd to see their much-lov'd country bleed.

O let such thoughts as these assuage your grief,
And stop the tear of sorrow as it flows,
Till Time's all powerful hand shall yield relief,
And shed a kind oblivion o'er your woes.

But oh thou Being infinitely just,
Whose boundless eye with mercy looks on all,

On thee alone thy humbled people trust,
On thee alone for their deliverance call.

Long did thy hand unnumber'd blessings shower,
And crown our land with liberty and peace;
Extend, O Lord, again thy saving power,
And bid the horrors of invasion cease.

But if thy awful wisdom has decreed
That we severer evils yet shall know,
By thy Almighty justice doom'd to bleed,
And deeper drink the bitter draughts of woe,

O grant us, Heaven, that constancy of mind
Which over adverse fortune rises still,
Unshaken faith, calm fortitude resign'd,
And full submission to thy holy will.

To Thee, Eternal Parent, we resign
Our bleeding cause and on thy wisdom rest;
With grateful hearts we bless thy power divine,
And own resign'd "Whatever is, is best."

Philadelphia, May 2, 1775   Sylvia

Sarah Wentworth Morton

(August, 1759-May 14, 1846)

Born in Boston to James and Sarah (Wentworth) Apthorp, young Sarah Apthorp enjoyed the prestige and economic security of two established merchant families. Afforded the luxury of a disciplined and unusually extensive education, she began writing verse as a child of ten, not long after her family moved to Braintree. Sarah Apthorp weathered the revolution as part of a family suspected of loyalist sympathies, but even in an ardently patriotic community she acquired a local reputation for her poetry. (Sarah herself seems to have been a patriot.) On February 24, 1781, she married Perez Morton, a young Boston lawyer and noted patriot. In 1784, the Mortons purchased and moved into the ancestral Apthorp House on State Street in Boston, thereby securing it from confiscation as loyalist property. Perez and Sarah Morton remained there until 1797 (at which time they moved to Dorchester), enjoying the rich social life of Boston, facilitating Perez Morton's rise to political prominence and raising five children.

Neither an active social life nor a growing family deterred Sarah Morton from pursuing her writing. Her home became a gathering place for the Boston literati. Her friends and acquaintances included John and Abigail Adams, Mercy and James Warren, Robert Treat Paine, Jr. and Joseph Dennie. In such an environment, encouragement for her writing was ready at hand. Unil 1788, most of Morton's work circulated in manuscript among friends; later she found periodicals, especially the *Columbian Centinel* and the *Massachusetts Magazine*, which would print her individual pieces. After a brief verse dialogue with Judith Sargent Murray over her use of Murray's pseudonym "Constantia," Morton signed her work as "Philenia." In 1790, Thomas and Andrews of Boston published her first book-length production, *Ouâbi: or the Virtues of Nature. An Indian Tale in Four Cantos.* Exploring native materials in borrowed forms, Morton's books, broadsides and periodical pieces appeared regularly for the next several years. Although the abstraction and conventionality of her images seldom move modern readers, "Philenia" was widely read in the new United States. Her prolific writing earned her such epithets as "the Sappho of America" and "the Mrs. Montagu of America."

These successes of Morton's literary career, however, could not compensate for the depressing events in her personal life. In the summer of 1788, an affair between Frances Apthorp, her sister, and Perez Morton (apparently never noted for his fidelity) became the gossip of Boston. Although Sarah Morton seemed to feel sympathy for Frances, who had borne a child by Perez, the censure of the rest of the Apthorp family was more than Frances could bear: she committed suicide soon after the affair was revealed. Several of Morton's poems, including "Stanzas to a Recently United Husband" printed here, may have been generated by the scandal. But whatever its impact, her marriage survived until Perez Morton's death in 1837. Ironically, a novel by William Hill Brown, *The Power of Sympathy*, using the Morton scandal for its plot, was erroneously attributed to Sarah Morton by nineteenth-century researchers.[1]

Not long after Frances' suicide, Sarah Morton gave birth to a son who lived only a few hours, another grief soon translated into verse. The premature deaths of her only other son Charles and of her youngest daughter Charlotte combined with earlier sorrows to prompt a melancholy note to *My Mind and Its Thoughts* (1823), her last major publication.

> A series of disappointments, with distress, cruelly aggravated by the premature death of very dear children, . . . left that stagnation of heart, and that pulsation of brain, which sometimes seems to precede the most deplorable of human miseries.[2]

Apparently to avoid a nervous breakdown, Sarah Morton had turned to her writing again, this time to a combination of prose and verse appropriately subtitled "In Sketches, Fragments, and Essays."

Reworking the themes of sorrow, betrayal and resignation which had been part of her message throughout her life, Sarah Morton returned less often to the pastoral themes of her earlier work. Preoccupied by the disintegration of family ties that had meant so much to her, she explained the fragmentary nature of *My Mind and Its Thoughts:*

> Thus occupied—with neither leisure, nor disposition, nor capacity to write a book, there has always been opportunity to pen a thought, or to pencil a recollection.[3]

Aware of her family heritage—perhaps extravagantly proud of it— Morton incorporated her mother's name into her own on the title page of this volume, signing her name to her work for the first time.

The melancholy preoccupations of *My Mind and Its Thoughts*, however, present only part of the Sarah Morton who often moved beyond personal and family themes into political and social issues. Despite unquestioningly conventional views regarding the participation of women in public affairs, she remained a moderate Federalist while her husband became a prominent member of the Democratic-Republican party in Boston. Furthermore, although Perez Morton joined Boston's so-called "Jacobin Club," Sarah wrote "Marie Antoinette" and "Batavia" to express her horror of the excesses of the French Revolution. Both Mortons were outspoken abolitionists; Sarah's "The African Chief" (included here) was frequently reprinted in contemporary anthologies for its anti-slavery sentiments.

Sarah Morton's denunciation of Mary Wollstonecraft's "pernicious precepts, and still more pernicious practice"[4] and of the "neglectful habits of some literary women"[5] mark her as a traditionalist regarding women's roles. But though she usually accepts the necessity for the submission of women, she sounds an impatient, even bitter, note in her essay on "The Sexes":

> To the mere superficial observer, it would seem that man was sent into this breathing world for the purpose of enjoyment—woman for that of trial and of suffering.... To man belong professions, dignities, authorities, and pleasures; for woman, there remain only duties, domestic virtues, and perhaps as the result of these, the happiness of tranquil submission....[6]

The price of that "tranquil submission" is unintentionally recorded in the melancholic, occasionally self-pitying, often cynical tone of Sarah Morton's verse. Outliving her children and her literary reputation, she died on May 14, 1846, in her childhood home at Braintree (by then part of Quincy).

Morton's manuscripts are in the collection of The Huntington Library in San Marino, California. Her major publications, some of which have already been enumerated, are listed in the checklist appended to this volume. *My Mind and Its Thoughts* (Boston, 1823) is readily available in facsimile edition (Delmar, N.Y., 1975). The most detailed secondary account of Morton's life is Emily Pendleton and Milton Ellis' *Philenia: The Life of Sarah Wentworth Morton* (Orono, Me., 1931), which includes a sizeable bibliography. Ola Elizabeth Winslow's "Sarah Wentworth Apthorp Morton" in *Notable American Women*, eds. Edward James, Janet Wilson James and Paul Boyer (Cambridge, Mass., 1971), II, 586-587, provides a useful snyopsis of her life and works.

Lines to the Breath of Kindness[7]

Sweet is the garden's breeze that flows,
With health and sweetness from the rose;
Charm'd was the strain Cecilia knew,
And with enrapturing finger drew;
So sweet the breath which kindness moves,
So charms the voice attention loves:
She, with the organ's lifted peal,
Could make a listening angel feel,
With floating wing from heaven descend,
And o'er her fine attractions bend;[8]
To thee a finer strain is given,
A strain that wins the heart to heaven.

What time the breath of kindness steals
O'er every pang that sorrow feels;
With all affection's hoarded stores,
How rich the balmy whisper pours,
Rich as the spring's first blossom blows,
Warm as the lip of summer glows;
Sweet as the morning's clovered vale,
And healthful as its zephyr'd gale,
More prized than wealth; than worlds more dear;
Still may that whisper loiter near;
Still to this trusting heart reveal
What only thou—loved friend! can'st feel.

To Constantia[9]

When press'd by ills, and sinking with despair,
When the cold friend with low'ring fortune frown'd,
When life hung quiv'ring on a single hair,
And midst a sea of grief my hopes were drown'd:

I dared not murmur;—Heaven allow'd the deed,
My dark horizon gave no sunny views,

For fate had destin'd that my heart should bleed,
And all my solace was the pensive muse.

One constant state my hapless life has known,
One constant love my changeless bosom moves,
Constant to virtue though oppression frown,
And constant to the friend my soul approves.

Thy name Constantia met my listening ear,
Unconscious of a theft I chose the lay.
Clouded with grief my gloomy strains appear,
Nor could thy genius lend its fervid ray.

The muse inspir'd, I touch'd the trembling string,
But how unlike the magic of thy line!
Could joyful light from sorrowing darkness spring,
Or streams of music from a plaint like mine.

Around thy head fair wreaths of myrtle blew,
Should I like envy tear those wreaths away!
And plant sad cypress where the laurel grew!
Or add dim tapers to the blaze of day.

Yet still to thee my wandering fancy clings,
Still on thy name would timid grief recline,
Attentive listen when Constantia sings,
And yield one tribute to her honor'd shrine.

                         Philenia Constantia

To Mr. Stuart. Upon Seeing Those Portraits Which were Painted by Him at Philadelphia, in the Beginning of the Present Century.

Stuart, thy portraits speak!—with skill divine
Round the light graces flows the waving line;
Expression in its finest utterance lives,

And a new language to creation gives.
Each varying trait the gifted artist shows,
Wisdom majestic in his bending brows;
The warrior's open front, his eye of fire—
As where the charms of bashful youth retire.
Or patient, plodding, and with wealth content,
The man of commerce counts his cent per cent.
'Tis character that breathes, 'tis soul that twines
Round the rich canvas, traced in living lines,
Speaks in the face, as in the form display'd,
Warms in the tint, and mellows in the shade.
Those touching graces, and that front sublime,
Thy hand shall rescue from the spoil of time.
Hence the fair victim scorns the threat'ning rage,
And stealing step, of slow advancing age.
Still on her cheek the bright carnation blows,
Her lip's deep blush its breathing sweetness shows.
For like the magic wand, thy pencil gives
Its potent charm, and every feature lives.

    Even as the powerful eye's transcendent ray
Bends its soft glance and bids the heart obey,
Thy fine perceptions flow, by heaven designed,
To reach the thought, and pierce the unfolded mind.
Through its swift course the rapid feeling trace,
And stamp the sovereign passion on the face.

    Even one, by no enlivening grace arrayed,
One, born to linger in affliction's shade,
Hast thou, kind artist, with attraction dressed,
With all that nature in her soul expressed.

    Go on, and may reward thy cares attend;
—The friend of genius must remain thy friend,
Though sordid minds with impious touch presume
To blend thy laurel with the cypress gloom,
With tears of grief its shining leaves to fade,
Its fair hope withering in the cheerless shade,
The well-earned meed of liberal praise deny,
And on thy talents gaze with dubious eye.

Genius is sorrow's child—to want allied—
Consoled by glory, and sustained by pride,
To souls sublime her richest wreath she owes,
And loves that fame which kindred worth bestows.

Sonnet To the Full Summer Moon

Thou silent traveller, of the glance benign,
    Who from yon crystal car on high
    Shedd'st the full luster of thy moving eye,
While the touched hills and vales reflective shine.

I love the wanderings of thy varied beam,
    What time the pale west bends thy silver wire—
    Till in the gorgeous east, thou bidst the sun retire,
Mingling warm blushes with his parting gleam.

He draws his crimsoned curtain round the main,
    And from the moist earth drinks refreshing dews;
Thou, gently bending o'er the child of pain;
    Canst charm the sadness of the mourning muse.

He, the proud emblem of oppressive power;
Thou, the mild sovereign of the pitying hour!

Stanzas to a Husband Recently United[10]

In vain upon that hand reclined,
    I call each plighted worth my own,
Or rising to thy sovereign mind
    Say that it reigns for me alone.

Since, subject to its ardent sway,
    How many hearts were left to weep,

To find the granted wish decay,
    And the triumphant passion sleep!

Such were of love the transient flame,
    Which by the kindling senses led,
To every new attraction came,
    And from the known allurement fled.

Unlike the generous care that flows,
    With all the rich affections give,
Unlike the mutual hope that knows
    But for a dearer self to live.

Was theirs the tender glance to speak
    Timid, through many a sparkling tear,
The ever changing hue of cheek,
    Its flush of joy, its chill of fear?

Or theirs the full expanded thought,
    By taste and moral sense refined,
Each moment with instruction fraught,
    The tutor'd elegance of mind?

Be mine the sacred truth that dwells
    On One by kindred virtues known,
And mine the chastened glance which tells
    That sacred truth to Him alone.

No sordid hope's insidious guise,
    No venal pleasure's serpent twine
Invites those soul-illumined eyes,
    And blends this feeling heart with thine.

Memento, for My Infant Who Lived But Eighteen Hours

As the pure snow-drop, child of April tears,
    Shook by the rough wind's desolating breath—

Scarce o'er the chilly sod its low head rears,
    And trembling dies upon the parent heath,

So my lost boy, arrayed in fancy's charms,
    Just born to mourn—with premature decay
To the cold tyrant stretched his feeble arms,
    And struggling sighed his little life away.

As not in vain the early snow-drop rose,
    Though short its date, and hard the withering gale;
Since its pale bloom ethereal balm bestows,
    And cheers with vernal hope the wasted vale.

My perished child, dear pledge of many a pain!
    Torn from this ruffian world, in yon bright sphere,
Joins with awakened voice the cherub train,
    And pours his sweet breath on a mother's ear.

Kind dreams of morn his fairy phantom bring,
    And floating tones of ecstacy impart,
Soft as when seraphs strike the heavenly string
    To charm the settled sorrow of the heart.

The African Chief

See how the black ship cleaves the main,
    High bounding o'er the dark blue wave,
Remurmuring with the groans of pain,
    Deep freighted with the princely slave!

Did all the Gods of Afric sleep,
    Forgetful of their guardian love,
When the white tyrants of the deep
    Betrayed him in the palmy grove?

A chief of Gambia's golden shore,
    Whose arm the band of warriors led,
Or more—the lord of generous power,
    By whom the foodless poor were fed.

Does not the voice of reason cry,
  Claim the first right that nature gave,
From the red scourge of bondage fly,
  Nor deign to live a burdened slave?

Has not his suffering offspring clung,
  Desponding round his fettered knee;
On his worn shoulder, weeping hung,
  And urged one effort to be free?

His wife by nameless wrongs subdued,
  His bosom's friend to death resigned;
The flinty path-way drenched in blood,
  He saw with cold and frenzied mind.

Strong in despair, then sought the plain,
  To heaven was raised his steadfast eye,
Resolved to burst the crushing chain,
  Or mid the battle's blast to die.

First of his race, he led the band,
  Guardless of danger, hurling round,
Till by his red avenging hand,
  Full many a despot stained the ground.

When erst Messenia's sons oppressed
  Flew desperate to the sanguine field,
With iron clothed each injured breast,
  And saw the cruel Spartan yield,

Did not the soul to heaven allied,
  With the proud heart as greatly swell,
As when the Roman Decius died,
  Or when the Grecian victim fell? [11]

Do later deeds quick rapture raise,
  The boon Batavia's William won,
Paoli's time-enduring praise,
  Or the yet greater Washington?

If these exalt thy sacred zeal,
  To hate oppression's mad control,

For bleeding Afric learn to feel,
  Whose Chieftain claimed a kindred soul.

Ah, mourn the last disastrous hour,
  Lift the full eye of bootless grief,
While victory treads the sultry shore,
  And tears from hope the captive chief.

While the hard race of pallid hue,
  Unpracticed in the power to feel,
Resign him to the murderous crew,
  The horrors of the quivering wheel,

Let sorrow bathe each blushing cheek,
  Bend piteous o'er the tortured slave,
Whose wrongs compassion cannot speak,
  Whose only refuge was the grave.

Ode Inscribed to Mrs. M. Warren[12]

Amid the splendor of that fame
  Immortal genius rais'd,
With all the love thy virtues claim,
  Virtues by envy prais'd,
The least of bright Apollo's choir
  Awakes the willing lyre;
And at thy feet the grateful tribute pays,
Due to thy matchless worth, thy fame-embellish'd lays.

Though o'er Columbia's plain,
  Fair science smil'd;
And many a muse-enraptur'd swain
  Lent music to the wild;
No fair one by Minerva led,
  Approach'd Pieria's spring,
Or dar'd the flow'ry paths to tread,
  Or tune the golden string.

But timid genius from herself retires,
Conceals her darting rays, and damps her kindling fires.

   Till bursting through the veil of night,
   Bright as the floating beams of light,
     Thy glowing strains appear;
   To lead the envied way is thine—
   Since only distant praise is mine,
     Ah! deign that praise to hear.
While o'er Parnassian heights thy muse ascends,
Low in the vale my humble genius bends.

   Not that round thy hallow'd brow,
   Fairest wreaths of laurel flow;
   That the graces of the Nine,
   Every power of song is thine;
   That Minerva leads the way,
   And thy ready steps obey:
   Not from these, alone, I raise
   All thy glory, all thy praise;
   Though to genius much is due,
   Brighter plaudits shine on you;
The heart, that melts at every woe,
   Which rends another's breast;
The mind, that feels th' enraptured glow,
   Whcne'er another's blest;
That o'er dejected virtue's sigh,
   Can pour the balm of care,
And from the magic of the eye,
   Lend patience to despair:
These are thy boast, and these shall grace thy name,
Beyond the glories of a deathless fame.

              Philenia Constantia

Part Two

Infrequent Poets

Sarah Goodhue

(1641-July 23, 1681)

A life-long resident of Ipswich, Massachusetts, Sarah Whipple Goodhue left a few verses to her family in her prose *Copy of a Valedictory and Monitory Writing* (1681). Sensing that her death was near as she approached childbirth, she desired to "declare something of [her] mind, lest [she] should afterwards have no opportunity."[1] Though the bulk of the *Writing* consists of consoling remarks for her family and spiritual admonitions to "hear the voice of the Lord," she doesn't neglect practical matters: she even names the families to which she felt her husband should send their children after her death. The comforting verses seem particularly appropriate since the title-page informs us that Sarah Goodhue "died suddenly (as she presaged she should) July 23, 1681, three days after she had been delivered of two hopeful children, leaving ten in all surviving." Goodhue's *Copy of a Valedictory and Monitory Writing* was first published in Cambridge, Massachusetts, in 1681. Reprints were made available in 1770, 1773, 1805 and 1850. Thomas F. Waters includes a full text in an appendix to *Ipswich in the Massachusetts Colony*, 2 vols. (Ipswich, Mass., 1905-1917), II, 519-524.

[Lines to Her Family]

My first, as thy name is Joseph, labor so in knowledge to increase,
As to be freed from the guilt of thy sins, and enjoy eternal peace.

Mary, labor so to be arrayed with the hidden man of the heart,
That with Mary thou mayst find thou hast chosen the better part.

William, thou hast that name for thy grandfather's sake,
Labor so to tread in his steps, as over sin conquest thou mayst make.

Sarah, Sarah's daughter thou shalt be, if thou continuest in doing well,
Labor so in holiness among the daughters to walk, as that thou may
                                                                excel.
So my children all, if I must be gone, I with tears bid you all farewell.
                                              The Lord bless you all.

Now, dear husband, I can do no less than turn unto thee,
And if I could, I would naturally mourn with thee:

    .   .   .   .

O dear heart, if I must leave thee and thine here behind,
Of my natural affection here is my heart and hand.

Anna Tompson Hayden

(1648-post 1720)

Anna Tompson Hayden, sister of the better-known poet Benjamin Tompson, was first noted as a writer with the publication in 1927 of the manuscript journal of Joseph Tompson of Billerica. Born in Braintree, Massachusetts, in 1648, Hayden leaves little record except two elegies (for only one of which the attribution is certain) copied into Tompson's journal sometime before 1715. Awkward syntax and pedestrian materials mark the poems as early (perhaps only) works. But an interesting aside, a parenthetical remark in Hayden's elegy to her brother, underscores contemporary attitudes regarding female intellectual capabilities. Noting the frequency with which she and her brother Benjamin "with discourse have pleased each other," Hayden mentions

> (Some that have wondered how I could find
> Discourse with you to please your mind.)

Apparently Joseph Tompson was a more astute judge of poetry than his limited education would indicate, for he includes Hayden's poems in his journal "not for the poetry, but for the love and . . . Christian spirit breathing in them."[1]

Anna Hayden's verse is included by Kenneth Murdock in his edition of Joseph Tompson's journal, *Handkerchiefs from Paul* (Cambridge, Mass., 1927), pp. 6-7, 20-22. Emily Stipes Watts discusses Hayden briefly in *The Poetry of American Women from 1632 to 1945* (Austin, Texas, 1977), pp. 23-25.

Upon the Death of that Desirable Young Virgin, Elizabeth Tomp-
son,[2] *Daughter of Joseph and Mary Tompson of Bilerika, Who*
Deceased in Boston Out of the House of Mr. Legg, 24 August, 1712,
Aged 22 Years

A lovely flow'r cropt in its prime
    By Death's cold fatal hand;
A warning here is left for all
    Ready prepar'd to stand.
For none can tell who shall be next,
    Yet all may it expect;
Then surely it concerneth all,
    Their time not to neglect.
How many awful warnings that
    Before us oft are set,
That as a flaming sword to mind
    Our youth hath often met,
To stop them in their course
    And mind them of their end,
To make them to consider
    Whither their ways to tend.
We see one suddenly taken hence
    That might have lived as long
For the few years she'd lived here
    As any she lived among.
Her harmless blameless life
    Will stand for her defence,
And be an honor to her name
    Now she is gone from hence.

A Supplement

Charity bids us hope that she'll among those virgins be,
    When Christ shall come to reign,
Whom he will own among the wise,
    And for his entertain.

[Verses on Benjamin Tompson] [3]

Ah, my dear brother, though your gone,
I do you often think upon,
Of your great kindness shown to me
In my greatest extremity.
You all ways had a friendly care
Of what might be for my welfare,
And often did me counsel give
How I should walk and happy live.
But now your gone, and left me here,
A place of sorrow, care and fear.
I hope that you've attain'd that rest
Where nothing there will you molest,
Where I do hope ere long to be,
Where's better times and company.
You've left me cause of great content:
Before your life was fully spent,
Many a time we walk't together
And with discourse have pleas'd each other.
(Some that have wondered how I could find
Discourse with you to please your mind.)
But we must now discourse no more,
As we were used to do before,
And mourn as much as any among;
But time is short, and then I'll sing another song.
You brought up many plants
That are plants of renown,
And, now that you are taken hence,
Add luster to your crown,
To our dear father show'd respect
And duty to him never did neglect.
He to his friends was all ways kind—
On all occasions they did find
A ready and comprising wit—
And all ways had [an] answer fit,
That sometimes 'maz'd the ignorant,
But pleasing to the wise,
That did his wit and learning highly prize.
"Speak well of the living, don't reproach the dead,"
This was his counsel might in his life be read;
Be not fond of living, yet prepar'd to die,

Was his advice to me in mine extremity.
Courteous to all, both high and low,
And due respect to all and every one did show.
Thus we daily drop away and take our flight
Both from each other's company and sight.
Did we but realize what we daily see,
Other manner of persons we should be:
Not so concern'd for things that's here below,
Not knowing how soon we from hence must go.
Here we have seen, within a little space,
Change upon change, and many run your race,
Who, may be, thought but little of death or dyin[g],
Or little minded how their time was flying.
O happy they, that are prepar'd to die,
And are convinc'd of this world's vanity,
And have made sure of a more happy pl[ace]!
Their souls are now in a most happy c[ase.]

Mary English

(1652?-1694)

The author of a single religious acrostic, Mary English is better known as a victim of the Salem witch trials than as a poet. Daughter of William and Elinor Hollingsworth, she married the well-to-do Salem merchant, Philip English, in 1675. Though her husband was staunchly Episcopalian, Mary English was admitted to Congregational church membership in 1681. Both Mary and Philip English were accused of witchcraft in April, 1692. They avoided execution by escaping to New York with the aid of friends, but affected by the strain of imprisonment, Mary English died in 1694.

Her only known verse is included on page 164 of George F. Chever's "A Sketch of Philip English . . . ," *Historical Collections of the Essex Institute*, 1 (1859), 157-181, which also includes a brief biography. Chever's article is part of a continuing series containing detailed information about the witchcraft trials. The sections which concern the Englishes are *EIHC*, 2 (1860), 137-139, 201-202, and *EIHC*, 3 (1861), 114.

[Acrostic]

May I with Mary choose the better part
And serve the Lord with all my heart,
Receive his word most joyfully
Y [And] live to him eternally.

Everliving God I pray,
Never leave me for to stray;
Give me grace thee to obey.
Lord grant that I may happy be
In Jesus Christ eternally.
Save me dear Lord by thy rich grace;
Heaven then shall be my dwelling place.

Elizabeth Bradford

(1663?-July 8, 1731)

If one judges from the arguments rather than the technique of her only published verse, Elizabeth Bradford was a devoted admirer of poetry. Born in London to the Quaker printer Andrew Sowle and his wife (whose identity is not available), she married her father's apprentice, William Bradford, in 1685. Emigrating to America the same year, the Bradfords settled temporarily in Philadelphia. They were permanently settled with a printing business in New York by 1693, Elizabeth dying there in 1731. When William Bradford published an edition of the Baptist divine Benjamin Keach's *War With the Devil* . . . in 1707, he and Elizabeth each supplied a prefatory poem. Although the poems are initialed rather than signed, A. S. W. Rosenbach includes the full attribution in *Early American Children's Books* (Portland, Me., 1933), p. 6.

To the Reader, in Vindication of this Book

One or two lines to thee I'll here commend,
This honest poem to defend
From calumny, because at this day,
All poetry there's many do gain-say,
And very much condemn, as if the same
Did worthily deserve reproach and blame.
If any book in verse, they chance to spy,
Away profane, they presently do cry:
But though this kind of writing some dispraise,
Sith men so captious are in these our days,
Yet I dare say, how e'er the scruple rose,
Verse hath express'd as secret things as prose.
Though some there be that poetry abuse,
Must we therefore, not the same method use?
Yea, sure, for of my conscience 'tis the best,
And doth deserve more honor than the rest.
For 'tis no humane knowledge gain'd by art,
But rather 'tis inspir'd into the heart
By divine means; for true divinity
Hath with this science great affinity:
Though some through ignorance, do it oppose,
Many do it esteem, far more than prose:
And find also that unto them it brings
Content, and hath been the delight of kings.
David, although a king, yet was a poet,
And Solomon, also, the Scriptures show it.
Then what if for all this some should abuse it?
I'm apt to think that angels do embrace it,
And though God giv't here but in part to some,
Saints shall hav't perfect in the world to come.

Sarah Kemble Knight

(April 19, 1666-September 25, 1727)

Except for her full and entertaining journal account of an arduous trip to New York in 1704, only fragmented records of Sarah Kemble Knight survive. She was born into the Boston merchant family of Thomas Kemble and Elizabeth Trerice on April 19, 1666. Although her published journal reveals her considerable cultivation, independence and wit, the source of her education is unknown. Sometime before her father's death in early 1689, she married Richard Knight, about whom little is known save that he died after 1706, leaving his widow with a single child, Elizabeth, who had been born on May 8, 1689. Soon after Elizabeth married John Livingston of New London, Connecticut, in 1713, Sarah Knight disposed of some of her Massachusetts property and resettled near her daughter. Continuing a variety of careers in her new residence, Knight was by turns shop-keeper, inn-keeper, tavern-keeper, farm manager and real estate speculator, earning a comfortable living that resulted in an estate worth over £1800 when she died in 1727. Dates of births and marriages, property transactions, court records (including a fine for selling liquor to Indians), a communion cup donated to the church in Norwich, Connecticut, a tombstone in New London, Connecticut—little else remains to complete our sketch.

Despite financial accomplishments remarkable for a colonial woman, Sarah Knight's literary efforts are more frequently remembered. Her journal account of a five-month, horseback trip from Boston to New York in 1704 discards religious interpretations that often shape journals of the period in favor of a realistic travelogue describing, among other things, inadequate lodging, difficult or non-existent roads, and indigent, drunken, or (occasionally) helpful people. The frankness and humor of her narrative portray an unusually resilient woman fully equal to the demands of colonial life.

All but one of Knight's extant poems are included in that journal; four lines apparently scratched by Knight with a diamond on a window of her Boston home form the exception. Combining warnings to future travelers with descriptions of romanticized scenes from nature and echoes of old nursery rhymes, Knight's verse presents a candor and variety uncommon among seventeenth and early eighteenth century American writers. From a formulaic ode to the moon to a witty invocation of "potent rum" to still a noisy inn, Knight mingles her verse with her prose, reacting to a conventionally-perceived natural world and an apparently more genuine human environment. A strong curse for a slovenly inn-keeper is quickly followed by a sympathetic glance at the rural poverty through which she passes.

> These indigents have hunger with their ease;
> Their best is worse behalf than my disease.

Such range of subject matter denotes a remarkable personality, if not an accomplished poet.

Knight's journal manuscript no longer exists; by one account it was accidently used to start a fire.[1] The frequent reprintings have usually been based on the first edition by Theodore Dwight, Jr., in 1825, well over a century after the journal had been written. Recent printings, New York in 1970 and Boston in 1972, make Knight's travelogue readily accessible to modern readers. A text for the poem Knight scratched on her window is included by "W. B. D." in "Madam Knights [sic]," *The Historical Magazine*, 9 (March, 1865), 93-94, in a note that draws extensively from "memoranda" of Hannah Mather Crocker, who had memorized the lines; Crocker's handwritten notes are bound into a copy of Knight's journal in the American Antiquarian Society.

Anecdotes (sometimes apocryphal) of Sarah Knight's life abound. Published resources include Frances Caulkin's *History of New London* (New London, Conn., 1852), pp. 364-365, 371-373, and her *History of Norwich* (Norwich, Conn., 1866), pp. 278, 283-284; Alice Morse Earle's *Colonial Dames and Good Wives* (Boston, 1895), pp. 135-159; Lucy Sayles' "A Brave Knight of the Seventeenth Century," *Connecticut Magazine*, 7 (1902), 334-338; and Harry C. Green and Mary W. Green's *Pioneer Mothers in America* (New York, 1912), I, 442-455. A collection by William R. Deane of rough biographical notes from the official records of several Massachusetts and Connecticut towns and from other published accounts was gathered for a study Deane never wrote; his notes are deposited in the New England Historic Genealogical Society. The most reliable biographical sketch is Malcolm Freiberg's "Sarah Kemble Knight" in *Notable American Women*, eds. Edward James, Janet Wilson James, and Paul Boyer (Cambridge, Mass., 1971), II, 340-342. Alan Margolies' carefully researched "Editing and Publication of 'The Journal of Madam Knight,' " Bibliographical Society of America *Papers*, 58 (1964), 25-32, traces the text of Knight's journal, superseding an earlier account by Anson Titus, "Madam Sarah Knight: Her Diary and Her Times, 1666-1726 [sic]," *Bostonian Society Publications*, 9 (1912), 99-126. Brief remarks by Moses Coit Tyler in his *History of American Literature, 1607-1765* (New York, 1883), II, 97-99, and by Harold Jantz in *The First Century of New England Verse* (Worcester, Mass., 1944), pp. 111-112, 225-226, discuss Sarah Knight as a literary figure.

["Fair Cynthia"]

Fair Cynthia, all the homage that I may
Unto a creature, unto thee I pay;
In lonesome woods to meet so kind a guide,
To me's more worth than all the world beside.
Some joy I felt just now, when safe got o'er
Yon surly river to this rugged shore,
Deeming rough welcomes from these clownish trees
Better than lodgings with Nereidees.
Yet swelling fears surprise; all dark appears—
Nothing but light can dissipate those fears.
My fainting vitals can't lend strength to say,
But softly whisper, O I wish 'twere day.
The murmur hardly warm'd the ambient air,
Ere thy bright aspect rescues from despair:
Makes the old Hag her sable mantle loose,
And a bright joy do's through my soul diffuse.
The boistero's trees now lend a passage free,
And pleasant prospects thou giv'st light to see.

["Here Stood a Lofty Church"]

Here stood a lofty church—there is a steeple,
And there the grand parade—O see the people!
That famous castle there, were I but nigh,
To see the moat and bridge and walls so high—
They're very fine! says my deluded eye.

["I Ask Thy Aid"]

I ask thy aid, O potent rum!
To charm these wrangling topers dumb.
Thou hast their giddy brains possest—

The man confounded with the beast—
And I, poor I, can get no rest.
Intoxicate them with thy fumes:
O still their tongues till morning comes!

[*"May All that Dread the Cruel Fiend"*]

May all that dread the cruel fiend of night
Keep on, and not at this curs't mansion light.
'Tis Hell; 'tis Hell! and devils here do dwell:
Here dwells the Devil—surely this's Hell.
Nothing but wants: a drop to cool yo'r tongue
Can't be procur'd these cruel fiends among.
Plenty of horrid grins and looks severe,
Hunger and thirst, but pity's banish'd here—
The right hand keep, if Hell on earth you fear!

[*"Though Ill at Ease"*]

Though ill at ease, a stranger and alone,
All my fatigues shall not extort a groan.
These indigents have hunger with their ease;
Their best is worse behalf than my disease.
Their miserable hut which heat and cold
Alternately without repulse do hold;
Their lodgings thin and hard, their Indian fare,
The mean apparel which the wretches wear,
And their ten thousand ills which can't be told,
Makes nature ere 'tis middle aged look old.
When I reflect, my late fatigues do seem
Only a notion or forgotten dream.

["Now I've Returned"]

Now I've returned poor Sarah Knight's,
Through many toils and many frights;
Over great rocks and many stones,
God has presar'ved from fractur'd bones.

Bathsheba Bowers

(1672?-1718)

An eccentric in colonial Philadelphia, Bathsheba Bowers'
unconventional life has attracted more interest than her writing.
She was born in Massachusetts to Benanuel Bowers and Elizabeth
Dunster, English Quakers who settled in Charlestown. Enduring the
Puritan persecution of Quakers themselves, the Bowers sent four
of their daughters, including Bathsheba, to Philadelphia to escape it.
Remaining single all her life, Bowers built a small house, which became known as "Bathsheba's Bower," at the corner of Little Dock
and Second Streets. (According to tradition, the house had a balcony
from which George Whitefield preached.) Furnishing her home with
books, a table, and little else, she became a vegetarian and as much
of a recluse "as if she had lived in a cave underground or on top of
a high mountain."[1]

Although Bathsheba Bowers was a Quaker by profession, her
niece Ann Bolton recorded in her diary that Bowers "read her Bible
much but I think sometimes to no better purpose than to afford
matter for dispute in which she was always positive."[2] Becoming a
Quaker preacher, Bowers later moved to South Carolina, where
she died in 1718. But her simple life in Philadelphia had allowed
much time for her "disputes" and her books. A voracious reader, she
owned several volumes "wrote by a female hand filled with dreams
and visions and a thousand romantic notions of her seeing various
sorts of beasts and bulls in the heavens."[3] The influence of these
books by women is conjectural, but it may have been from them that
Bowers developed her own desire to write.

Bathsheba Bowers is said to have written a number of books,
for only one of which we have records today. Her spiritual autobiography, *An Alarm Sounded to Prepare . . . the World to Meet the
Lord* (which includes her few rough verses) was published in New

York in 1709, probably by William Bradford. Printed accounts of Bowers are rare and brief, but William John Potts draws useful references together in "Bathsheba Bowers," *Pennsylvania Magazine of History and Biography*, 3 (1879), 110-112. His narrative includes extracts from Ann Bolton's mansucript diary.

[Lines Written in a "Sharp Hour of Temptation"]

> That once again the Lord discover'd his grace,
> And openly shew'd to me his face.

[Lines From her Spiritual Autobiography]

> Who can know Heaven's blest continent,
>   Till they, with me,
>   Be made to set,
> That 'tis in Love's sweet cement.
> Or who can tell the depth of Hell,
>   Whilst they, as I,
>   Be made to cry,
> Where raging [horrors?] dwell.

Rev[elation] XXII V[erse] 17.

> The Spirit saith, come,
> And the Bride saith, come,
> And let all that hear, come,
> And take of the water of life freely.

> But Lord, if they will not come
> Without sin, to salvation, do thou come,
> And compel them to come,
> That we may altogether come,
> And forever sing hallelujah to Thee,
> In the 1st, 2d, 3d, 4th, 5th, 6th and 7th degree.
>   Amen, saith my soul.

Susanna Wright

(August 4, 1697-December 1, 1784)

Born in Warrington, England, to the Quaker household of Patience Gibson and John Wright, Susanna Wright received much of her formal education before her emigration to America. In later years, she was noted for her fluency in French, her competency in Italian and Latin and her background in natural philosophy. Perhaps the foundation for that learning had been set before Wright moved to Chester, Pennsylvania, where her father had established himself as a shopkeeper by 1714. With the death of her mother in 1722, she assumed responsibility for her father's household and her seven younger brothers and sisters. By 1728, the Wrights had moved to the Pennsylvania frontier, establishing Wright's Ferry in the Susquehanna Valley. Sometime after 1745, Susanna Wright moved with her brother James and his family into a nearby house and estate that had been bequeathed to her for life by Samuel Blunston. Although Wright never married, tradition has it that Blunston had been her suitor, a legend given credence by the fact of her inheritance. A remarkably active woman, Susanna Wright experimented with the cultivation of silkworms and with the medicinal uses of herbs, engaged in a variety of home manufactures, served her neighbors as occasional apothecary, physician, scrivener and arbiter, championed the causes of local Indian tribes and acquired a considerable reputation for her hopsitality and wit.

But Wright's accomplishments were intellectual as well as pragmatic. A voracious reader, she confided to Benjamin Rush shortly before her death "that she still retained her relish for books—'that she could not live without them'—and that . . . 'the pleasure of reading was to her a most tremendous blessing.' "[1] Carrying on an extensive correspondence, Wright counted among her friends such Pennsylvania notables as Benjamin Franklin, James Logan, Charles Norris and Isaac Norris. She exchanged letters and verses with

Elizabeth Graeme Fergusson (see pages 101-111), Hannah Griffitts (see pages 55-69) and Deborah Logan (whose poetry is post-Revolutionary, too late for inclusion here). Known to her contemporaries as a prolific writer and a skilled artist (though none of her drawings have been found), Susanna Wright apparently had little regard for preserving her poetry: only two manuscript poems are available. Circulating her occasional pieces among friends, she seems to have kept no personal copies; at least none have survived. (Margaret Wright and Elizabeth Heistand note that "in some of the old magazines" Wright's verses may be found "with her name attached,"[2] but I have been unable to discover any evidence of her verse being published.) Wright's poem on her 64th birthday, "My Own Birth-Day, August, 1761," may partly explain her disregard for preserving her work. Noting that few are granted so many years of life, she shrugged them off in an expression of the impermanence of temporal things:

> And what are they—a vision all the past,
> A bubble on the water's shining face,
> What yet remain, till the first transient blast,
> Shall leave no more remembrance of their place.

Characteristically, Wright framed her experience with religious interpretations that reflect her lifelong affiliation with the Society of Friends. A Quaker women of considerable cultivation, Susanna Wright was known by her contemporaries as "the famous Suzey Wright, a lady who has been celebrated above a half a century for her wit, good sense and valuable improvements of mind."[3]

Wright's extant correspondence and poetry are housed in the Historical Society of Pennsylvania. Since the manuscripts provide a spotty record at best, the material for much of Wright's biography comes from two early nineteenth-century accounts, both of which draw on an anonymous contemporary sketch, probably by Deborah Logan: "Some Account of the Early Poets and Poetry of Pennsylvania," *Register of Pennsylvania*, ed. Samuel Hazard, 8 (September 17, 1831), 177-178, and Samuel Knapp, *Female Biography* (Philadelphia, 1836), pp. 484-487. Wright's correspondence with Franklin has been published in *The Papers of Benjamin Franklin*, eds. Leonard W. Labaree et. al. (New Haven, Conn., 1959-   ), IV, 210-211; VI,

23-24; George L. Heiges summarizes the Wright-Franklin corre-
spondence in "Benjamin Franklin in Lancaster County," Lancaster
Co. (Pa.) Historical Society *Papers,* 61 (1957), 3-6, Lyman H.
Butterfield's text of "Dr. Benjamin Rush's Journal of a Trip to
Carlisle in 1784," *Pennsylvania Magazine of History and Biography*,
74 (October, 1950), 455, outlines Rush's impression of Wright.
Other biographical sketches are available in M. Katherine Jackson's
Outlines of the Literary History of Colonial Pennsylvania (Lancaster,
Pa., 1906), pp. 154-155, Gertrude Biddle and Sarah Lowrie's *Notable
Women of Pennsylvania* (Philadelphia, 1942), pp. 24-25, and the
Lancaster Co. (Pa.) Historical Society *Papers*, 26 (1922), 193; 52
(1948), 216-217. The most full and reliable accounts are those by
Marion Reninger, "Susanna Wright," Lancaster Co.(Pa.) Historical
Society *Papers*, 63 (1959), 183-189, and Frederick B. Tolles,
"Susanna Wright," *Notable American Women*, eds. Edward James,
Janet Wilson James and Paul Boyer (Cambridge, Mass., 1971), III,
688-690.

On the Death of a Young Girl, 1737

The little bird, at break of day,
   That wak'd us with its song,
And fondly hopp'd from spray to spray
   The music to prolong

Ere evening came ill fated fell,
   Struck by a hand unseen,
Resign'd that breath which pleas'd so well,
   And flutt'red on the green.

The lambs that wont to bleat and play,
   And bask in sunshine air,
That danc'd the fleeting hours away,
   And knew not want or care,

As night her sable curtain spread
   Fell to the wolf a prey,
And here—and there, (dispers'd and dead)
   The scatter'd fragments lay.

The blossoms which to vernal air
   Their fragrant leaves unfold,
And deck the spreading branches fair,
   In purple, white, and gold,

Defuse[4] their sweets, and charm the eye
   And promise future store,
Nipp'd by a frost, untimely die,
   And shed perfumes no more.

T'was thus, the poppet ceas'd to breathe,
   The small machine stood still,
The little lungs no longer heave,
   Nor motion follows will,

No more that flattering voice we hear,
   Soft as the linnet's song,
Each idle hour to sooth and cheer,
   Which slowly rolls along;

That sprightly action's past and gone,
    With all its tempting play,
Sprightly as lambs that tread the lawn
    Along a summer's day.

The dawn of reason we admir'd
    As opening blossoms fair;
Now to the silent grave retir'd
    Its organs molder there;

Flowers on thy breast, and round thy head,
    With thee their sweets resign,
Nipp'd from their tender stalks, and dead,
    Their fate resembles thine,

Just as their charms allure the eye
    And fragrant leaves unfold,
Clos'd in eternal night they lie
    To mix with common mold.

Thy harmless soul, releas'd from earth,
    A cherub sings above,
Immortal in a second birth
    By thy Redeemer's love.

My Own Birth-Day, August, 1761[5]

"Few and evil have the days of the years of my life been."—Genesis

Were few and evil, [illegible] the patriarch's days,
Extended to a length of years, unknown
In this luxurious age, whose swift decays
Allow to few, so many as my own;

And what are they—a vision all the past,
A bubble on the water's shining face,
What yet remain, till the first transient blast,
Shall leave no more remembrance of their place.

Still few and evil, as the days of old,
Are those allotted to the ease of man,
And threescore years, in sounding numbers told,
Where's the amount—a shadow, and a span;

Look back through this long tide of rolling years,
Since early reason gave reflection birth,
Recall each sad occasion of thy tears,
Then say, can happiness be found on earth?

Pass former strokes—the recent only name,
A brother, whom no healing art cou'd save,
In life's full prime, unnerv'd his manly frame,
From wasting pain, took refuge in the grave;

A darling child, all lovely, all admir'd,
Snatch'd from our arms, in youth's engaging bloom,
A Lazar tomb'd, ere his short date expir'd,
And laid a piteous object, in the tomb;

A sister, who long causeless anguish knew,
A tender parent, and a patient wife,
Calmly, she bore the bitter lot, she drew,
And clos'd her sorrows, with her close of life;

Your memories from my breast shall never stray,
Shou'd years to patriarchal age extend,
Through glooms of night, through social hours of day,
The starting tear stands ready to descend;

But though I mourn, not without hope, I mourn,
Dear kindred shades, though all unknown your place,
Though to these eyes, you never must return,
You are safe in the infinitude of space;

One all-disposing God, who gave you birth,
That life sustain'd, which his good pleasure gave,
Then cut you off, from ev'ry claim on earth,
Is the same guardian God, beyond the grave;

Though by impenetrable darkness veil'd,
Your separate state lies hid from human sight,

The Savior, friend of man, Messiah hail'd,
Brought life and immortality to light;

Rest then my soul, in these appointments rest,
And down the steep of age pursue thy way,
With humble hope, and faith unfailing blest,
The mortal shall surpass thy natal-day.

Mary French

(fl. 1703)

    Taken captive by the Indians during a raid on Deerfield, Massachusetts, in August, 1703, Mary French and her fellow prisoners were held among the French in Canada. The prisoners were forbidden to meet together for worship and were apparently pushed by their captors to accept Catholicism. In his *Good Fetch'd Out of Evil* [Boston, 1706], Cotton Mather compiled some of the captives' writings and stories, among them Mary French's 104-line poem to her sister. Rehearsing conventional Puritan precepts, French cautioned her sister "that earthly things are fading flow'rs," that she must trust "the mighty hand of God" in her captivity. No complete copy of the 1706 edition is reported, but Mather's *Good Fetch'd Out of Evil* was republished at Boston in 1783; French's poem appears on pages 22-25. *Good Fetch'd Out of Evil* is also available as part of the *Narratives of North American Indian Captivities*, ed. Wilcomb E. Washburn (New York, 1975), IV.

From *A Poem Written By a Captive Damsel, About Sixteen or Seventeen Years of Age, Who Being [Told?] That Her Younger Sister at a Distance From Her [Would?] Be Led Away by the Popish [Demons?], Address'd Her in these Lines*

Dear sister, Jesus does you call
  To walk on in his ways.
I pray make no delay at all,
  Now in your youthful days.
O turn to him, who has you made,
  While in your tender years,
For as the withering grass we fade,
  Which never more appears.
But if that God should you afford
  A longer life to live,
Remember that unto the Lord
  The praises you do give.

. . . .

That earthly things are fading flow'rs
  We by experience see;
And of our years and days and hours
  We as observers be.
Of all degrees, and every age,
  Among the dead we find;
Many there fell by bloody rage,
  When we were left behind.
Let us be silent then this day
  Under our smarting rod.
Let us with patience meekly say,
  It is the will of God.
Of friends and parents we're bereaved,
  Distresst and left alone;
Lord, we thy spirit oft have grieved:
  And now as doves we moan.

. . . .

Dear sister, bear me in your mind;
  Learn these few lines by heart;
Alas, an aching heart I find,

Since we're so long to part.
But to the care of God on high
Our cause we will commend.
For your soul sake these lines now I
Your loving sister send.

December 23d, 1703

Mercy Wheeler

(b. 1706)

Born in 1706 to Isaac and Sarah Wheeler of Plainfield, Connecticut, Mercy Wheeler was agile and healthy until 1726, when she "was taken sick of the burning ague."[1] Never fully recovering, she became totally bedridden in 1727. Slowly wasting away, feeling herself near death, Wheeler nevertheless experienced periods of revitalization that allowed her to give a conventional deathbed *Address to Young People, Or ... Warning from the Dead*. The address was taken down by Samuel Stearns, also of Plainfield, who supplied a brief biographical note dated July 10, 1732. A spirtual message to her contemporaries, Wheeler's *Address* is in prose, but Stearns preserved eight lines of her verse by quoting them in his preface. He established a context for the stanza by noting that

> in one of [his] last conferences with her, [he] could not but take peculiar notice of a sad surprise she seemed to be in from her being informed of some families which lived in the neglect of family prayer; so affected was she in her meditation on it, that she versified upon it; and rehearst to me several of the verses she had composed: one of which I will here record, hoping that it may jog some of 'em that lie snoring in such a shameful omission. . . .[2]

Spending her last years as a complete invalid, Mercy Wheeler was apparently still alive when her *Address* was published in 1733.

[*"Poor, Wretched and Vile Sinners All"*]

Poor, wretched and vile sinners all
Rank'd with the heathen nation,
Who unto God ne'er pray nor call,
For pardon and salvation.

What dreadful threats, O direful wrath!
    Such families fall under,
Who will tread that forbidden path
    Full strow'd with bolts of thunder.

Lydia Fish Willis

(April, 1709-January 25, 1767)

The scanty records of the life of Lydia Fish Willis were gathered by an anonymous editor with the publication, perhaps in 1767,
of a selection of her personal letters. Born in Duxborough, Massachusetts, in April, 1709, Willis apparently developed her meager
opportunities for education, discovering in the process that her cultivation gave her access to "the best society that her rural situation
and times afforded."[1] "A gentleman of her intimate acquaintance"
reported that her "natural genius was above the common size—her
taste for reading was almost singular, and she excelled most of her
sex in a relish for works of genius, books written in taste. She had a
quick sense of the charms of imagination and beauties of expression."[2]

After her marriage to the Reverend Mr. Eliakim Willis, she
lived for a time in Dartmouth, New Hampshire, later moving with
her husband to his new post as pastor of the second church of
Malden, Massachusetts. They had three children, a daughter who
died in infancy and twin sons who were stillborn. Particularly close
to a niece (unidentified by name in the letters), perhaps as a result
of these losses, Willis leaves her only extant verse stanza in a letter
to her. Most of the published letters record family deaths, personal
illness, sorrow, and other unidentified family troubles, possibly
financial. Conventionally religious, occasionally self-pitying, the
letters may reveal more about the editor's criteria for selecting materials than about Lydia Willis. Published originally as *Rachel's
Sepulchre; Or, a Memorial of Mrs. Lydia Willis, taken, Chiefly, from
her Letters to Friends* ... (Boston? 1767?), the materials were later
republished as *Madam Willis's Letters and her Character. With some
Strictures of Madam Ann Stockbridge's and the Character of Madam
Sarah Page* ... (Boston, 1788).

[Lines From an Undated Letter to her Niece]

The gate is straight,—the way is narrow,—my heart is hard,—my
sins are great,—my strength is weak,—my faith is so benighted with
doubts, that I am ready to cast all offered good away.—

Such languid, faint desires I feel,
Within this wicked, stupid heart,
I should, I would, but that, I will,
   I hardly dare (with truth) assert.

Susanna Rogers

(b. 1711?)

A minister's daughter living in Boxford, Massachusetts, Susanna Rogers became engaged to Jonathan Frye, chaplain to Captain Lovewell's military unit. Apparently Frye's family objected to the union because of her "want of property and education."[1] Our only record of Rogers derives from her "Mournful Elegy of Mr. Jona[than] Frye," a piece composed after she had received news of her fiance's death in action with Lovewell's men. Engaging a band of Indians on May 8, 1725, at Pigwacket in Maine, Lovewell's unit was forced to retreat, leaving the wounded Frye behind. The anonymous ballad that records "Lovewell's Fight" notes that Frye's wound did not inhibit his participation in the battle:

> . . . he many Indians slew,
> And some of them he scalped when bullets round him flew.[2]

Fourteen-year-old Susanna Roger's sentimental elegy focuses more on the bravery than the brutality of the encounter, seeking to comfort Frye's parents for the loss of their only son.

Since the manuscript of the elegy has been lost, the text used here was printed in the *New England Historical and Genealogical Register*, 15 (January, 1861), 91. Samuel Knapp discusses the poem briefly in his *Lectures on American Literature* (New York, 1829), which is available in facsimile as *American Cultural History 1607-1829*, eds. Richard Beale Davis and Ben Harris McClary (Gainsville, Fla., 1961), p. 157. Perry Miller's *The New England Mind: From Colony to Province* (Boston, 1953), p. 369, uses Roger's elegy as an example of the movement toward secularism in popular expression of the early eighteenth century. No other writings by Susanna Rogers are known.

The Mournful Elegy of Mr. Jona[than] Frye, 1725

Assist ye muses, help my quill,
Whilest floods of tears does down distill,
Not from mine eyes alone, but all
That hears the sad and doleful fall
Of that young student, Mr. Frye,
Who in his blooming youth did die.
Fighting for his dear country's good,
He lost his life and precious blood.
His father's only son was he,
His mother loved him tenderly:
And all that knew him loved him well,
For in bright parts he did excel
Most of his age, for he was young,
Just entering on twenty-one:
A comely youth and pious too,
This I affirm, for him I knew.
He served the Lord whilst he was young,
And ripe for Heaven was Jonathan.
But God did take him from us all,
And we lament his doleful fall.
Where'er I go I hear this cry:
Alas! alas! good Mr. Frye.
Wounded and bleeding he was left,
And of all sustenance bereft,
Within the howling desert great,
None to lament his dismal fate.
A sad reward you'll say, for those
For whom he did his life expose:
He listed out with courage bold,
And fought the Indians uncontrolled;
And many of the rebels slew,
While bullets thick around him flew.
At last a fatal bullet came,
And wounded this young son of fame,
And pierced him through and made him fall;
But he upon the Lord did call.
He prayed aloud, the standers by
Heard him for grace and mercy cry:
The Lord did hear and raised him so,
That he enabled was to go,

For many days he homewards went,
Till he for food was almost spent,
Then to the standers by declared,
"Death did not find him unprepared."
And there they left him in the wood,
Some scores of miles from any food;
Wounded and famishing all alone,
None to relive[3] or hear his moan,
And there without all doubt did die.
And now I'll speak to Mr. Frye.
Pray Sir be patient, kiss the rod,
Remember this the hand of God
Which has bereft you of your son,
Your dear and lovely Jonathan;
Although the Lord has taken, now
Unto himself, your son most dear,
Resign your will to God, and say,
"Tis God that gives and takes away;"
And blessed be his name, for he
For he has caused this to be.
And now to you, his mother dear
Be pleased my childish lines to hear;
Mother, refrain from flowing tears,
Your son is gone beyond your cares,
And safely lodged in Heaven above,
With Christ, who was his joy and love.
And, in due time, I hope you'll be
With him, to all eternity.
Pray Madam, pardon this advice,
Your grief is great, mine not much less,
And if these lines will comfort you,
I have my will,—farewell,—adieu.

Grace Smith

(fl. 1712)

Seeking to leave her children "a perpetual monitor," Grace Smith of Eastham, Massachusetts, directed the transcription of her deathbed message to her family. Her published statement, *The Dying Mother's Legacy. Or the Good and Heavenly Counsel of the Eminent and Pious Matron, Mrs. Grace Smith* (1712), contains instructions (largely in prose) regarding religious precepts and proper conduct. Only the introductory call for her children's attention and the concluding prayer are in verse. The role of the transcriber in casting the form of the published *Legacy* is uncertain, but the work is typical of many puritan deathbed statements in admonishing survivors to "remember [their] baptismal vows and covenant."[1]

From *The Dying Mother's Legacy*

My children dear, whom I did bear,
   O lend your ear to my instructions:
[Let] not vain toys nor worldly joys
   Shut out these my directions:
[Sil] ver and gold, such glistering mold,
   Tis not my chief care to leave you:
[But] riches sure, that will endure,
   Whereof this world can't rob you.
[Th] ose I covet, you to inherit,
   That each enjoy both grace and glory:
[Af] ter few days might sing J A H's praise,
   In blest Heaven's highest story.
[Unt] o this end, I do commend,
   These dying words you'd bear in mind:
[Oh?] hear their voice, therein rejoice,
   Whenas you hear no more me find.
[Le] t not me see, one of you be
   Mongst goats standing at Christ's left hand.
[On?] Judgment-Day, oh! that I may
   Find you heirs of Immanuel's land.

. . . .

These dying groans and hearty moans,
   Let them be laid up in your mind.
Oh! Jesus dear, do thou me hear,
   According to thy mercies kind:
My children all I have, and shall
   Unto thy tender mercies leave:
Them keep and teach, and save them each,
   From sin and Hell do them reprieve.
And now I rest; for me 'tis best
   To bid vain sinful world farewell:
Here's vanity, sin and misery;
   Glory, glory with Christ doth dwell.
Oh! There's my hope, those doors will o[pe,]
   My longing soul to entertain;
For bridegroom's face, that mansion-place,
   Oh! Ever there for to remain.

Esther Hayden

(1713?-February 14, 1758)

Wife of Samuel Hayden of Braintree, Massachusetts, and mother of nine children, Esther Hayden left a deathbed message in verse to her family and friends. The concern for their religious condition expressed in that message was apparently as much a theme of her life as of her verse. Exhibiting "a clear relish for all the duties of religion,"[1] Hayden inspired "a near relative" to eulogize her as "a precious saint."

> Great blessings we enjoy from God
>   In a true faithful wife:—
> So saying, diligent and neat,
>   She well adorn'd her place.[2]

But despite her relative's conviction of her saintliness (based on her womanly "meek and quiet sp'rit"[3]), Hayden seems less sure. In addition to her concern for others, she continually returns in the poem to her fear of death and her struggle to believe in her salvation. The excerpts printed here from the original 167-line poem illustrate both themes. Omitted from Charles Evans' *American Bibliography* and the Shipton-Mooney *National Index of American Imprints through 1800, A Short Account of the Life, Death and Character of Esther Hayden* (1759) is available in the Harris Collection at Brown University. Emily Stipes Watts includes Hayden in her survey of *The Poetry of American Women from 1632 to 1945* (Austin, Texas, 1977), p. 25.

From *[Lines "Composed About Six Weeks Before Her Death, When Under Distressing Circumstances"]*

> O come ye near, my friends around,
>   And see my great distress;
> God doth afflict me very sore
>   In days of weariness.
> I on a bed of languishing,
>   And wasting sickness, lie:
> Oh! may God's love come from above,
>   That I mayn't fear to die;
> But, O! that horr'r and grievous sorr'w
>   Me often doth invade;
> And Satan's darts, with all his arts,
>   Temptations sore hath laid.—
> O whether! whether[4] shall I fly!
>   Lord Jesus, bow thine ear!
> Thy blood alone it can atone,
>   And bring salvation dear!—
> That all those shades, which me invades,
>   May all away depart;
> O may that dove come from above,
>   And set and warm my heart!
> God, if he please, can give pure ease
>   Unto his creatures here:
> O may I wait in this estate,
>   And not so greatly fear!
>
> .   .   .   .
>
> My dearest friends! I with concern
>   And pity do it speak.
> My husband dear, that is so near,
>   O do Jehovah seek;
> I wish you grace and happiness
>   In this world and above,
> For all unwearied kindnesses
>   Done unto me in love:
> Oh! part we must;—but fain I first
>   My children dear would teach
> The fear of God, who when they die

The happiness may reach:—
My children dear! the Lord O fear,
    And seek him in your youth,
And daily pray, that so you may
    Be made to seek in truth;
Come, draw you near, Jehovah fear,
    And daily do him seek:
O that he would his blessing give,
    And place you with the meek.—

.   .   .   .

O that Jehovah would appear,
    And satisfy me with
His loving-kindness! so that I
    Mayn't fear the pow'r of death:—
And oh! that I assurance had
    Of any grace in me!
I would it then declare to Thine,
    The glory give to Thee!

Abigail Colman Dennie

(January 14, 1715-May, 1745)

In the local notoriety accorded Jane Turell (see pages 43-54) for her poetry, it is usually overlooked that Turell's sister, Abigail Colman Dennie, also wrote verse. Unlike her submissive and devout sister, Abigail rebelled against the strictures of their Puritan father, Benjamin Colman. Though he continually praised Jane as an example to her, Abigail sought independence. In 1732 her grandfather left her a bequest that removed economic barriers to freedom. A year later, Abigail transferred control of her property from her father to her merchant uncle, John Colman. The estrangement that resulted in this transfer was temporary; Benjamin Colman reassumed responsibility for his daughter's affairs in 1734. But it was during this period of separation that Abigail's only extant piece was written, a letter in verse to her sister ("Delia"). (Her other poems have disappeared, though Colman mentions sending some of them to Isaac Watts, lamenting that her verse was not "as magnetically turned on heaven" as Jane's.) 1

The reconciliation with her father was short-lived. In September, 1737, Abigail Colman eloped with Albert Dennie after her father had refused to sanction their marriage. Dennie proved to be as irresponsible as Colman had feared: he left Abigail in November to return to his family home in Connecticut. Their son John was born in December, and was baptized by his grandfather Colman. Though Abigail remained loyal to her husband, Colman viewed the marriage as a punishment of her penchant for reading novels and romances.2 Growing ill health, a scandal-prone husband and new financial difficulties eventually led Abigail to seek a rapprochement with her father. Living with the father she had fought so hard to escape, Abigail Dennie died in May, 1745. After her death, Benjamin Colman expressed his sense of the paradox his two daughters represented: "My Turell died in fear, who never offended anyone, and if she knew her own heart, had a thousand times given herself to God. My Dennie dies in peace and transports, that had made the greatest breaches on me, and had given scandal and offence to all in point of filial duty."[3]

The text of Abigail Dennie's verse letter to her sister was inserted by the Reverend Elias Nason of Medford in the *New England Historical and Genealogical Register*, 14 (1860), 169-170. It was reprinted by the *North American Review*, 93 (1861), 32-33, in an anonymous article on Jane Turell. Clayton Harding Chapman's "Benjamin Colman's Daughters," *New England Quarterly*, 26 (1953), 169-192, gives a full account of both women, especially emphasizing Benjamin Colman's domination of their lives.

[Lines From a Letter to Her Sister, Jane Colman Turell, March 23, 1733]

Not all my woes can make me wretched while
My Delia does vouchsafe on me to smile.
Though Alps and oceans keep you from my arms,
Deprive me of the bliss to view those charms,
Yet still my fate permits me this relief,
To write to lovely Delia all my grief.
To you alone I venture to complain;
From others hourly strive to hide my pain.
But Celia's[4] face dissembles what she feels;
Affected looks her inward pain conceal.
She sings, she dresses, and she talks and smiles,
But these are all spectators to beguile.
But when alone, and from restraint she's free,
What undissembled sorrows would you see
Could you then view her. In her pensive face
You might a thousand woes and miseries trace;
Amidst a thousand sighs and flowing tears,
She has recourse to write to you her fears.
My tenderest love unto the beauteous boy,[5]
Vouchsafe a line, nor all my hopes destroy.

The unfortunate Celia

Deborah Prince

(December 23, 1723-July 20, 1744)

The oldest daughter of Deborah Denny and Thomas Prince, minister of the Old South Church of Boston, Deborah Prince was devoutly religious even as a child. She was moved "to study the Bible, and the best of authors, both of history and divinity; among the latter of which, Dr. Watts' and Mrs. Rowe's writings were very agreeable and familiar to her."[1] Influenced by her study, she entered into full communion in the church with a public declaration of her faith on July 19, 1739. But even that declaration apparently could not resolve her struggle to believe in her salvation, a struggle that preoccupied much of her short life; she contracted a fever that ended her life on July 20, 1744.

A few of her papers, including her only extant poem (of uncertain authenticity), are appended to Thomas Prince's *Sermon Occasioned by the Decease of Mrs. Deborah Prince* (1744), but most of her writings she destroyed, "it being one of her infirmities to be too reserved."

> And the reason she gave to an intimate companion and one of the female society to which she join'd for the most endearing exercise of social piety, was, because, in case she should be suddenly taken away, her friends would think her to be as good as those writings represented."[2]

In addition to Prince's *Sermon*, material concerning Deborah and her sister Sarah (see pages 253-254) was published in the *Dying Exercises of Mrs. Deborah Prince and Devout Meditations of Mrs. Sarah Gill . . .* (Edinburgh, 1784; Newburyport, Mass., 1789). Extracts from Thomas Prince's *Sermon* for his daughter were reprinted in Boston in 1804 and approximately 1810.

*[Lines . . . "Found in her Pocket Book in her Own Hand-writing,
After her Decease"]*

> Go careless mortal, view that withered flower;
> Fresh in the morn it bloom'd, a beauteous hue
> Sat on its smiling bosom; all around
> Diffus'd, its cheering odor fill'd the air;
> But ere the sun reach'd the meridian height
> And in full glory shone, a mortal pale
> Seiz'd the fair flower and robb'd it of its charms;
> See how it fades, it droops, it bows, and dies!

Bridget Richardson Fletcher

(1726-1770)

Published posthumously, the *Hymns and Spiritual Songs* (1773) of Bridget Fletcher seem to trace a personal rather than a poetic development. Containing eighty-three hymns (although the volume I examined appeared to be missing pages at the end), Fletcher's collection moves from an abstract melancholy into gratitude for God's specifically-enumerated mercies. The contrast, for example, between the simple thanks of "Hymn LXXVII: God's Protecting Hand Shown in Deliverance, When in Danger of Fire" and the self-pity of the apparently earlier "Hymn XXXIII: No Darkness to be Compared With Spiritual Darkness, No Sorrow Like Soul Sorrow" suggests Fletcher's spiritual development, but the uniform ballad stanzas reveal little growth in poetic technique. A religious poet, she dedicates her song-writing to the service of God; yet a note of secular pleasure in her compositions surfaces occasionally.

> I'd have you know, I'd rather go,
>   And a new song record,
> Than to eat here, the best of cheer,
>   That the whole earth affords.[1]

Religious themes of redemption, God's glory and human sin predominate, but many of the songs adopt a lighter tone for the consideration of more temporal subjects, such as marriage, prosperity and proper conduct.

Never intending her work for publication, Bridget Fletcher "was deprived of an opportunity of revising, or so much as giving titles to many of [her hymns]," [2] by her death in 1770. Cautioning her readers "to make allowances for the many inaccuracies of a female pen," [3] Fletcher's anonymous editor prepared the volume at the request of her friends, "hoping that none will be so disingenuous

as to criticize, upon the poetry or composition, which may be ser-
viceable and instructive to some, but injurious to none."[4]

Hymn II. On the Author's Proceeding on this Work

1

Things new and old I'd now unfold,
    Out of Christ's treasures bring,
Which when you hear, I hope they'll cheer,
    And make you glory sing.

2

If wonders here, which I declare,
    If wonders which I bring,
Should you surprise, by faith then rise,
    And glory give to him.

3

Now at his throne, let him alone,
    Let him exalted be,
Because that I am unworthy,
    Don't give it unto me.

4

Oh! if much good by the great God
    To me is surely giv'n,
O not to me, but glory be,
    Unto the God of Heaven.

5

If God you love, praise him above,
    Let him exalted be,
And do not tell that I do well,
    'Tis not I say of me.

6

A tear I'd drop now if I thought
    That I should surely rob,
Oh! the most high, of his glory,
    From whence comes all my good.

7

With Amos, sir, I'd now answer,
    That I no proph'tess am,
Of prophet's line I ne'er did spring,
    Only of an herdsman.

8

I am, dear sir, a fruit gatherer,
  If not of the sycamore,
It is from these the apple trees,
  Which here we have in store.

*Hymn XXXVI. The Greatest Dignity of a Woman, Christ Being
Born of One*

1

God's only son by woman came,
  To take away our shame;
And so thereby, to dignify,
  Also to raise our fame.

2

Did Christ our friend, thus condescend,
  Of woman to be born;
Did one so high, so dignify,
  Those that you treat with scorn?

3

What man is there, that shall thus dare
  Woman to treat with scorn,
Since God's own son, from heav'n did come,
  Of such an one was born.

4

Did one so high, thus dignify,
  And here do such a thing;
Shall we now fear, those that live here,
  Although it was a king.

Hymn LXX. The Duty of Man and Wife.

1

You gentlemen and who are friend
   To your own happiness,
Come now and hear or stop your ear,
   As it shall please you best.

2

To every head that is married,
   This song is now entail'd;
If any hiss, I say at this,
   Then let him be expell'd.

3

The matter here, which I'll declare
   I hope will end much strife;
I wish it might, each man invite,
   To love and prize his wife.

4

Let women fair, also take care
   And see they do submit,
As reason there, shall say is fair,
   And as it shall seem fit.

5

Would man and wife, live free from strife,
   How happy might they be,
If they would try, in harmony
   To live in unity.

6

As bone of bone, they should be one
   In heart so in pretence;
For 'tis a shame, if they are twain,
   Since join'd by providence.

7

Their hands and hearts, their skill and arts,
   Should combine together,
Thus join they must, and so one purse
   Hold all they do gather.

8

The poor that come you must give some,
   With kindness treat each friend;
And all your store, will be bless'd the more,
   Likewise the better spend.

9

Strict care pray take, least you do break,
   The bond of unity,
For if that's broke it makes sad work,
   Soon ends prosperity.

Sarah Prince Gill

(July 16, 1728-August 5, 1771)

Daughter of minister-bibliophile Thomas Prince and sister of poet Deborah Prince (see pages 245-246), Sarah Gill was known to her contemporaries as a woman of cultivation and talent. Her funeral sermon noted that she had been

> placed under the forming hand of an indulgent parent, who made it no more the business than the pleasure of his life to instill in her mind those principles of knowledge and piety, which were so conspicuous in himself.... Her natural inclination led her to books, and her many private papers discover a good acquaintance with them.[1]

Married to merchant Moses Gill in 1759, Sarah Gill apparently kept a diary from 1743 until shortly before her death. Her "Devout Meditations," published posthumously, were selected from "papers ... which she was willing to save from ruin, having put an end to many of her writings with her own hands...."[2]

These extant meditations are largely prose, but occasionally Gill casts her thoughts in verse. (The quotation marks in the published "Meditation" may indicate that the verse is borrowed, but I have located no source for the borrowing.) Integrating her verse lines with her prose, sometimes switching modes mid-sentence, Gill develops the personal religious themes that are commonplace in colonial New England. A woman on whom "the great Author of Nature had bestowed ... a genius uncommonly strong and penetrating,"[3] she leaves the scanty traces of her life and work in the *Dying Exercises of Mrs. Deborah Prince and Devout Meditations of Mrs. Sarah Gill* . . . (Edinburgh, 1784; Newburyport, Mass., 1789).

[Lines From Her "Devout Meditations"]

—Thou, thou art all!
My soul flies up and down in thoughts of thee,
And finds herself but at the center still!
I AM, thy name! Existence, all thine own!
Creation's nothing to Thee, the great Original!

.   .   .   .

Now at thy feet with awful fear,
   Adoring low I'll fall;
With joy I shrink to nothing here,
   Before th' eternal All!

.   .   .   .

How most exact is nature's frame!
How wise th' Eternal Mind!
His counsels never change the scheme
That his first thoughts design'd.

.   .   .   .

I know I've made my refuge God,
And found a most secure abode;
Have walk'd all day beneath his shade,
And there at night rested my head.
Now I will say, my God, thy pow'r
Shall be my refuge and my tow'r,
I, that am form'd of feeble dust,
Make thine Almighty arm my trust;
How happy I! my Maker's care
Shall keep me from the fowler's snare.

Lucy Terry

(1730-1821)

Kidnapped in Africa as a young child and brought to Rhode Island, Lucy Terry (or Luce Bijah, as she was called) was purchased by Ebenezer Wells of Deerfield, Massachusetts. Arriving in Deerfield as a slave child about five years old, she gradually developed a local reputation as a story-teller. On May 17, 1756, Lucy Terry married Abijah Prince, a free black man who became a successful entrepreneur. Though no extant records confirm the transaction, Prince was apparently able to purchase his wife's freedom after their marriage. Receiving a gift of land in 1762, he parlayed it into larger holdings in Guilford and Sunderland, Vermont. In 1764, Prince and Terry moved to Vermont, where they lived for the rest of their lives, working their land and raising their six children. They once fought a successful court battle with their neighbor, Colonel Eli Bronson, over his attempt to encroach on their holdings. The case went to the United States Supreme Court, where Terry apparently argued part of their case herself, receiving commendation from Justice Samuel Chase of Maryland. She was less successful in her attempt to get permission to enroll one of her sons at Williams College.

Terry composed the only one of her verses still extant in 1746, making her the first black American poet. "Bars Fight" is a rough but factual account of an Indian attack on a group of workers in a hay meadow near Deerfield. It was handed down orally in the Deerfield community for over a hundred years before Josiah Holland printed it in his *History of Western Massachusetts* (Springfield, Mass., 1855), II, 360. (The text given here is taken from Holland.) As late as 1893, Harriet Hitchcock of Deerfield remembered two lines from what may be another version of Terry's poem, although Bernard Katz argues that the couplet is rightfully lines five and six of the fuller text.

Twas nigh unto Sam Dickinson's mill,
The Indians there five men did kill.[1]

The rest of this version (if there was more) has been lost.

Most of our information regarding Lucy Terry has been preserved in nineteenth-century local histories such as Holland's. George
Sheldon's "Negro Slavery in Old Deerfield," *New England Magazine*, 8 (March, 1893), 49-60, contains an account of Terry and a
variant text of her poem. He includes almost identical comments in
his *History of Deerfield, Massachusetts* ([Greenfield, Mass.], 1895-
1896; facsimile rpt., Somersworth, N.H., 1972), II, 898-901. Lor-
enzo Greene's *The Negro in Colonial New England, 1620-1776*
(New York, 1942), pp. 242-243, 248, 314-315, bases its account of
Terry on Sheldon, but is more easily obtainable.

Terry is also frequently mentioned in black histories and anthologies of black poetry. Sidney Kaplan's *The Black Presence in
the Era of the American Revolution* (New York, 1973), pp. 209-211,
includes a copy of her poem with a biographical sketch. Bernard
Katz's "A Second Version of Lucy Terry's Early Ballad?" *Negro
History Bulletin*, 29 (Fall, 1966), 183-184, investigates textual
variants. William H. Robinson's *Early Black American Poets* (Du-
buque, Iowa, 1969), pp. 3-4, and Langston Hughes and Arna Bon-
temps' *The Poetry of the Negro: 1746-1970* (Garden City, N.Y.,
1970), p. 3, are two of the many recent anthologies that include
Terry's poem. More notable for being a "first" than for its poetic
qualities, "Bars Fight" is still "the fullest and best contemporary
account of that bloody tragedy which has been preserved."[2]

Bars Fight[3]

August, 'twas the twenty-fifth,
Seventeen hundred forty-six;
The Indians did in ambush lay,
Some very valiant men to slay,
The names of whom I'll not leave out.
Samuel Allen like a hero fout,[4]
And though he was so brave and bold,
His face no more shall we behold.
Eleazer Hawks was killed outright,
Before he had time to fight,—
Before he did the Indians see,
Was shot and killed immediately.
Oliver Amsden he was slain,
Which caused his friends much grief and pain.
Simeon Amsden they found dead,
Not many rods distant from his head.
Adonijah Gillett, we do hear,
Did lose his life which was so dear.
John Sadler fled across the water,
And thus escaped the dreadful slaughter.
Eunice Allen see the Indians coming,
And hopes to save herself by running,
And had not her petticoats stopped her,
The awful creatures had not catched her,
Nor tommy hawked her on her head,
And left her on the ground for dead.
Young Samuel Allen, Oh lackaday!
Was taken and carried to Canada.

Consider Tiffany

(1733-1796)

Consider Tiffany of Hartland, Connecticut, took reports of deaths by lightning in June, 1767, as an occasion for her verse, published in broadside as a "Relation of the Melancholy Death of Six Young Persons Who Were Kill'd by Lightning. . . ." Conventionally interpreting the deaths as signs from Providence to an erring, sinful community, Tiffany combined in her poem a memorial to the dead with exhortations to the living to "submit unto [God's] rod,/ And bow at his command." The original broadside, a copy of which is located in the Connecticut Historical Society in Hartford, is in poor condition, but much of the poem is still decipherable.

From *Relation of the Melancholy Death of Six Young Persons Who were Kill'd by Lightning in the Month of June, 1767*

.   .   .   .

The angel he sent to destroy
   The brutal herds below;
God sent them grief instead of joy,
   That man his pow'r might know.

Electric streaks, with loud amaze,
   Were seen and heard by all,
The Heavens seem'd to be on blaze,
   And thunder-bolts did fall;

.   .   .   .

May old and young prepare for death
   Before this life doth end.
And may we spend our latest breath
   In making Christ our friend.

Let's not forget to drop a tear
   On William Burt's urn,
Who was killed by lightning,
   While others it did burn.

.   .   .   .

Let us remember the great God,
   Who rules the sea and land;
May we submit unto his rod,
   And bow at his command.

What shall we say,—Is God austere?
   No!—He has mercy free;
Yet he is just and not severe
   To those that humble be.

.   .   .   .

Elizabeth Drinker

(1734-November 24, 1807)

Born into the well-to-do Philadelphia merchant family of William and Sarah Jervis Sandwith, Elizabeth Sandwith Drinker was educated by Anthony Benezet at a school which offered girls much the same curriculum available to boys in other schools. A devout Quaker, she married Henry Drinker, owner of a Philadelphia shipping and import business, in a Friends' ceremony on January 13, 1761. Nine children, four of whom died in infancy or early in childhood, resulted from their marriage.

In October, 1758, Elizabeth Drinker began a diary, a record which she kept faithfully until shortly before her death on November 24, 1807. The diaries detail the minute and the important events of her life, ranging from the casual visits of friends to a journey she undertook during the Revolution to George Washington's headquarters at Valley Forge to secure the release of her husband and others who had been exiled to Virginia for refusing as Quakers to swear allegiance to the new government. (Henry Drinker was released after eight months without coming to trial.) Elizabeth Drinker's verses are interspersed throughout the thirty-six volume account of her daily activities. Written strictly for her own amusement, they are frequently humorous, rough in rhythm, playing with alliteration and internal rhyme. Usually quatrains and couplets recalling a particular event, occasionally the poems are longer pieces more general in theme.

Drinker's manuscript diary is preserved in the Historical Society of Pennsylvania. Exerpts from it have been published in *Extracts from the Journal of Elizabeth Drinker*, ed. Henry Drinker Biddle (Philadelphia, 1889); Cecil Drinker's *Not So Long Ago: A Chronicle of Medicine and Doctors in Colonial Philadelphia* (New York, 1937); "Extracts from the Journal of Mrs. Henry Drinker, of

Philadelphia, from September 25, 1777, to July 4, 1778," *Pennsylvania Magazine of History and Biography*, 13 (1889), 298-308; and "Verses by Elizabeth Drinker," *Pennsylvania Magzine of History and Biography*, 15 (1891), 246. Harold Eberlin and Cortlandt Hubbard's "The American 'Vauxhall' of the Federal Era," *Pennsylvania Magazine of History and Biography*, 68 (1944), 155, prints a poetic excerpt from Drinker's diary as do Carl and Jessica Bridenbaugh in their *Rebels and Gentlemen* (New York, 1942), p. 114.

["I Stay Much at Home"]

I stay much at home, and my business I mind,
Take note of the weather, and how blows the wind,
The changes of seasons, sun, moon, and stars,
The setting of Venus, and rising of Mars.
Birds, beasts, and insects, and more I could mention,
That pleases my leisure, and draws my attention.
But respecting my neighbors, their egress and regress,
Their coaches and horses, their dress and their address,
What matches are making, who's plain, and who's gay,
I leave to their parents or guardians to say:
For most of those things are out of my way.
But to those, where my love and my duty doth bind,
More than most other subjects engages my mind.

Lines Verging Somewhat on the Bath(os), But Intended as a Tribute of Gratitude to our Landlord B. Wister, for his Kindness in Building us a Bath-House

Hail! thou noblest of landlords who'rt worthy to stand,
On a par, any day, with the knights of the land!
'Mongst the minions of monarchs, no man, surely hath
Half the claim to the title of Knight of the Bath!

Thee I hereby do dub, who to tub us hast deigned,
And cry hail to the man who his favors has rained,
On a house that had else been a great deal too dry,
Though containing of Drinkers a dozen or nigh.

Not a step shall we stir, not a ride shall we take,
But a feeling of thanks in our hearts shall awake,
For thou'st come like the spring, sung by poets in odes,
And thy showers refreshing hast shed on the Rhoads!

And each sultry day when emerged from the tub,
I sit down with friends to partake of a rub(ber);
My skin shall be cool which the heat else would blister,
And the pleasures of whist be made greater by Wister.

Rebecca Richardson

(fl. 1738)

Rebecca Richardson's case is known only in the barest outline. The poem she published in the *American Weekly Mercury* for January 10, 1738, alludes to legal problems that are further developed in a prose footnote to the piece. Forced to flee Philadelphia for England to obtain justice in her suit (never clearly specified), Richardson records that "it was his most gracious Majesty's pleasure in Council, to grant an order for repealing that unjust Act of Assembly, which so unmercifully cut the widow and fatherless from their lawful possessions. . . ."[1] Upon her return to Philadelphia, however, she notes that her "Writ of Execution, . . . though authorized by the King's Seal, has been contemptibly looked upon and slighted by the very person that is commanded to comply with it."[2] Despite the discrepancies in publication dates, it is possible that the Richardson of the poem is the same Rebecca Richardson who published in prose *A True State of the Case of R. R., Widow* [1755], a copy of which is located in the Library Company of Philadelphia. This small volume concerns Richardson's title to a house and lot that she alleged was fradulently taken from her.

["Do Thou, O God, in Mercy Help"]

Do thou, O God, in mercy help,
    For man my life pursues:
To crush me with repeated wrongs,
    He daily strife renews.
Continually my spiteful foes
    To ruin me combine:
Thou see'st who sits enthron'd on high,
    What naughty number join.
But though sometimes STruth surpris'd by fear,
    On danger's first alarm;
Yet still for succor I depend
    On thy Almighty Arm.
God's faithful promise I shall praise,
    On whom I now rely:
In God I trust, and trusting him,
    The arm of flesh defy.
They wrest my words and make 'em speak
    A sense they never meant.
Their thoughts are all with restless spite
    On my destruction bent.
In close assemblies they combine,
    And wicked projects lay.
They watch my steps and lie in wait
    To make my soul their prey.
Shall such injustice still escape!
    O righteous God arise;
Let thy just wrath (too long provok'd)
    This impious race chastise.
Thou numb'rest all my steps since first
    I was compell'd to flee:
My very tears are treasur'd up,
    And registered by thee.
When therefore I invoke thy aid,
    My foes shall be o'erthrown;
For I am well assur'd that God
    My righteous cause will own.
I'll trust God's word, and so despise
    The force that man can raise:
To thee, O God, my vows are due,
    To thee I render praise.

Thou hast retriev'd my soul from death,
And thou will still secure
The life thou hast so oft preserv'd;
And make my footsteps sure.
That thus protected by thy pow'r
I may this life enjoy;
And in the service of my God,
My lengthened days employ.

Sarah Parsons Moorhead

(fl. 1741-1742)

Wife of the Reverend John Moorhead of Boston, Sarah Parsons Moorhead wrote her verse during the controversies engendered by "the Great Awakening." Addressing a verse pamphlet "To the Reverend Mr. James Davenport on His Departure from Boston, By Way of a Dream," (1742) Moorhead sounded a note of caution for supporters of the revival. Although she professed to admire "the zeal that fires good Davenport's breast," she warned that

> Conversion is become the drunkard's song;
> God's glorious work, which sweetly did arise,
> By this unguarded sad imprudence dies. . . .

The "Lines . . . Humbly Dedicated to the Rev. Gilbert Tennent" appearing on the front page of the *New England Weekly Journal* for March 17, 1741, expressed the same concern for the excesses of the "Awakening."

> Welcome, dear thund'ring herald of the Lord;
> God prosper in thy hand the flaming sword,
>
> . . . .
> Yet, O dear sacred Tennent, pray beware,
> Least too much terror, prove to some a snare.
> Least stupid scoffers be provok'd to say,
> They were by awful curses drove away.[1]

Although the author of these "Lines . . . to . . . Gilbert Tennent" is identified only as "Mrs. S. M.," it seems almost certainly to be the work of Sarah Moorhead. Publication dates and locations combine with the subject matter and tone to indicate a single author for both publications.

From *To the Reverend Mr. James Davenport on his Departure From Boston, By Way of a Dream*

> Assist, celestial Powers, my grieved heart,
> For love and sorrow bear an equal part;
> I love the zeal that fires good Davenport's breast,
> But his harsh censures give my soul no rest;
> Our worthy guides whom God has much inflam'd,
> As unexperienc'd souls, alas, be nam'd;
> Hence giddy youth a woeful license take;
> A mock at reverend hoary heads they make;
> Despise the blest instructions of their tongue,
> Conversion is become the drunkard's song;
> God's glorious work, which sweetly did arise,
> By this unguarded sad imprudence dies;
> Contention spreads her harpy claws around,
> In every church her hateful stings are found,
> But as these thoughts my troubled mind opprest,
> Sleep, sweet cessation, instantly refresh'd,
> My tumults calm, and new-born pleasure rise,
> A charming vision swims before my eyes.
>
> The sacred man is to his shade convey'd,
> On camomile his aching temples laid;
> Here roses, honey-suckles, jessamine
> In beauteous arches o'er the champion twine;
> . . . .
> Now as the shining warriors watch his bed,
> Those gentle checks they whisper in his head;
> "Favorite of Heaven! How came it in thy mind
> "That grace was so much to thy self confin'd?
> "Crush the proud thought, and kill it in the bud;
> "Too long you have in this sad error stood;
> "Let charity unclose thy drowsy eyes;
> "You'll see a train of faithful pastors rise,
> "Thousands of happy souls surround their feet,
> "Which you in realm[s] of glory soon shall meet;
> "The timorous christian to his great surprise,
> "Sees himself there though he himself despis'd;
> "So the censorious wonders when he views
> "Souls there he thought God surely would refuse:
> "What has the enemy provok'd you too?
> "Success is not confin'd, dear man, to you;

"O let not fancy turn thy zeal aside,
"Free grace in others must not be deny'd;
"No more attempt to touch the Judgment Throne,
"Soul secrets to the Lord alone are known."
    The heralds rise and touch him with their wings;
Now in his breast a holy shame there springs;

. . . .

In lovely language here his lips impart
The blest contrition of his pious heart;
His shining guardians listen to his tongue,
And smiling upwards bear his mournful song;
I'll hearken too, as yet he does not cease;
"Father," he cries, "creator of my peace,
"Forgive my guilt, I'll censure so no more;
"Thy pardon on my knees I here implore;
"Unite the churches I have rashly rent,
"To heal the breaches O let some be sent;
"My error in my mind I ever keep,
"Unhappy shepherd thus to scatter sheep;
"Colman and Sewall I in hast[2] exprest,
"I clasp as first rank worthies to my breast;
"Now all I've wrong'd, or have too rashly nam'd,
"Freely forgive, as I myself have blam'd:"
In folded arms of love the prophets meet,
God's work goes on by unity most sweet.

. . . .

    But I must leave the pleasures of my dream,
And turn my thoughts to a more awful theme,
To souls immers'd in the black gulf of sin,
Who [opening?] drink the deadly poison in;

. . . .

Dare you appear before th' eternal throne
In this vile cob-web garment of your own!
Oh no! my friends, repent, reform ye must,
And trust free grace, or be forever curst. . . .

Milcah Martha Moore

(1740-1829)

Milcah Martha Hill was born in 1840, the daughter of Dr. Richard Hill. Little is known of her early years, but in 1767 she married Dr. Charles Moore of Philadelphia. Because the Moores were first cousins, the Philadelphia Monthly Meeting of Friends to which they belonged disowned them for an improperly consanguineous marriage. Despite their official exclusion, the Moores continued to worship as Friends throughout their lives; Milcah was eventually readmitted in 1811. Even with so inauspicious a beginning, the marriage was apparently a happy one.

At the outbreak of the Revolutionary War, the Moores left Philadelphia for their country home at Montgomery Square. They lived there, except for short periods in the city, until Charles Moore's death in 1801. Both Charles and Milcah seemed to enjoy rural life, especially the leisure it provided for reading and writing. Much of Milcah's commonplace book records her life at Montgomery Square. While Charles kept a small medical practice, Milcah opened a school for poor girls in the area. She gradually acquired a minor reputation for her teaching and writing, much of it based on the popular interest accorded her compilation of *Miscellanies, Moral and Instructive* (1787). Benjamin Franklin warmly recommended the collection. Four American imprints were issued and several reprints were published in London and Dublin as well. After her husband's death in 1801, Moore moved to Burlington, New Jersey, to live with a sister. She remained in New Jersey, except for brief visits to her old home, until her death in 1829.

Because Moore's papers were unavailable to me, much of this biographical information was furnished by Whitfield J. Bell, Jr., who read Moore's commonplace book and some of her letters in 1967. He recalled the existence of a number of verses in the commonplace book, some of them surely of Moore's composition because of their personal character. The text of "The Female Patriot" from Moore's commonplace book was printed in the *William and Mary Quarterly*, third series, 34 (April, 1977), 307-308. Variations between the manuscript text printed there and the published text in the *Pennsylvania Chronicle*, 3 (December 18-25, 1769), 392, are substantial enough to suggest that the piece is of Moore's composition. The *Pennsylvania Chronicle* text has been used here.

*The Female Patriots. Address'd to the Daughters of Liberty in
America, 1768*[1]

Since the men, from a party or fear of a frown,
Are kept by a sugar-plum quietly down,
Supinely asleep—and depriv'd of their sight,
Are stipp'd of their freedom, and robb'd of their right;
If the sons, so degenerate! the blessings despise,
Let the Daughters of Liberty nobly arise;
And though we've no voice but a negative here,
The use of the taxables, let us forbear:—
(Then merchants import till your stores are all full,
May the buyers be few, and your traffic be dull!)
Stand firmly resolv'd, and bid Grenville to see,
That rather than freedom we part with our tea,
And well as we love the dear draught when a-dry,
As American Patriots our taste we deny—
Pennsylvania's gay meadows can richly afford
To pamper our fancy or furnish our board;
And paper sufficient at home still we have,
To assure the wiseacre, we will not sign slave;
When this homespun shall fail, to remonstrate our grief,
We can speak viva voce, or scratch on a leaf;
Refuse all their colors, though richest of dye,
When the juice of a berry our paint can supply,
To humor our fancy—and as for our houses,
They'll do without painting as well as our spouses;
While to keep out the cold of a keen winter morn,
We can screen the north-west with a well polished horn;
And trust me a woman, by honest invention,
Might give this state-doctor a dose of prevention.
    Join mutual in this—and but small as it seems,
We may jostle a Grenville, and puzzle his schemes;
But a motive more worthy our patriot pen,
Thus acting—we point out their duty to men;
And should the bound-pensioners tell us to hush,
We can throw back the satire, by biding them blush.

Barbara Leininger

(fl. 1755-1759)

Emigrating from Germany to Pennsylvania with her family in 1748, Barbara Leininger is chiefly remembered for the story of her captivity among the Indians from October, 1755, until her escape with Marie le Roy, Owen Gibson and David Breckenreach in March, 1759. The published account of their captivity is a story of hunger, hard work, atrocities and plans for escape. The only poem attributed to Leininger was occasioned by their flight from the Indians. Fearful of being retaken and tortured, the group had to cross the Muskingum River on the first night of their freedom. Barbara Leininger apparently adapted an old hymn to their predicament, using it as a verse prayer. *Die Erzehlungen von Maria Le Roy und Barbara Leininger, welche vierthalb Jahr unter den Indianern gefangen gewesen* (Philadelphia, 1759) was translated into English as *The Narrative of Marie Le Roy and Barbara Leininger. . .* (Harrisburg, Pa., 1878). An English text has been printed in the *Pennsylvania Magazine of History and Biography*, 29 (1905), 407-420, and the original German edition is available as part of the *Narratives of North American Indian Captivities*, ed. Wilcomb E. Washburn (New York, 1975), VIII.

["If We Were Only Across the Tide"] 1

If we were only across the tide,
My deepest fears do cry.
I see approaching woeful distress,
On all sides stands death:
Oh, what is yet at hand!
In those barren lands
There is no water, meat, or bread.
Every morning a cruel new dread.
Hunger I would suppress,
If I could only flee
The cruel host in the wilderness,
The fearful band that tortures and chides,
While Satan himself stands at its side.
And should the hoard come too near,
Then help us God, do not let us fear:
We trust in you, stay in our hearts,
And always be our Joshua.

—translated by George Mason Vaught, 1979

Anna Green Winslow

(November 29, 1759-July 19, 1780)

    Born in Nova Scotia to Anna Green and Joshua Winslow, Commissary-General of the British forces there, Anna Green Winslow was sent to Boston as a young girl to attend a "finishing" school. During her separation from her family (who later moved to Marshfield, Massachusetts), Winslow kept a diary of her daily activities as a running letter to her parents. Her diary minutely records the details of a life carefully circumscribed by traditional female roles. Filled with sermon notes, descriptions of parties and clothing, and records of domestic tasks rather than with references to the surrounding political and social turmoil that later resulted in Joshua Winslow's exile from Massachusetts as a Tory, Anna Winslow's diary has two entries that contain verse she had "transcribed from [her] copy book."[1] While the original manuscript of the diary is privately owned, Alice Morse Earle makes the text accessible in her *Diary of Anna Green Winslow: A Boston School Girl of 1771* (Boston, 1895). Earle's edition was reprinted in facsimile by Detroit's Singing Tree Press in 1970.

[On the Death of Mr. Stephen March, Diary Entry for March 14, 1772]

> Stoop down my thoughts, that use to rise,
> Converse a while with death;
> Think how a gasping mortal lies,
> And pants away his breath.

[To her Parents, Diary Entry for March 17, 1772]

> Next unto God, dear parents I address
> Myself to you in humble thankfulness,
> For all your care and charge on me bestow'd;
> The means of learning unto me allow'd,
> Go on I pray, and let me still pursue
> Those golden arts the vulgar never knew.

Mary Nelson

(fl. 1769)

Using verse for practical purposes, Mary Nelson of Philadelphia offered a reward for a thief, in hopes of recovering her lost property. She inserted her rhymned advertisement in the *Pennsylvania Chronicle* twice, in the issues for January 9-16, 1769, and January 23, 1769. Whether anyone was able to claim her reward is unknown.

Forty Shillings Reward

Last Wednesday morn, at break of day,
From Philadelphia run away,
An Irish man, nam'd John M'Keoghn,
To fraud and imposition prone;
About five feet five inches high,
Can curse and swear as well as lie;
How old he is I can't engage,
But forty-five is near his age;
He came (as all reports agree)
From Belfast town in sixty-three,
On board the Culloden, a ship
Commanded by M'Lean that trip;
Speaks like a Scotchman, very broad,
Is round shoulder'd, and meagre jaw'd;
Has thick short hair, of sandy hue,
Breeches and hose of maz'reen blue;
Of lightish cloth an outside vest,
In which he commonly is dress'd;
Inside of which two more I've seen,
One flannel, th'other coarse nankeen.
He stole, and from my house convey'd,
A man's blue coat, of broadcloth made;
A grey great coat, of bearskin stuff,
(Nor had the villain yet enough;)
Some chintz (the ground was pompadour)
I lately purchas'd in a store,
Besides a pair of blue ribb'd hose,
Which he has on as I suppose.
He oft in conversation chatters,
Of scripture and religious matters,
And fain would to the world impart,
That virtue lodges in his heart;
But take the rogue from stem to stern,
The hypocrite you'll soon discern,
And find (though his deportment's civil)
A saint without, within a devil.
Whoe'er secures said John M'Keoghn,
(Provided I should get my own)

Shall have from me, in cash paid down,
Five dollar-bills, and half-a-crown.

Water-street, Jan[uary] 10, 1769

Jane Dunlap

(fl. 1771)

Signing herself "a daughter of liberty and lover of truth," Jane Dunlap of Boston produced a handful of *Poems Upon Several Sermons Preached by the Rev'd . . . George Whitefield . . .* (1771). Seemingly oblivious to the tensions of the impending revolution, Dunlap restricts herself in the volume to religious themes developed in a uniform ballad stanza. She acknowledges that "some may sneer and others laugh" at her "little book";

> But those that truly fear the Lord,
> They will it not despise. [1]

Citing her "obscure station of life" [2] since the death of her husband, she asks her readers to "overlook what errors and mistakes they may find," [3] adding that if the reception of her lines is favorable, she will write more on the subject. Though records of the response to her work are unavailable, no additional verses appeared.

Another [Poem on the Reverend George Whitefield]

Shall his due praises be so loudly sung
By a young Afric damsel's virgin tongue,[4]
And I be silent and no mention make
Of his blest name, who did so often speak.

To us, the words of life,
Fetch'd from the fountain pure,
Of God's most holy sacred truths,
Which ever shall endure.

But Oh! should I attempt the praise
Of that most blessed man,
I should but darken his bright rays,
Which none in justice can.

His worthy deeds, and holy life,
The brightest luster casts,
Upon his worthy name which shall
To endless ages last.

O may we all, when God shall call
Us to resign our breath,
Arise like him, on angel's wings,
To worlds of peace and rest.

Those blissful mansions, yet unseen
To any mortal eye,
With cherubims, and seraphims,
To praise our God most high.
And to sing praises to the Lamb,
To all eternity.

Revelation Chap[ter] 2. Ver[ses] 4-5.

Nevertheless, I have somewhat against thee, because thou hast left thy
first love.

Remember therefore from whence thou art fallen, and repent, and do
the first works; or else I will come unto thee quickly, and will remove
thy candlestick out of his place, except thou repent.

New-England churches, O how fair,
How bright thou once did'st shine;
Sure few with thee, there could compare,
But now on sad decline.

O where's that love, you once exprest,
When after Christ you came,
Into this howling wilderness,
For love of his great name.

Your blessed Lord, does not forget,
But kindest mention makes,
Of all you do, from love to him,
He gracious notice takes.

Take Jesus's counsel, and advice,
By his dear servants sent;
Many of whom, of late deceas'd,
The Lord hath call'd them hence.

But still the call to you is sent,
Repent! repent! and turn;
Lest God remove you, far from hence,
And you your folly mourn.
In that you have forsaken God,
That's always took such care,
In all your griefs, to send reliefs,
When him, you sought by prayer.

O seek him now, and he'll return,
Do good, and build us up,
And make our peace, like rivers run,
Or waves, o'er mountain's tops.

Part Three

Anonymous Poets

Anonymous Poets

The growth of periodicals and the widespread use of broadside publication in eighteenth-century America enormously expanded markets for women writers, particularly in the southern colonies, where publishing was slow to develop. With such notable exceptions as the prose of Ann Eliza Bleecker and Judith Sargent Murray, women's publications in these ephemeral vehicles were usually in verse. Editors apparently welcomed didactic or entertaining pieces by women, perhaps hoping they would attract a female audience for the periodicals. Soon after the establishment of the original *South-Carolina Gazette* in 1732, for example, a verse riddle by a "Fair Correspondent" was inserted in the paper with editor Thomas Whitmarsh's note that "the ladies may be assur'd that whatever we are favored with, in their hand-writing, may claim a place in our paper, without any other introduction."[1] Many other colonial periodicals followed similar editorial policies if we may judge from the number of published poems that had been written by "a female hand," sent from "a lady," or ascribed to a female pseudonym. Perhaps the accepted practice of publishing verse anonymously seemed sufficiently safe for women otherwise unwilling to risk public censure by stepping outside traditional roles. Or perhaps the appearance of women's work in widely distributed publications stimulated literary efforts by others. Whatever the reasons, the number of women publishing their verses increased exponentially with the growth of eighteenth-century periodicals.

As with newspapers and magazines today, colonial periodicals addressed a broad audience, usually with materials of immediate or topical concern. Not surprisingly, the verse favored by periodicals was often inferior as literature to verse published in more permanent vehicles. But if we assume that periodical verse accurately reflects contemporary tastes and interests, the dozens of colonial women poets whose work appeared in periodicals have a collective importance. Like their male contemporaries, they outline a movement toward the secularization of American culture.

Growing secular interests among poets should not obscure, of course, the religious materials that remained a staple of colonial verse. Eugenia's "A Hymn; or, An Attempt to Versify the 104th Psalm" (*American Magazine and Historical Chronicle*, Boston, October, 1746), for example, emphasized her concern for human salvation:

> If vent'rous man, lur'd by the hopes of gain,
> Shall boldly tempt the dangers of the main,

how can he expect God's mercy? The later broadside "Address to New-England" (Boston, 1774) by "a Daughter of Liberty" took the political turmoil of the impending Revolution as an occasion to turn to a similar religious theme. The broadside examined Boston's plight almost exclusively for the divine message it contained.

> Unhappy Boston! wherefore doth thy God,
> Thus scourge thee with a tyrant's iron rod?
>
> .   .   .   .
>
> Consider now when God thus loudly calls,
> Before the final storm upon thee fall.
> What sins, what crying sins did God provoke,
> To cause his wrath against this land to smoke?

Implying that Boston's unrest was no more than its residents deserved for "rejecting Christ" and harboring "wanton passions and unchaste desires," this "Daughter of Liberty" seemed less concerned for New England's political future than for its spiritual well-being.

Without ignoring these religious interpretations of colonial events or the continuing appeal of sacred themes, American periodicals gradually opened their columns to secular verse as well. As the Revolution approached, dozens of colonial women tested their poetic skills on social and increasingly political materials. Courtship rituals like that of "Florella to Damon" (*South-Carolina Gazette*, Charlestown, June 17, 1732) developed the familiar "absent lover" theme. Writing of a suitor who had traveled to England, Florella worried aloud about his constancy:

> O killing thought! but harder still,
> Shou'd, with resistless art,
> Some dang'rous, courtly, British belle
> Seduce my wand'rer's heart!

She may have had good reason to be anxious, for she added from her own experience that

> Dang'rous indeed! for ah! my own [heart],
> (Dar'd it the truth disclose)
> Cou'd tell how oft (yet fixt on none)
> 'Twou'd flutter at their beaux.

(Perhaps Damon was fortunate that it was he and not his lover who journeyed to England.) Occasionally such courtship themes were attended by a less bantering tone, as in "The Maid's Soliloquy" (*South-Carolina Gazette*, Charlestown, March 4, 1751):

> Marriage! thou pleasing and yet anxious thought!
> Through what variety of hopes and fears,
> Through what new scenes, and changes, must we pass:
> . . . .
> For the great end of nature's law, is bliss.
> But yet—in wedlock—women must obey.

Afraid to be at the mercy of a tyrant husband, yet "longing after something unpossess'd," the anonymous author of "The Maid's Soliloquy" seemed more apprehensive than Florella about court-ship games.

Other secular forms and themes also became commonplace in periodical verse by women. Noting the influences of Milton, Dryden, Swift, and "Homer's high page in Pope's illustrious dress,"[2] women poets (like their male contemporaries) adopted British secular models. The satire of "On a Late Representation to the Lords of the Admiralty" (*Virginia Gazette*, ed. Hunter, April 22, 1757), for example, sported with military courage—or the lack of it. Addressing a court martial, the poem's narrator summed up the case of "Admiral Byng":

. . . 'twas prov'd he ne'er shew'd any tokens of fear,
(And how the plague should he, so far in the rear?)

Odes to charity, virtue, friendship and love, elegies and other occasional poems, riddles and epigrams, pastorals, songs and light verse,
translations, paraphrases—all were used for secular ends by women
writers who appeared in eighteenth-century periodicals. Their explor-
ation of social and political materials for verse marked a discernible
shift in public taste.

    This secularization of American culture, however, was not the
only development perceptible in colonial periodical verse. A growing recognition of common national concerns complemented region-
al diversity as the colonies reluctantly considered a revolution.
"Verses Addressed by the Ladies of Bedford, [Virginia] at their
Meeting to Resolve Against Tea" (*Virginia Gazette*, ed. Purdie and
Dixon, March 17, 1774), for example, was prefaced by an anecdote
from Newport, Rhode Island, in which a "countryman," attempting
to smuggle a small quantity of tea into the colonies "fell" into the
harbor, "for the salt water seems of late to attract [tea] as a lodestone attracts iron." Further indication of the growth of nationally
shared concerns is evident from the number of poems published
more than once. "A Lady's Adieu to Her Tea-Table" appeared in
the *Virginia Gazette*, ed. Purdie and Dixon, on January 20, 1774;
just a few weeks later, on February 2, 1774, the same piece was
printed in the *Pennsylvania Gazette*. The feminist themes of "The
Lady's Complaint" found publication in three different colonies.
While such borrowings were accepted editorial practice from the
beginnings of periodical literature, the reprinted pieces indicate a
similarity of interests and tastes which increasingly bound the colonies together.

    Both women and men who published verses in colonial period-
icals shared in the movements towards secularization and national
identity. Using materials and modes accessible to all literate colonists, they wrote of friendship, love, death, grief, of battles and dan-
ces, Indians and fashions. But far more frequently than their male
peers, colonial women poets wrote of gender-bound expectations
and roles. Lines "On the Noted and Celebrated [English] Quaker

Mrs. Drummond," for example, articulated a common frustration:

> Too long indeed our sex has been denied,
> And ridicul'd by men's malignant pride;
> Who fearful of a just return forbore,
> And made it criminal to teach us more.
> That woman had no soul, was their pretense,
> And woman's spelling, past for woman sense;
> 'Till you most generous heroine stood forth,
> And show'd your sex's aptitude and worth.[3]

Much of the dissatisfaction expressed by women poets focused on the educational restrictions that kept their "minds in fetters." One poet who had shrewdly calculated the motives of her male audience wrote an "Impromptu, on Reading an Essay on Education" that pleaded for more intellectual advantages for women Note her argument:

> Be it your task our intellects to aid,
> And you with tenfold interest shall be paid.

The true beneficiary of women's education, she argued, would be the man with whom such an intellectual woman lived as "faithful counselor" and "loving wife." Other women were less concerned with educational equality than with legal redress.

> Then equal laws let custom find,
>   And neither sex oppress;
> More freedom give to womankind,
>   Or give to mankind less.

Whatever concerns they shared with male counterparts, women poets writing for colonial periodicals took some themes for their own.

Periodicals (and an occasional broadside or anthology) proved rich in verse by anonymous or pseudonymous women. More such verse remains to be explored, much of it only available by the laborious process of leafing through entire issues of colonial publications. (I have paged through more than twenty-five periodical issues and followed leads in perhaps fifteen others.) Microformed resources, especially the American Periodical Series, make many such materials readily accessible. Other research aids include J. A. Leo Lemay's *Calendar of American Poetry in the Colonial Newspapers and Magazines and in the Major English Magazines Through 1765* (Worcester, Mass., 1970), a useful reference for identifying individual pieces in major colonial periodicals. Indexes for individual publications, such as *The Virginia Gazette Index*, eds. Lester J. Cappon and Stella F. Duff, 2 vols. (Williamsburg, Va., 1950), and studies such as Hennig Cohen's *The South Carolina Gazette, 1732-1775* (Columbia, S. C., 1953) furnish references to poems as well as detailed background to give them context. Lyon N. Richardson's *History of Early American Magazines, 1741-1789* (New York, 1931) gives scant attention to the beginnings of southern periodicals, but provides useful sketches for New England and middle-colony publications. Frank Luther Mott's *History of American Magazines 1741-1850* (Cambridge, Mass., 1939) devotes most of its space to the nineteenth century but includes a useful summary of the rise of eighteenth-century magazines.

A Riddle[4]

Who dare affirm my pow'r is weak,
Whilst I instruct the dumb to speak?
And, what's confess'd a greater deed,
Bestow new life upon the dead!
The things most valu'd here below,
To me their preservation owe.
Things past, with me, as present are;
And thousand fancies that ne'er were.
Nay more, in my capacious womb,
Are treasur'd up events to come.
Futurity I penetrate,
And shew the dark designs of fate.
Thoughts never utter'd I can tell,
Imaginations can reveal.
Each syllable I can repeat,
In all the volumes ever writ.
Estates I give to whom I please,
Transferring that man's land to this.
I'm conversant the earth throughout,
From splendid court to humble cot.
I ratify the leagues of princes,
And mine, their solemn treaty's fence is.
My birth no human skill can trace,
But, that I'm not of heav'nly race,
Is easily discern'd by this:
In me, both truth and error is;
And though my counsel he that takes,
Shall certainly avoid mistakes;
Yet whoso follows all I say,
Perplex'd in endless doubts shall stray.
    Who in good verse explains me clear,
    Shall have this Gazette, free, one year.

—from the *South-Carolina Gazette*
(January 15-22, 1732), p. [4] ; rpt.
Pennsylvania Gazette (June 15-19,
1732), p. [4].

Answers to the Riddle in Our Last[5]

The pow'r of letters can't be weak,
When they instruct the dumb to speak;
And, when form'd into words, and read,
Bestow new life upon the dead.
The things most valu'd here below,
To these their preservation owe.
Things past and present they compare;
And whims and fancies that ne'er were.
Nay more, in their capacious womb,
Are treasur'd up events to come.
Futurity they penetrate,
And shew the dark designs of fate.
Thoughts never utter'd they can tell,
Imaginations can reveal.
Each syllable they can repeat,
In all the volumes ever writ.
They ratify the leagues of princes,
In them their solemn treaty's fence is.
Their birth no human skill can trace,
For they're as old as human race.
They're not descended from the skies,
Because they tell both truth and lies;
And though their counsel he that takes,
Shall frequently avoid mistakes;
Yet whoso follows all they say,
Perplex'd in endless doubts shall stray.
  Your Gazette thus this verse secures,
  For they're at least as good as yours.

—from the *Pennsylvania Gazette*
(June 19-26, 1732), p. [4].

Florella to Damon[6]

Say, I conjure thee, Damon, say,
    What happier Nymph can lure
My am'rous swain from Charlestown Bay
    To Britain's distant shore?

Must thy Florella, in her turn,
    For many tedious moons,
Her fav'rite Damon's absence mourn
    In fruitless sighs and groans?

O killing thought! but harder still,
    Shou'd, with resistless art,
Some dang'rous, courtly, British belle
    Seduce my wand'rer's heart!

Dang'rous indeed! for ah! my own
    (Dar'd it the truth disclose)
Cou'd tell how oft (yet fixt on none)
    'Twou'd flutter at their beaux.

Guard him, ye pow'rs, against the fair,
    My Damon constant keep,
Not all my other foes I'll fear,
    The perils of the deep.

But hope some friendly eastern gale,
    Propitious to my love,
May soon the spreading canvas fill,
    Nor long will let thee rove.

—from the *South-Carolina Gazette*
(June 17, 1732), p. [3].

The Lady's Complaint

Custom, alas! doth partial prove,
    Nor gives us equal measure;
A pain for us it is to love,
    But is to men a pleasure.

They plainly can their thoughts disclose,
    Whilst ours must burn within:
We have got tongues, and eyes, in vain,
    And truth from us is sin.

Men to new joys and conquests fly,
    And yet no hazard run:
Poor we are left, if we deny,
    And if we yield, undone.

Then equal laws let custom find,
    And neither sex oppress;
More freedom give to womankind,
    Or give to mankind less.

—from the *Virginia Gazette*,
ed. Parks (October 22, 1736),
p. [3] ; rpt. *South-Carolina
Gazette* (August 15, 1743),
p. [4] ; rpt. as "The Maiden's
Complaint," *Essex Almanack
for . . . 1773* (Salem: S. and E.
Hall, 1773), pp. [12-13] .

Written Under a Libel Upon a Deceased Gentleman. By a Lady

And lives there one, by canker'd malice led
T'arraign the innocent defenceless dead?
With vulture's rage await the parting breath,
To all humanity's soft pleadings deaf?
Lost to the motions of a generous heart,

The stings of meditated fury dart?
With spleen unsated bid foul slander live,
And endless hate at such an hour revive?
　　The Lion, gentler savage, through the wood
Wild though he roves, adust, and dry for blood,
Yet if he chance where death, with friendly care,
Has just reliev'd the painful traveller,
With rough compassion stern he stalks away,
And scorns to tear the unresisting prey.

—from the *Virginia Gazette*,
ed. Parks (July 15-22, 1737),
p. [2] .

Verses Written by a Young Lady, on Women Born to be Controll'd!

How wretched is a woman's fate,
　　No happy change her fortune knows,
Subject to man in every state.
　　How can she then be free from woes?

In youth a father's stern command,
　　And jealous eyes control her will;
A lordly brother watchful stands,
　　To keep her closer captive still.

The tyrant husband next appears,
　　With awful and contracted brow;
No more a lover's form he wears,
　　Her slave's become her sov'reign now.

If from this fatal bondage free,
　　And not by marriage chains confin'd;
But blest with single life can see,
　　A parent fond, a brother kind;

Yet love usurps her tender breast,
　　And paints a Phoenix to her eyes,

Some darling youth disturbs her rest,
  And painful sighs in secret rise.

Oh, cruel pow'rs! since you've design'd,
  That man, vain man! should bear the sway;
To a slave's fetters add a slavish mind,
  That I may cheerfully your will obey.

—from the *South-Carolina Gazette*
(November 21, 1743), p. [3] ; rpt.
*American Magazine and Historical
Chronicle* (June, 1744), p. 435;
*American Magazine, or General Re-
pository* (August, 1769), p. 271.

*To ********* Desiring to Borrow Pope's Homer. From a Lady*

The muse now waits from ***'s hands to press
Homer's high page, in Pope's illustrious dress:
How the pleas'd goddess triumphs to pronounce,
The names of ***, Pope, Homer, all at once!

—from *A Collection of Poems. By
Several Hands* (Boston: B. Green
and D. Gookin, 1744), p. 44.

A Hymn; or, an Attempt to Versify the 104th Psalm

Arise, my soul, and in harmonious lays
Proclaim thy glorious God's immortal praise.
When rob'd in light, as in the clouds he rode,
All trembling nature own'd the voice of God.
With sov'reign pow'r, and awful justice join'd,
Lo! where he comes, borne by the wings of wind.

Heav'n, like a curtain, shades his radiant head,
And his throne beams arc in the waters laid.
His flaming ministers around him wait,
Perform his will, "for what he wills is fate."
Fix'd at his word, behold the beauteous earth,
And creatures, by his will, spring forth to birth.
From the high hills imprison'd waters flow,
Whose gentle waves enrich the plains below.
Fruit, and sweet springing grass, the valley yields,
And flow'ry herbs adorn the verdant fields.
There the wild asses quench their thirst, and there
From mountain tops the wanton goats repair.
The beasts and fowls his providence supplies,
Nor ought that's needful to their life denies;
The warbling birds, the cedar trees among,
Hail the creator in their tuneful song.
On man a golden harvest he bestows,
Whilst from the vine a sprightly nectar flows;
For him the corn, the fig, the olive grows,
'Tis God appoints the sun his constant course,
And bids the moon assist the water's force.
With sable night this world he mantles o'er;
Then tigers prey, and hungry lions roar.
"Now tim'rous grown, at sight of new born day,
"They sculk to dens, and quit the savage fray."
Soon as the morn her fragrant sweets disclose
Man, born to labor, leaves his soft repose:
Various the toils his mind and body share,
Till dewy night brings his release from care.
O wisdom infinite! by all ador'd,
Whose wond'rous works confess Jehovah Lord.
If vent'rous man, lur'd by the hopes of gain,
Shall boldly tempt the dangers of the main,
When billows roll, and blust'ring winds arise,
The frighted sailor his last refuge tries;
God hears, at length, his supplicating cries.
Myriads of angels his commands obey,
He rules the storm, and bounds the foaming sea;
A calm ensues, then all the finny train
Renew their sport amidst the wat'ry plain:
Huge leviathan, monarch of the sea,
Depends for food, O mighty God, on Thee.
O source of all true happiness below,

From whom alone immortal pleasures flow,
If Thou, indignant, turn away thy face,
Provok'd to punish man's untoward race,
That sad reverse of happiness they mourn,
They droop, they die, and to their dust return.
All-gracious God, since by thy pow'r I live,
The humble tribute of my praise receive.
What time of life thy bounty gives to me,
Those future days I consecrate to Thee:
Thy truth and mercy shall my songs proclaim,
And heathens learn to bless thy holy name.

Eugenia

—from the *American Magazine and
Historical Chronicle* (October, 1746),
pp. 470-471.

By a Lady on the Loss of her Son at Sea

Thou'rt gone, dear prop of my declining years;
No more for thee I'll weary Heav'n with prayers:
Ere while, the purple morn, the sable night,
The glorious sun in his meridian height,
With every shining star of paler light,
Still saw me prostrate on the earth for thee,
With prayers and tears implore the diety.
But, oh! diffus'd in unresisting air,
They never pierc'd the skies, nor reach'd th' Almighty's ear.
For thou art gone, and I am left to mourn;
Nor ever shalt thou to these arms return,
Or thy dear image from my soul depart,
While life's warm spring beats at my tortur'd heart.
    Upon the fatal deck I see thee stand;
I feel the bulging vessel strike the sand;
I hear the cries of death, the wild affright,
The dreadful scene is present to my sight:

It strikes again; mercy, great God! he cries;
The vessel splits; he falls, he sinks, he dies!
    And do I live! Thus Heav'n asserts its pow'r,
Enjoins me life beyond this fatal hour.
By nature soft, I ne'er unmov'd could hear
The sound of woe, or view the falling tear:
What feel I now, when, at one dreadful cast,
My life, my joy, my hopes, my treasures lost?
My hopes, my joys, were center'd all in thee;
And only God was more belov'd by me.
    Ah! had my trembling hand thy eye lids clos'd,
Thy manly limbs with decent care compos'd;
Had I with pious tears bath'd thy lov'd face;
Obtain'd one fond, one dear, one last embrace!
From thy pale lips receiv'd one parting kiss,
Ere angels bore thee to celestial bliss;
Catch'd thy last breath, and instantly expir'd,
Oh! happy fate, and much by me desir'd.
But Heav'n has lengthen'd my unhappy days,
For various woes dispens'd in various ways;
Doom'd from my early years to misery,
Unheard I mourn, and unregarded sigh.
    What have I said?—Tumultuous passions cease,
In resignation we alone have peace.
Shall a poor worm omnipotence arraign?
Shall animated dust of God complain?
Yet, awful power, whom Heaven and earth obey,
Who stills the tempests, and who calms the sea,
Command the deep his body to restore;
Winds gently waft it to its native shore:
Let these poor arms clasp, in one last embrace,
The dear remains of what my darling was:
To my pain'd heart I'll press his breathless clay,
And weep my sorrows and my soul away.
Th' enlarged soul, from prison thus set free,
Shall seek thee in the realms of liberty,
Of light, and love, and everlasting peace,
Where all our pains, where all our sorrows cease.
No shipwreck there shall snatch thee from my arms,
No fears of raging seas, or war's alarms.
In these calm regions of eternal rest,
For ever blessing, and for ever blest,

We'll sing his praises whom all worlds adore,
And sorrow, sin, and death shall be no more.

—from the *Independent Advertiser*
(June 12, 1749), pp. [1-2].

The Maid's Soliloquy[7]

It must be so—Milton, thou reas'nest well,
Else why this pleasing hope, this fond desire,
This longing after something unpossess'd?
Or whence this secret dread and inward horror
Of dying unespous'd? Why shrinks the soul
Back on itself, and startles at the thought?
'Tis instinct! faithful instinct stirs within us,
'Tis nature's self that points out an alliance,
And intimates an husband to the sex.
      Marriage! thou pleasing and yet anxious thought!
Through what variety of hopes and fears,
Through what new scenes, and changes, must we pass:
Th' important state in prospect lies before me,
But shadows, clouds and darkness, rest upon it.
Here will I hold—if Nature prompts the wish,
(And that she does is plain, from all her works)
Our duty and our interest, bid indulge it:
For the great end of nature's law, is bliss.
But yet—in wedlock—women must obey:
I'm weary of these doubts—the priest must end them.
      Thus, rashly do I venture loss and gain,
Bondage and pleasure, meet my thoughts at once;
I wed——my liberty is gone for ever:
If happy—then I'm still secure in life.
Love, will then recompense my loss of freedom;
And when my charms shall fade away, my eyes
Themselves grow dim, my stature bend with years,
Then virtuous friendship, shall succeed to love.

Then pleas'd, I'll scorn infirmities, and death,
Renew'd immortal, in a filial race.

—from the *South-Carolina Gazette*
(February 25-March 4, 1751), p. [1].

On a Late Representation to the Lords of the Admiralty—(By a Young Lady of Fifteen)[8]

My Lords,
'Tis the humble opinion of us the court martial,
(A court of all courts, most surely impartial)
That Admiral Byng his utmost did not,
T'engage—And adjudge him for that to be shot;
But to palliate his crime, with deference we shew,
In our sentence, distinctions quite subtle and new:
That 'twas prov'd he ne'er shew'd any tokens of fear,
(And how the plague should he, so far in the rear?)
That clearly to us, he appears in this light,
Not a coward,—but only damn'd backward to fight;
Or more clear to refine it, we've shewn in effect,
To be backward in fighting, is—but a neglect.
And though we've condemn'd him, for mercy we pray,
Lest his case be our case, as it certainly may.

—from the *Virginia Gazette*, ed.
Hunter (April 22, 1757), p. [2].

Golden Age Fabulous (Said to be Wrote by a Lady of New-York)[9]

The Golden Age, a specious cheat.
No Age of Gold was ever yet.
Amusing dream! and unbeliev'd
By those who would not be deceiv'd.

The first-born man, with envy warm'd,
Against a harmless brother arm'd;
The victim bled, to quench his rage;
Could this be call'd the golden age?
So fast the spreading evil grew,
That God abhor'd his work to view;
And much incens'd, his work defac'd,
And nature floats a watery waste;
A scene too dreadful to behold:
Was this the boasted age of gold?
The rescu'd patriarch's rising race,
Let Babel witness their disgrace.
Her horrid flames while Sodom rears,
No golden age as yet appears.
The trembling Lot with awe retires
From neighborhood of vengeful fires;
His daughters' conduct plainly prove
Incestuous dealings, lawless love:
A thousand mischiefs, here untold,
Postpone this boasted age of gold;
And Pharoah's Egypt, Israel's crimes
Proclaim that this was not their times.
Let Median, Persian, Trojan, Greek,
Roman, or Carthaginian speak;
Let learned Athens bring her claim,
Or Europe's sons the period name;
Let the united world engage
To fix this boasted happy age:
But since there never was a clime
Could boldly say, that age was mine;
The unfix'd date this truth maintains,
It iron was, and so remains.

—from the *New-England Magazine*,
1 (October, 1758), 56-57.

The Rake. By a Lady in New England

—Video meliora proboque,
Deteriora sequor.

Hor[ace]

An open heart, a generous mind,
But passion's slave, and wild as wind:
In theory, a judge of right;
Though banish'd from its practice quite;
So loose, so prostitute of soul,
His nobler wit becomes the tool
Of every importuning fool:
A thousand virtues misapply'd;
While reason floats on passion's tide:
The ruin of the chaste and fair:
The parent's curse, the virgin's snare:
Whose false example leads astray
The young, the thoughtless, and the gay:
Yet, left alone to cooler thought,
He knows, he sees, he feels his fault;
He knows his fault, he feels, he views,
Detesting what he most pursues:
His judgment tells him, all his gains
For fleeting joys, are lasting pains:
Reason with appetite contending,
Repenting still, and still offending:
Abuser of the gifts of nature,
A wretched, self-condemning creature,
He passes o'er life's ill-trod stage;
And dies, in youth, the prey of age!
The scorn, the pity of the wise,
Who love, lament him—and despise!

—from *A Collection of Poems . . .
By Several Hands*, ed. Robert
Dodsley (London: J. Hughs
for R. and J. Dodsley, 1758),
IV, 318-319.

From *An Answer to a Piece, Entituled a Line Drawn Between Christ, and Anti-Christ*[10]

. . . .

That evil time we now behold,
Which was to Timothy foretold:
There was a people to arise,
As should all government despise.
These people having itching ears,
The emblem of such people bears,
Their ears from truth they turn away,
And are by fables led astray.
Desiring men the law to teach,
Saying that God sends them to preach,
Yet knowing not what they affirm,
And so their hearers do much harm.

. . . .

Now let us one and all look back,
And see wherein we have been slack,
That God should suffer at this day,
The flock out from their fold to stray.
A short address to you my friend,
And so I draw unto an end,
To answer you I did not seek,
But to defend the truth must speak.
You have a sentence on me past,
I shall to the left hand be cast,
But I believe wise Solomon,
The curse that's causeless shall not come.
And as you drew unto a close,
You said that such as did oppose
These lines, should go to the left side,
But I by you shall not be tried.
Did you help God make his decree?
How do you know who sav'd shall be?
You many put to the left hand,
Take care you do not with them stand.
Is this your manner, now my friend,
Who so much zeal for God pretend,
Throughout the land to sow discord,
Strictly forbidden in the Word?
There was another thing you wrote,

About some men who wore a coat,
But you its color truly show,
Pray tell what fashion if you know.
Or let your writings quite alone,
Enough besides you, strifes have sown.
Lest peradventure you complain,
Your words are by a WOMAN slain.
How blind alas! mistaken people are,
Who to these party zealots do adhere.

—from H. W., *An Answer to a Piece,
Entituled a Line Drawn Between Christ,
and Anti-Christ* (Providence? William
Goddard? 1765), pp. 3-4, 11-12.

A Song

I.
Shall I forsak'n ever mourn,
My much lov'd absent swain,
Impatient wait his long return,
And bear each tort'ring pain.

II.
The woods o'er which we used to stray,
A desert doth appear,
No more the lark perch'd on the spray
Delights my ravish'd ear.

III.
The flow'rs and fields, their verdure loose,
Nor can delight my eye;
To please me nature doth refuse,
When Damon is not by.

IV.
Old Time with ling'ring motion flow,
Each morning lets me see

How long it is before he'll show
His much lov'd face to me.

Florella

—from the *American Magazine,
or General Repository* (February,
1769), p. 56.

Impromptu, on Reading an Essay on Education. By a Lady

Yes, women, if they dar'd, would nobly soar,
And every art and science would explore;
Though weak their sex, their notions are refin'd,
And e'er would prove a blessing to mankind.
If they our free-born minds would not enslave,
No other boon of Heaven they need to crave;
But while our minds in fetters are enchain'd,
On it rely your hearts will e'er be pain'd:
While dissipation fondly we pursue,
Believe we small regard can have for you.
Be it your task our intellects to aid,
And you with tenfold interest shall be paid;
Improve our morals, us to honor guide,
And teach us vice from virtue to divide,
And, far as our weak geniuses can go,
Let us each useful theme of learning know:
'Tis then, and then alone, you'll surely prove
There is no blessing like conjugal love.
Thus form'd, the humble friend you'll find, for life,
The faithful comforter, and loving wife.
Should sickness come, she will attend you still,
And ever be obedient to you will.
Should cares attend (as who from cares are free)
A faithful counselor she'll prove to thee;
Though every friend thy sufferings should desert,
In her thou'lt find a true and honest heart,
Who all thy woes will cheerfully partake,
And suffer all for thy beloved sake.

Be generous then, and us to knowledge lead,
And happiness to you will sure succeed;
Then sacred Hymen shall in triumph reign,
And all be proud to wear his pleasing chain.

—from the *Virginia Gazette*, ed.
Purdie and Dixon (February 11,
1773), p. [4].

A Letter From Miss ***** to Her God-Mother

Dear Madam, you need not be told
That—whether they be young or old,
Rich, poor, lame, lazy, sick or well,
Since Adam and his help-mate fell,
Mankind incessantly pursue
The chase of something strange or new.
Wou'd you awaken their attention?
Amuse them with some rare invention;
Promise to captivate their ears
With music of the rolling spheres;
Exhibit to their gazing eyes
The ocean spouting to the skies;
Let dolphins quit their native seas,
And flounce aloft among the trees;
Let lowing herds and bleating sheep,
For pasture, plunge into the deep;
In short—turn nature topsy-turvy,
And you may cure the spleen or scurvy.
No doctor can be disconcerted,
Whose patients are so well diverted!

Since novelty and wonder, then,
Can thus delight the sons of men,
O what a pleasure must it be,
To read a letter writ by me!
'Twould make you stare as much, almost,
As if you saw the Cock-lane ghost!

'Tis not a quarter of a year,
Since first I came, a stranger, here;
Who, all my life before, had been
Secluded from this busy scene,
Debarr'd all commerce with mankind,
And in a narrow cell confin'd,
Where never sun nor moon appear'd,
Nor human voice was ever heard.
But though it's such a little while
I've had to cultivate my style,
Yet I will venture to defy
The spleen and microscopic eye
Of every critic gnat or fly.
If any one despise my letter,
Let him attempt to write a better;
Or if another, with surprise,
Should praise my letter to the skies,
Tell him that he shall find my skill
In other matters greater still.

Untaught in languages, I speak
Italian, Latin, French, or Greek,
As glibly as my mother-tongue!
And this, methinks, for one so young,
And one who never was at school,
May show, at least, that I'm no fool.

In arts and sciences my knowledge
Might shame the lads of Princeton college.
I can explain the globes and maps,
As readily as pin my caps;
Mechanics too, and hydrostatics,
Astronomy and mathematics,
Discoveries by sea and land;
I know them all—and understand
The works of Newton, Boyle, and Locke,
As well as—how to make a smock,
Or fix a tucker to my frock!

But, what is more than all beside,
I've neither vanity nor pride;
For, though they praise me every day,

Yet I regard not what they say;
At least no further than to show
That I have sense enough to know
How much to complaisance I owe.
And here, O let me not forget
A far, far more endearing debt!
A triple debt, dear Madam, due
To your associates and to you,
The guardians of my tender youth,
The vouchers for my faith and truth,
Whose solemn promise has been given
In my behalf, and heard in heav'n!
For this kind office, please to take
The best return that I can make:
May you, ere long, rejoice to see
The plant you've water'd, grown a tree,
Deep-rooted in a fertile ground,
And with unfading honors crown'd!
Ere long may your adopted prove
Not undeserving of your love.

May 25, 1772

—from the *Pennsylvania Magazine*,
1 (August, 1775), 374.

A Lady's Adieu to her Tea-Table

Farewell the tea board, with its gaudy equipage,
Of cups and saucers, cream bucket, sugar tongs,
The pretty tea chest also, lately stor'd
With Hyson, Congo, and best Double Fine.
Full many a joyous moment have I sat by ye,
Hearing the girls tattle, the old maids talk scandal,
And the spruce coxcomb laugh at—may be—nothing.
No more shall I dish out the once lov'd liquor,
Though now detestable,
Because I'm taught (and I believe it true)

Its use will fasten slavish chains upon my country,
And Liberty's the Goddess I would choose
To reign triumphant in America.

—from the *Virginia Gazette*, ed.
Purdie and Dixon (January 20,
1774), p. [2] ; rpt. *Pennsylvania
Gazette* (February 2, 1774), p. [3] .

*Verses Addressed by the Ladies of Bedford, at their Meeting to
Resolve Against Tea, to the Gentlemen of That Place*[11]

What you can raise upon your farms
We'll eat and drink with hearts so free;
The coarsest food we choose to eat,
Before we'll lose our liberty.
Don't cast reflections on our sex,
Because the weaker sort we be;
We'll work our fingers to the bone,
Before we'll lose our liberty.
Our honest hearts abound with zeal,
We'll fight it out with courage free;
And bid adieu to India stuff,
Before we'll lose our liberty.

—from the *Virginia Gazette*, ed.
Purdie and Dixon (March 17,
1774), p. [2] .

From *An Address to New-England: Written by a Daughter of Liberty*

Mourn, mourn O Heavens, and thou O earth bewail,
And weep ye saints, 'till all your spirits fail!
Once happy land, I grieve at thy sad fate,

Thy breach is like the sea, exceeding great.
Boston! thou brave illustrious city fair,
How art thou on the brink of black despair?
I see thy ruin where I turn mine eyes,
Thy trade is gone, thy gainful merchandise,
Kind Heaven assist my pen, inspire my muse,
While I rehearse the melancholy news:
Heaven clothes itself in blackness all around,
While I lament thy deep and dangerous wound;
The sun's enwrapt in clouds, and hides its head,
Darkness its sable mantle now has spread.
Heaven astonish'd now in dreadful forms,
Groans loud with thunder, weeps with wat'ry storms;
The blooming groves forgetting nature's laws,
Withhold their fragrance, wonder at the cause,
The troubled seas with angry billows roar,
That thy destroyers now invade her shore!
The angel strong foretold in holy Writ,
Has loos'd the door of the infernal pit.
See! how the locusts in huge swarms ascend,
New England's fall and ruin they intend.
Thy passages are stopt,—this murd'rous brood,
Thirst for our lives to wash their hands in blood!
Devils incarnate, worst of human kind,
Who can in Hell such brutish monsters find!
Witness, O King Street, how thy sons once fell
A bleeding victim to those hounds of Hell!

. . . .

Unhappy Boston! wherefore doth thy God,
Thus scourge thee with a tyrant's iron rod?
How art thou spoil'd, O city of renown?
Thy sceptre broke, where hast thou lost thy crown?
To deprecate thy loss, who can refuse?
Is there no healing for thy mortal bruise?
Is there no balm in Gilead for thy wound,
That thou sit'st desolate upon the ground?
Consider now when God thus loudly calls,
Before the final storm upon thee fall.
What sins, what crying sins did God provoke,
To cause his wrath against this land to smoke?
Rejecting Christ when offer'd you refus'd,
His gracious calls and warnings you abus'd.

Like Sodom you declare your sins at large,
An awful roll is writ, an heavy charge:
Among professors and among profane,
Such sins abound as heathen count a stain.
What wanton passions and unchaste desires,
With which our youth with Hell are set on fire?
Vice goes unmask'd and rages to excess,
Pride, envy, malice, anxious worldliness;

. . . .

New England, now to meet thy God prepare,
Awake repentance, faith and earnest prayer.
For who can tell but God may stay his hand,
And send salvation to our ruin'd land:
The darkest midnight is his usual time
Of rising and appearing in his prime;
When we of human succor shall despair,
And to the Lord alone for help repair. . . .

—printed in broadside,
Boston, 1774

Ode to Charity

Come Charity! celestial maid,
    Thy influence I adore,
Descend unto thy votary's aid
    Who bows before thy pow'r.

Teach me to feel another's smart,
    And teach my tears to flow;
Teach me to soothe the sorrowing heart,
    And give relief to woe.
Surely with joy I may dispense
    The little fate has given

When promis'd such a recompense
A Savior and a Heaven.

Philadelphia, February 9.   Delia

—from the *Pennsylvania Magazine*,
1 (February, 1775), 87.

Notes

Notes/Introduction

[1]Virginia Woolf, "Professions for Women," *Death of the Moth and Other Essays* (New York: Harcourt Brace Jovanovich, 1970), pp. 235-236.

[2]Useful anthologies of colonial poetry have been provided by Harrison Meserole, ed., *Seventeenth-Century American Poetry* (New York: New York University Press, 1968), and by Kenneth Silverman, ed., *Colonial American Poetry* (New York: Hafner Publishing Company, 1968). But even in these period collections, the only women represented are Anne Bradstreet and Sarah Knight.

[3]Cotton Mather, *Awakening Thoughts on the Sleep of Death* (Boston: Timothy Green, 1712), pp. iii-iv.

[4]Cotton Mather, *Ornaments for the Daughters of Zion* (Cambridge, Mass.: Samuel and Bartholomew Green, 1692), p. 74.

[5]G. Hayden, "The Choice of a Husband," *North-Carolina Magazine* (September 7, 1764), p. 108.

[6]Benjamin Rush, *Thoughts Upon Female Education* (Philadelphia: Prichard and Hall, 1787), p. 25.

[7]Mary Astell, *Reflections on Marriage* (London: R. Wilkin, 1706), preface.

[8]Several useful studies of colonial education are available for further reference, the fullest and most recent being Lawrence A. Cremin's *American Education: The Colonial Experience, 1607-1783* (New York: Harper and Row, 1970), which includes a lengthy bibliographical essay. Bernard Bailyn's provocative *Education in the Forming of American Society* (Chapel Hill, N.C.: University of North Carolina Press, 1960) was among the earliest studies to expand the definition of education beyond public school systems to encompass other transmitters of culture such as family, church and community. A more concise account of colonial concern for education is provided by Louis Wright's *The*

Cultural Life of the American Colonies 1607-1763 (New York: Harper and Brothers, 1957), pp. 98-125. Thomas Woody's *A History of Women's Education in the United States* (New York: The Science Press, 1929), 2 vols., surveys the origins of schooling for women. Educational opportunities for working class and poor children are detailed in Marcus W. Jernegan's 1931 study *Laboring and Dependent Classes in Colonial America 1607-1738* (New York: Frederick Ungar Publishing Co., 1960), pp. 59-171.

   9Ann Eliza Bleecker, *The Posthumous Works of Ann Eliza Bleecker in Prose and Verse. . .*, ed. Margaretta Faugeres (New York: T. and J. Swords, 1793), p. 240.

   10Quoted by Roger Thompson, *Women in Stuart England and America: A Comparative Study* (Boston: Routledge and Kegan Paul, 1974), p. 10.

   11Among those historians favorably comparing the position of American women with that of British women are Ann Gordon, Mary Jo Buhle and Nancy Schrom, "Women in American Society: An Historical Contribution," *Radical America*, 5 (July-August, 1971), 3-74; Thompson, *Women in Stuart England and America;* Page Smith, *Daughters of the Promised Land: Women in American History* (Boston: Little, Brown and Co., 1970); Mary S. Benson, *Women in Eighteenth Century America* (New York: Columbia University Press, 1935); and Elisabeth Dexter, *Colonial Women of Affairs* (Boston: Houghton-Mifflin Co., 1924). Richard Morris' more specialized *Studies in the History of American Law* (New York: Columbia University Press, 1930), pp. 126-200, details the legal advantages (especially recognition of the marriage contract as a reciprocal agreement and greater proprietary capacity) that distinguished American women from their British contemporaries.

   12Thelma M. Smith, "Feminism in Philadelphia, 1790-1850," *Pennsylvania Magazine of History and Biography*, 68 (1944), 243-268. See also Ann Douglas, *The Feminization of American Culture* (New York: Alfred A. Knopf, 1977).

   13Patricia Branca and Peter Stearns, "On the History of Modern Women, a Research Note," *AHA Newsletter*, 12 (September, 1974), 6.

   14"Advice to a Young Lady," *The American Magazine, or General Repository* (July, 1769), p. 224. The poem was reprinted as "Advice to the Ladies," *Virginia Gazette*, ed. Purdie and Dixon (May 16, 1771), p. [4].

   15John Winthrop, *The History of New England from 1630-1649*, ed. James Savage (Boston: Little, Brown and Co., 1853), II, 265-266.

[16]James Fordyce, "On Female Virtue, with Intellectual Accomplishments," *Sermons to Young Women* ([Boston: Mein and Fleeming], 1767), II, 15.

[17]Thomas Parker, *The Copy of a Letter Written by Mr. Thomas Parker . . . to His Sister, Mrs. Elizabeth Avery . . . Touching Sundry Opinions by Her Professed and Maintained, November 22, 1649* (London: John Field, 1650), p. 13.

[18]*Boston Weekly Magazine* (March 2, 1743), p. 7.

[19]Bathsheba Bowers, *An Alarm Sounded to Prepare the Inhabitants of the World to Meet the Lord . . .* [New York: Bradford, 1709], pp. 4-5.

[20]"To the Visitant, from a Circle of Ladies, on Reading his Paper, No. 3 . . . ," *Pennsylvania Chronicle*, 2 (March 7-14, 1768), 50; rpt. *American Museum*, 4 (December, 1788), 491.

[21]*American Weekly Mercury* (April 8-15, 1736), pp. [1-2].

[22][Antoine Léonard Thomas], "An Occasional Letter on the Female Sex," *Pennsylvania Magazine*, 1 (August, 1775), 362-364. See Frank Smith, "The Authorship of 'An Occasional Letter on the Female Sex,' " *American Literature*, 2 (November, 1930), 277-280, for evidence establishing Antoine Thomas as the source of this letter; Thomas Paine has often been mistakenly identified as the author.

[23]"To a Poetical Lady," *Boston Weekly Magazine* (March 2, 1743), p. 6.

[24]John Duncombe, "The Feminead; or, Female Genius," *Boston Magazine*, 2 (December, 1785), 470. Duncombe's piece had been printed in London as a book by 1754.

[25]Edward Johnson, *Wonder-Working Providence of Sion's Saviour in New England 1628-1651*, ed. J. Franklin Jameson (New York: Charles Scribner's Sons, 1910; rpt. New York: Barnes and Noble, 1959), p. 28.

[26]Nathaniel Ward, *The Simple Cobler of Aggawam in America*, ed. P. M. Zall (Lincoln, Neb.: University of Nebraska Press, 1969), p. 26.

[27]Nathaniel Ward, [Commendatory Poem], *The Works of Anne Bradstreet in Prose and Verse*, ed. John H. Ellis (New York: Peter Smith, 1932), p. 85.

28Judith Sargent Murray, "On the Equality of the Sexes," *Massachusetts Magazine*, 2 (March, 1790), pp. 133-134.

29Jane Turell to Abigail Colman, 1727, in *Reliquiae Turellae, et Lachrymae Paternae: . . .Two Sermons Preach'd at Medford, April 6, 1735, by Benjamin Colman . . . After the Funeral of His Beloved Daughter, Mrs. Jane Turell. To Which Are Added, Some Large Memoirs of Her Life and Death, by her Consort, the Reverend Mr. Ebenezer Turell . . .* (Boston: S. Kneeland and T. Green, 1735), p. 95.

30Bridget Richardson Fletcher, *Hymns and Spiritual Songs . . .* (Boston: I. Thomas, 1773), p. [iii] .

31Sarah Wentworth Morton, *Ouâbi: Or the Virtues of Nature. An Indian Tale* (Boston: Thomas and Andrews, 1790), p. viii.

32Studies of the work load and responsibilities typically undertaken by colonial women are provided by Carl Holliday, *Woman's Life in Colonial Days* (Boston: Cornhill Publishing Co., 1922; rpt. New York: Frederick Ungar Publishing Co., 1960), and Julia C. Spruill, *Women's Life and Work in the Southern Colonies* (1938; rpt. New York: Russell and Russell, 1969).

33John Woodbridge, "Epistle to the Reader," *Works of Anne Bradstreet*, p. 84.

34Sarah Wentworth Morton, *Beacon Hill. A Local Poem* (Boston: Manning and Loring, 1797), p. ix.

35Ellen Moers, *Literary Women* (Garden City, N. Y.: Doubleday, 1976), passim.

36Probate Records, Northampton, Massachusetts, January 13, 1729/30.

37Cotton Mather, *Magnalia Christi Americana*, ed. Kenneth B. Murdock (Cambridge, Mass.: Harvard University Press, 1977), II, 233.

38The Prince Library, *A Catalogue of the Collection of Books and Manuscripts which Formerly Belonged to the Reverend Thomas Prince . . .* (Boston: Alfred Mudge and Son, 1870), p. 8.

39Ann Bolton, unpublished diary, quoted by William John Potts, "Bathsheba Bowers," *Pennsylvania Magazine of History and Biography*, 3 (1879), 112.

[40]Publication data for any volume printed in colonial America can be obtained from Clifford K. Shipton and James E. Mooney's *National Index of American Imprints through 1800* (Barre, Mass.: American Antiquarian Society, 1969). J. A. Leo Lemay's *Calendar of American Poetry in the Colonial Newspapers and Magazines* (Worcester, Mass.: American Antiquarian Society, 1970) is useful for investigating British reprints in periodicals, though often such reprints will be anonymous and difficult to trace.

[41]Useful studies of contemporary British women are available in Doris Stenton's *The English Woman in History* (New York: Macmillan, 1957), and Myra Reynold's *The Learned Lady in England, 1650-1760* (Boston: Houghton-Mifflin, 1920). See also *The Female Spectator: English Women Writers before 1800* (Bloomington: Indiana University Press and Old Westbury, N. Y.: The Feminist Press, 1977).

[42] [Lady Mary Lee Chudleigh] , "A Caveat to the Fair Sex," *Pennsylvania Evening Post*, 1 (February 18, 1775), 47. See also Lady Mary Lee Chudleigh, *Poems on Several Occasions* (London: W. B. for Bernard Lintott, 1703), p. 40.

[43]Anne H. Wharton, *Salons Colonial and Republican* (Philadelphia: J. B. Lippincott Co., 1900), p. 15.

[44]See pp. 67-69 for the text of the poem.

[45]See pp. 190-191 for the text of the poem.

[46]Judith Sargent Murray, "Lines to Philenia," *Massachusetts Magazine*, 2 (April, 1790), 248-249; the poem is reprinted here on pp. 135-136. Sarah Wentworth Morton's reply "To Constantia" was published in the *Massachusetts Magazine*, 2 (May, 1790), 309-310; see pp. 183-184 in this volume for the text of the poem.

[47]See pp. 95-96 for the text of the poems.

[48]"Misericordus," *Pennsylvania Chronicle*, 6 (July 6-13, 1772), [1] .

[49]Quoted by Alice Morse Earle, *Colonial Dames and Good Wives* (Boston: Houghton-Mifflin, 1895), p. 232.

[50]Hannah Griffitts, "On Reading Some Paragraphs in 'The Crisis,' April, '77," manuscript poem in the Historical Society of Pennsylvania. See pp. 64-65 for the full text of the poem.

51Anna Young Smith, "On Reading Swift's Works," *Universal Asylum and Columbian Magazine*, 5 (September, 1790), 185. The complete poem is printed on page 173 of this volume.

52Bleecker, *Posthumous Works of Ann Eliza Bleecker*, p. 241.

53Ann Stanford, *Anne Bradstreet: The Worldly Puritan* (New York: Burt Franklin and Company, 1974).

54Judith Sargent Murray, *The Gleaner* (Boston: Thomas and Andrews, 1798), I, 13.

55Martha Brewster, *Poems on Divers Subjects* (New London: [John Green], 1757), p. [2].

56Anne Bradstreet, "In Honor of DuBartas, 1641," *The Works of Anne Bradstreet in Prose and Verse*, pp. 353-356.

57Jane Turell, [Lines on Childbirth], in Benjamin Colman, *Reliquiae Turellae, et Lachrymae Paternae. . .*, p. 103. See page 52 of this volume for the complete text of the poem.

58Annis Stockton, "An Extempore Ode in a Sleepless Night . . . ," appended to Rev. Samuel Stanhope Smith, *Funeral Sermon on the Death of the Hon. Richard Stockton . . .* (Trenton, N. J.: Isaac Collins, 1781), p. 48.

59"The Lady's Complaint," *Virginia Gazette*, ed. Parks (October 22, 1736), p. [3].

60Murray, "On the Equality of the Sexes," p. 132.

61Bradstreet, "The Prologue," *Works of Anne Bradstreet*, p. 101.

62Hannah Griffitts to Susanna Wright, February 6, 1763. The letter is with the Norris Papers at the Historical Society of Pennsylvania.

63Katherine Philips, the "matchless Orinda."

64Elizabeth Singer Rowe.

65Jane Turell, "To My Muse, December 29, 1725," in Benjamin Colman, *Reliquiae Turellae, et Lachrymae Paternae . . .* , pp. 74-75.

Anne Bradstreet

[1]Cotton Mather, *Magnalia Christi Americana*, ed. Kenneth B. Murdock (Cambridge, Mass.: Harvard University Press, 1977), II, 230. A complete account of Bradstreet's ancestry and life is available in Elizabeth Wade White's *Anne Bradstreet: The Tenth Muse* (New York: Oxford University Press, 1971).

[2]Anne Bradstreet, *The Works of Anne Bradstreet in Prose and Verse*, ed. John Harvard Ellis (New York: Peter Smith, 1932), p. 5.

[3]Samuel Kettell, ed., *Specimens of American Poetry* (Boston: S. G. Goodrich, 1829; rpt. New York: B. Blom, 1967), I, xxvii-xxviii; Harold S. Jantz, *The First Century of New England Verse* (Worcester, Mass.: American Antiquarian Society, 1944; rpt. New York: Russell, 1962), pp. 38-39.

[4]John Woodbridge, *Works of Anne Bradstreet*, ed. Ellis, pp. 83-84.

[5]Texts reprinted here are based on those established by John Harvard Ellis in *The Works of Anne Bradstreet in Prose and Verse*, pp. 100-102, 389-390, 393-395, 398-403, 40-44.

[6]Bradstreet, *Works of Anne Bradstreet*, ed. Ellis, p. 47.

[7]Ann Stanford, *Anne Bradstreet: The Worldly Puritan* (New York: Burt Franklin and Co., 1974), p. i.

[8]John Harvard Ellis, in his edition of *The Works of Anne Bradstreet*, p. 400, notes that this date "is clearly wrong, as events are referred to in the course of the poem which took place more than a year later." He surmises that the date should be 1658, while Jeannine Hensley's edition of *The Works of Anne Bradstreet* (Cambridge, Mass.: Harvard University Press, 1967), p. 232, gives the date as 1659.

[9]Her oldest son Samuel, who went to England in 1657 and returned home in 1661.

[10]Her daughter Dorothy, who married the Reverend Seaborn Cotton in 1654. Living for a time in Wethersfield, Connecticut, in 1660 they moved to Hampton, New Hampshire.

[11]Her daughter Sarah, who married Richard Hubbard of Ipswich.

[12]Her son Simon, who graduated from Harvard College in 1660.

[13]Probably her son Dudley. Although he is the seventh rather than the fifth child, Dudley is the next son after Simon.

[14]The "other three" are Hannah, Mercy and John.

Jane Colman Turell

[1]*Reliquiae Turellae, et Lachrymae Paternae: . . . Two Sermons Preach'd at Medford, April 6, 1735, by Benjamin Colman. . . .After the Funeral of His Beloved Daughter, Mrs. Jane Turell. To Which Are Added, Some Large Memoirs of Her Life and Death, by her Consort, the Reverend Mr. Ebenezer Turell . . . .* (Boston: S. Kneeland and T. Green, 1735), p. 61.

[2]Turell, *Memoirs of . . . Jane Turell*, signatured with Colman, *Reliquiae Turellae*, p. 78.

[3]Turell, *Memoirs of . . . Jane Turell*, signatured with Colman, *Reliquiae Turellae*, p. 64.

[4]Turell, *Memoirs of . . . Jane Turell*, signatured with Colman, *Reliquiae Turellae*, p. 86.

[5]Turell, *Memoirs of . . . Jane Turell*, signatured with Colman, *Reliquiae Turellae*, p. 78.

[6]Elizabeth Singer Rowe.

[7]Huldah (Ebenezer Turell's note).

[8]Katherine Philips.

[9]Elizabeth Singer Rowe.

[10]"Delia" is the pseudonym Turell adopted for referring to herself in verse.

[11]"Philander" is the pseudonym Turell used for her husband Ebenezer.

[12]Turell's mother, Jane Clark Colman, died on October 28, 1730.

Hannah Griffitts

[1]Hannah Griffitts to Susanna Wright, February 6, 1763. Griffitts' manuscript correspondence may be consulted in the Historical Society of Pennsylvania.

[2]Hannah Griffitts to General Anthony Wayne, July 13, 1777. This letter has been published in the *Pennsylvania Magazine of History and Biography*, 27 (1903), 110-111. Handwritten marginal notes in "Letters and Communications Addressed to John F. Watson on the Subject of his *Annals of Philadelphia*," I, 29, in the Historical Society of Pennsylvania, call Hannah Griffitts a "strenous whig," while Anne Wharton in *Through Colonial Doorways* (Philadelphia, 1893), p. 54, refers to her as an "ardent loyalist." Much of the political poetry seems to support Wharton. "On Reading Some Paragraphs in 'The Crisis,' April, '77," for example, points to Thomas Paine as a fraud and a "fibber." Yet the letter to General Wayne leaves little doubt that Griffitts was a whig.

[3]Hannah Griffitts to Susanna Wright, November, 1762.

[4]Deborah Logan, Griffitts' cousin and a poet herself, pictured Griffitts as "averse to her pieces appearing in print, which they sometimes did, though without her knowledge," in an account printed in the *Register of Pennsylvania*, ed. Samuel Hazard, 8 (September 17, 1831), 178. I have located no trace of the publications Logan mentions.

[5]"On the Anniversary Day of the Death of my Only Attachment to Life, My Beloved Parent, February 13, 1751," manuscript poem in the Historical

Society of Pennsylvania. This is the first of a series of such "anniversary poems" written regularly from 1751 to 1803 in memory of Griffitts' mother.

[6]Hannah Griffitts to Susanna Wright, April 15, 1763.

[7]Hannah Griffitts to Susanna Wright, November, 1762.

[8]Hannah Griffitts to Susanna Wright, February 6, 1763.

[9]Griffitts' earliest extant poem. "This verse was composed as I stood at the window about an hour before the earthquake which happened the 7th, 10 mo[nth], 11 at night, 1737." (Griffitts' note)

[10]Probably an error for Sinai.

[11]"Wrote, in the spring, perhaps 1765, in a most violent storm, through the morning, and did considerable damage to the stores, on the water—but suddenly ceased to a perfect calm; and a beautiful appearance 'of the setting sun' occasion'd the following lines." (Griffitts' note) The manuscript from which the text is taken was copied by Griffitts in 1799.

[12]The manuscript is a 1773 copy in Griffitts' hand. Samuel Fothergill (1715-1772) was a Quaker minister who travelled widely in Wales, Ireland, Scotland and North America.

[13]"Wrote on the 28th of Feb[ruar]y, 1775." (Griffitts' note)

[14]Frederick North, second Earl of Guilford (1732-1792), England's first lord of the treasury from 1770 to 1782. Lord North was a supporter of the Stamp Act and of Charles Townshend's tea duty.

[15]The authorship of the "Inscription on a Curious Chamberstove..." is uncertain, but as the earliest datable copy is in Griffitts' hand, I include it among her pieces. Griffitts' manuscript is a copy dated November, 1776. But the "Inscription" was attributed to Jonathan Odell on its first publication, in *The Gentleman's Magazine and Historical Chronicle*, 47 (April, 1777), 188.

[16]The word "defend" is less legible than the rest of the manuscript. Perhaps to avoid confusion, Griffitts footnoted it: " 'defend' was, I suppose, intended, but I don't believe such virtue was lodg'd in the man or his art."

[17]As part of an organized persecution of Quakers, John Roberts and Abraham Carlisle were tried and convicted of treason during the Revolution. They were hanged on November 4, 1778.

[18]"Mat[thew] 18th chap[te]r, from the 23d verse to the 35th." (Griffitts' note)

[19]"Gray's Church-Yard." (Griffitts' note)

[20]"See a piece she [Susanna Wright] wrote on her own birthday, which closes with the above last line." (Griffitts' note)

Mercy Otis Warren

[1]Mercy Warren, ["While Life's Encumber'd Stage I Tread"], manuscript poem. Mercy Warren Papers, Massachusetts Historical Society.

[2]Mercy Warren to John Adams, January 30, 1775. *Warren-Adams Letters*, I, Massachusetts Historical Society *Collections*, 72 (1917), 37.

[3]John Adams to Mercy Warren, March 15, 1775. *Warren-Adams Letters*, I, 42.

[4]Mercy Warren to "Betsey," undated. This and all subsequent references to unpublished Warren correspondence are taken from the Mercy Warren Papers at the Massachusetts Historical Society.

[5]Mercy Warren to Winslow Warren, December 24, 1779. The letter was printed in the *Independent Chronicle*, 13 (January 18, 1781), [2], and reprinted by the *Massachusetts Magazine*, 2 (January, 1790), 37.

[6]Katharine Anthony, *The First Lady of the Revolution* . . . (Garden City, N. Y.: Doubleday and Co., 1958), p. 163.

[7]John Adams to Mercy Warren, December 26, 1790. *Warren-Adams Letters*, II, Massachusetts Historical Society *Collections*, 73 (1925), 324.

[8]James Warren to Mercy Warren, June 28, 1790.

[9]Mercy Warren to Elbridge Gerry, December 25, 1793.

[10]Rufus Griswold, *The Female Poets of America* (Philadelphia: Carey and Hart, 1849), p. 23.

[11]James Otis, Jr., Mercy Warren's oldest brother, who apparently experienced increasingly numerous periods of insanity as he grew older. The texts of the poems printed here, unless otherwise noted, have been taken from Warren's manuscripts in the Massachusetts Historical Society or from *Poems, Dramatic and Miscellaneous*.

[12]Taken from the Adams manuscripts, "To Mr. Adams" is printed in the *Warren-Adams Letters*, II, 402-403. The poem is addressed, of course, to John Adams.

[13]An unidentifiable word. Cf. entheus, inspiration.

[14]Ecstatics?

[15]An obscure form of reaved; despoiled, plundered.

[16]The "H" is nearly erased in the manuscript. It refers to Thomas Hutchinson, the Rapatio of Mercy Warren's early plays.

[17]Dr. Joseph Warren (1741-1775), noted Boston physician and ardent Whig, abandoned his medical practice to join the colonial army in 1775. See page 93 for Annis Stockton's eulogy on the same occasion.

[18]"Burning of Charlestown." (Warren's note)

[19]James Warren, Mercy's husband.

[20]Richard Montgomery (1738-1775), commander of the American assault on Montreal during the Revolution. Montgomery was killed during the assault on Quebec. See pages 145-146 for Ann Eliza Bleecker's eulogy to Montgomery.

[21]Janet Livingston Montgomery, wife of Richard Montgomery and correspondent of Mercy Warren.

[22]Mercy Warren's pen name.

[23]Mercy Warren's son, who died in Spain of tuberculosis.

[24]Elizabeth Robinson Montagu (1720-1800), according to Abigail Adams in a letter from London to Mercy Warren, May 14, 1787, "a violent anti-American." *Warren-Adams Letters*, II, 287. Warren sent a copy of her *Poems, Dramatic and Miscellaneous* to Montagu, eventually receiving a warm response that particularly praised her dramas.

Annis Boudinot Stockton

[1]Annis Stockton, "The Dream. An Ode." The manuscript text is in the Princeton University Library.

[2]Elizabeth Fergusson's commonplace book is on deposit with the Dickinson College Library.

[3]The Esther Burr journal is located in the Beinecke Library at Yale University.

[4]Annis Stockton to Elias Boudinot, May 1, 1789. (The endorsement reads May 10, 1789.) The letter is located at the Historical Society of Pennsylvania; it was published in Lyman H. Butterfield's "Annis and the General: Mrs. Stockton's Poetic Eulogies of George Washington," *Princeton University Library Chronicle*, 7 (November, 1945), 39.

[5]Annis Stockton to Elias Boudinot, October 23, 1781. A photostat of the letter is held by the Princeton University Library; the original is in private hands. The letter was printed by Butterfield in "Annis and the General," p. 25.

[6]Unless otherwise noted, the texts printed here have been drawn from the Annis Stockton manuscripts in the Princeton University Library.

[7]*New-York Mercury* (January 9, 1758), p. [1]; reprinted by the *New American Magazine* (January, 1758), p. 16. The manuscript version in the Princeton University Library misspells Schuyler's name as "Scuyler" and includes a headnote identifying the occasion of the poem more precisely: the lines celebrate "his return to Jersey after two years captivity in Canada—he was taken at Fort William Henry and maintained out of his own private fortune the

most of his regiment during their confinement." A headnote to the printed text also notes the occasion of the poem, but goes on to inform Hugh Gaine, editor of the *New-York Mercury*, that as the lines "discover so fruitful and uncommon a genius in their fair author, . . . their communication to the public, through the channel of your paper, will be acceptable to all, but more especially to your female readers." The manuscript and published texts differ slightly.

[8]*Pennsylvania Magazine*, 1 (June, 1775), 280-281. This poem is a revision of Stockton's manuscript "To Mr. Stockton in England, An Epistle, 1769" in the Princeton collection.

[9]Dr. Joseph Warren (1741-1775), noted Boston physician and ardent Whig, abandoned his medical practice to join the colonial army in 1775. See pages 80-81 for Mercy Warren's eulogy on this same occasion.

[10]Stockton makes reference to nineteen resolutions formulated by delegates of towns in Suffolk County, Massachusetts, on September 9, 1774. The resolutions denounce the authority of the British Parliament over the colonies and recommend preparations for armed resistance.

[11]*Columbian Magazine*, 1 (January, 1787), 245. The printed text is substantially different from the Princeton manuscript.

[12]Elizabeth Graeme Fergusson of Philadelphia (see pages 101-111).

[13]Reprinted from an appendix to the Reverend Samuel Stanhope Smith's *Funeral Sermon on the Death of the Hon. Richard Stockton* . . . (Trenton, N. J.: Isaac Collins, 1781), pp. 47-48. The title and subjoined date are from the Princeton manuscript text. Much of the poem was reworked for publication.

[14]Reprinted from an appendix to Smith, *Funeral Sermon on . . . Richard Stockton* . . . , pp. 45-47. The title is taken from the Princeton manuscript text. Discrepancies between the two versions are slight.

[15]Pseudonym for Stockton's husband Richard.

Elizabeth Graeme Fergusson

[1]Elizabeth Fergusson to Mrs. Campbell, May 9, 1779. The manuscript is in the collection of the Historical Society of Pennsylvania; it has been published by Simon Gratz, "Material for a Biography of Mrs. Elizabeth Fergusson, née Graeme," *Pennsylvania Magazine of History and Biography*, 41 (1917), 388.

[2]Nathaniel Evans, *Poems on Several Occasions* (Philadelphia: John Dunlap, 1772), pp. 149-150.

[3]Unless otherwise noted, the texts used here have been taken from the Fergusson manuscripts in the Historical Society of Pennsylvania. The Mr. Herschel of this poem is Sir William Herschel (1738-1822), noted astronomer and discoverer of the planet Uranus in 1781. Herschel at first took his discovery for a comet, but when he realized his error, he designated the planet as the "Georgium Sidus," in honor of George III.

[4]"This line has an immediate allusion to the shocks that this globe has sustain'd by the late dreadful earthquakes in many parts of the world as it is reported the very poles of the earth are mov'd." (Fergusson's note)

[5]*Columbian Magazine*, 1 (December, 1786), 198.

[6]" 'God-like died' may not be proper, as God cannot die; but it has a reference to our Savior dying for man." (Fergusson's note)

[7]*Columbian Magazine*, 1 (September, 1787), 667.

[8]*Columbian Magazine*, 3 (May, 1789), 312.

[9]*Columbian Magazine*, 3 (July, 1789), 437-438.

[10]The manuscript text is located in the Princeton University Library. Fergusson reacts to the occasion of the poem in a note: "Gracious Heaven! Were these barbarities which would disgrace savages committed by French men, by that lively and ingenious people."

Martha Brewster

[1]Martha Brewster, *Poems on Divers Subjects* (New London, Conn.: [John Green], 1757), p. 22.

[2]Brewster, *Poems on Divers Subjects*, p. [2].

Judith Sargent Murray

[1]*Massachusetts Magazine*, 6 (June, 1794), 369.

[2]Boston poet Sarah Wentworth Morton.

[3][Judith Sargent Murray], *The Gleaner* (Boston: Thomas and Andrews, 1798), I, 14-15.

[4][Murray], *The Gleaner*, I, vi.

[5][Murray], *The Gleaner*, I, vii-viii.

[6][Murray], *The Gleaner*, III, 217.

[7][Murray], *The Gleaner*, III, 188.

[8][Murray], *The Gleaner*, III, 189.

[9][Murray], *The Gleaner*, III, 313.

[10]Judith Sargent Murray to Winthrop Sargent, August 30, 1802. The manuscript letter is in the Massachusetts Historical Society.

[11]*Massachusetts Magazine*, 2 (February, 1790), 120.

[12]*Massachusetts Magazine*, 2 (January, 1790), 57-58. The occasion of the poem was the death of Murray's son George, born in 1789.

[13]*Massachusetts Magazine*, 3 (May, 1791), 307-308.

[14] [Murray], *The Gleaner*, I, 180. All subsequent poems by Murray (unless otherwise noted) are taken from the three volumes of *The Gleaner*.

[15]*Massachusetts Magazine*, 2 (April, 1790), 248-249. Murray directed this tribute to Sarah Wentworth Morton after the resolution of their confusion over Morton's accidental use of Murray's pseudonym "Constantia."

Ann Eliza Bleecker

[1]Ann Eliza Bleecker, *The Posthumous Works of Ann Eliza Bleecker* . . . , ed. Margaretta Faugeres (New York: T. and J. Swords, 1793), p. 118.

[2]I have been unable to positively identify "Mr. L*****," though four of the poems in the *Posthumous Works* are written to him. Perhaps he is the Edmund Ludlow listed among the subscribers to the volume; certainly he had initiated a verse correspondence with Bleecker. She addresses "Mr. L*****" only in her pastoral voice, perhaps echoing Milton's "Lycidas."

[3]Archaic form of lyre.

[4]"On the Immensity of Creation" appeared originally in the *New-York Magazine*, 1 (June, 1790), 364.

[5]"Written in the Retreat from Burgoyne" had been printed earlier in the *New-York Magazine*, 1 (March, 1790), 184-185. John Burgoyne (1722-1792) was given command of 6400 British soldiers for a march from Canada into New York to meet a division under Sir William Howe. At first successful, Burgoyne was forced to surrender on October 17, 1777.

[6]Bleecker's half-sister, who lived with the Bleeckers in Tomhanick before the Revolution.

[7]Richard Montgomery (1738-1775), commander of the American assault on Montreal during the Revolution. Montgomery was killed during the assault on Quebec. See pages 81-82 for Mercy Warren's eulogy to Mongomery.

8"Recollection" first appeared in the *New-York Magazine*, 1(February, 1790), 118.

9"On Reading Dryden's Virgil" was first published in the *New-York Magazine*, 2 (November, 1791), 670.

10Probably Margaret Van Wyck, Bleecker's cousin.

Phillis Wheatley

1John Wheatley, Letter to A. Bell, Publisher, November 14, 1772, *Poems on Various Subjects, Religious and Moral* (London: A. Bell, 1773), p. [vi].

2An explanation for the disappearance of some of Wheatley's manuscripts was offered by Margaretta Matilda Odell, "a collateral descendant of Mrs. Wheatley," in *Memoir and Poems of Phillis Wheatley*, 2nd edition (Boston: Light and Horton, 1835), p. 36. She noted that although other poems and letters certainly existed at one time, John Peters had received his wife's papers after her death from a relative of Susanna Wheatley to whom they had been entrusted. He took them south with him, where they have apparently disappeared.

3Phillis Wheatley to Samson Occom, February 11, 1774, *Boston Post-Boy* (March 21, 1774), p. [3]. This letter was reprinted in the *Massachusetts Spy* (March 24, 1774), p. [3], and the *Providence Gazette* (March 26, 1774), p. [2]. Many of Wheatley's other letters can be found in Julian D. Mason, Jr.'s *Poems of Phillis Wheatley* (Chapel Hill: University of North Carolina Press, 1966), pp. 103-111. Newly discovered materials are available from Kenneth Silverman, "Four New Letters by Phillis Wheatley," *Early American Literature*, 8 (1974), 257-271, Sarah D. Jackson, "Letters of Phillis Wheatley and Susanna Wheatley," *Journal of Negro History*, 57 (1972), 211-215, and Mukhtar Ali Isani, "Phillis Wheatley in London: An Unpublished Letter to David Wooster," *American Literature*, 51 (May, 1979), 255-260. An additional letter to the Reverend Samuel Hopkins is reprinted by Carter G. Woodson in the preface to *The Mind of the Negro as Reflected in Letters Written During the Crisis 1800-1860* (Washington, D. C.: The Association for the Study of Negro Life and History, Inc., 1926; rpt. New York: Russell and Russell, 1969).

[4][Margaretta Matilda Odell]. "Memoir of Phillis Wheatley." *Memoir and Poems of Phillis Wheatley*, 3rd edition (Boston: Isaac Knapp, 1838: rpt. Miami, Fla.: Mnemosyne Publishing Company, 1969), p. 35.

[5]The text for "America" is taken from a manuscript in the Historical Society of Pennsylvania. It was first published by Robert C. Kuncio in "Some Unpublished Poems of Phillis Wheatley," *New England Quarterly*, 43 (1970), 293. Although the manuscript is undated, Kuncio places its composition between 1768 and 1770.

[6]Probably a mistake for "flood."

[7]Probably "Reach O."

[8]Three versions of this poem (with varying titles) are extant, one published in *Poems on Various Subjects, Religious and Moral* (1773) and two in manuscript. One manuscript version, in the possession of the Massachusetts Historical Society, was published in an appendix to William H. Robinson's *Phillis Wheatley in the Black American Beginnings* (Detroit: Broadside Press, 1975), pp. 75-76, though Robinson's printed text is unfortunately error-ridden. The text used here is from the manuscript in Harvard University's Houghton Library. The differences between this and the Massachusetts Historical Society text are slight.

[9]The text for this poem, and for all subsequent Wheatley poems, is from Mason's *Poems of Phillis Wheatley*. "To the University of Cambridge" was written in 1767, and revised for inclusion in *Poems on Various Subjects, Religious and Moral.*

[10]Addressed to William Legge, Second Earl of Dartmouth (1731-1801), who served as Secretary of State for the Colonies and President of the Board of Trade and Foreign Plantations in Lord North's administration from 1772-1775, the poem was sent in a letter dated October 10, 1772.

[11]Archaic for "temple."

[12]Originally published in 1784, this is one of only two poems that Wheatley published under her married name. The other was "An Elegy . . . To . . . Dr. Samuel Cooper," published in 1783.

Anna Young Smith

[1]Elizabeth Fergusson's commonplace book, now on deposit with the Dickinson College Library, has an interlinear notation that incorrectly assigns the Smiths' marriage to 1774. Handwritten notes in the Graeme-Smith family Bible, privately owned, list the correct date.

[2]Some confusion exists as to the date of Anna Young Smith's death. The Fergusson commonplace book notes that "this dear child died April the 3, 1780, in the child bed of her third child very sudden." The Douglas C. Turnbull, Jr. family tree places her death on April 4, 1783, while the Graeme-Smith family Bible lists her death on March 22, 1780, just a few days after the birth of her fifth child. Presumably Fergusson is the most reliable of the sources.

[3]Elizabeth Fergusson's political labels for her niece and nephew are attached as annotations to her transcription of Smith's "An Elegy to the Memory of the American Volunteers . . ." in Fergusson's commonplace book.

[4]Texts used here, unless otherwise noted, are from the Fergusson commonplace book, now on deposit with the Dickinson College Library.

[5]"Written by Anna Young at eighteen, three years after the death of Dr. Graeme." (Elizabeth Fergusson's note)

[6]Anna Young Smith's pseudonym for William Smith, her husband.

[7]*Universal Asylum and Columbian Magazine*, 5 (September, 1790), 185. A variant text is available in Elizabeth Fergusson's commonplace book.

[8]"Written a year before her marriage with Damon." (Elizabeth Fergusson's note)

[9]*Pennsylvania Magazine*, 1 (June, 1775), 278-279. A manuscript copy in Elizabeth Fergusson's commonplace book differs only slightly from the published text.

Sarah Wentworth Morton

[1]The error was finally corrected by Milton Ellis, "The Author of the First American Novel," *American Literature*, 4 (January, 1933), 359-368.

[2]Sarah Wentworth Morton, *My Mind and Its Thoughts* (Boston: Wells and Lilly, 1823; rpt. Delmar, N. Y.: Scholars' Facsimiles and Reprints, 1975), p. 287.

[3]Morton, *My Mind and Its Thoughts*, p. xvi.

[4]Morton, *My Mind and Its Thoughts*, p. 156.

[5]Morton, *My Mind and Its Thoughts*, p. 159.

[6]Morton, *My Mind and Its Thoughts*, pp. 219-220.

[7]Morton, *My Mind and Its Thoughts*, pp. 32-33. Morton introduced her "Lines to the Breath of Kindness" with this note: "The following lines being, as their style imports, a production of early youth, are here inserted, not surely for poetic merit, but rather for the grateful sentiment at that period felt, uttered, and inscribed to the kindest of the kind" (p. 32). Unless otherwise noted, the Morton poems reprinted here were obtained from *My Mind and Its Thoughts*.

[8]"In the legends of the saints, it is written that saint Cecelia, the inventress of the organ, drew an angel from heaven by the melody of that divine instrument." (Morton's note)

[9]*Massachusetts Magazine*, 2 (May, 1790), 309-310.

[10]The Huntington Library manuscript is the source for this text of Morton's "Stanzas to a Husband Recently United." Another version is included in Morton's *My Mind and Its Thoughts*, pp. 182-183.

[11]"Leonidas." (Morton's note)

[12]*Massachusetts Magazine*, 2 (July, 1790), 437. A much different version of this poem is preserved in the Morton manuscripts at the Huntington Library.

Sarah Goodhue

[1]Sarah Goodhue, *The Copy of a Valedictory and Monitory Writing* (New London, Conn.: James Allen, 1773), p. 3.

Anna Tompson Hayden

[1]*Handkerchiefs from Paul*, ed. Kenneth Murdock (Cambridge, Mass.: Harvard University Press, 1927), p. 22.

[2]Hayden's niece.

[3]These lines are "headed in Joseph Tompson's journal: 'sent unto me by a friend.' " Murdock, *Handkerchiefs from Paul*, p. 20.

Sarah Kemble Knight

[1]Alan Margolies, "Editing and Publication of 'The Journal of Madam Knight,' " Bibliographical Society of America *Papers*, 58 (1964), 30.

Bathsheba Bowers

[1]Ann Bolton, manuscript diary, quoted in William John Potts, "Bathsheba Bowers," *Pennsylvania Magazine of History and Biography*, 3 (1879), 111.

[2]Bolton, in Potts, "Bathsheba Bowers," p. 111.

3Bolton, in Potts, "Bathsheba Bowers," p. 112.

Susanna Wright

1Lyman H. Butterfield, "Dr. Benjamin Rush's Journal of a Trip to Carlisle in 1784," *Pennsylvania Magazine of History and Biography*, 74 (October, 1950), 455.

2Margaret Wright and Elizabeth Heistand, "Susanna Wright," *Notable Women of Pennsylvania*, eds. Gertrude Biddle and Sarah Lowrie (Philadelphia: University of Pennsylvania Press, 1942), p. 25.

3Butterfield, "Dr. Benjamin Rush's Journal," p. 455.

4Probably "diffuse."

5The Historical Society of Pennsylvania has two manuscript copies of this poem; the texts differ only slightly.

Mercy Wheeler

1Samuel Stearns, "To the Reader," *An Address to Young People, Or Warning to them from One Among Them, Yet May Be Called Warning From the Dead, Given by Mercy Wheeler* . . . (Boston: n. p., 1733), p. ii.

2Stearns, "To the Reader," *An Address to Young People . . . by Mercy Wheeler*, p. iv.

Lydia Fish Willis

[1]Anonymous editor, *Rachel's Sepulchre; Or, A Memorial of Mrs. Lydia Willis* . . . (Boston? Coverly? 1767?), p. 4.

[2]"A gentleman," *Rachel's Sepulchre* . . . , p. 38.

Susanna Rogers

[1]T. C. Frye, [Headnote to "The Mournful Elegy of Mr. Jona[than] Frye, 1725"], *New England Historical and Genealogical Register*, 15 (January, 1861), 91.

[2]Anonymous, "Lovewell's Fight," *American War Ballads and Lyrics*, ed. George Cary Eggleston (New York: G. P. Putnam's Sons, 1889), p. 18.

[3]Probably "relieve."

Grace Smith

[1]Grace Smith, *The Dying Mother's Legacy. Or the Good and Heavenly Counsel of the Eminent and Pious Matron, Mrs. Grace Smith* (Boston: Timothy Green, 1712), p. 1.

Esther Hayden

[1]*A Short Account of the Life, Death and Character of Esther Hayden* . . . (Boston: Fowle and Draper, 1759), p. 3.

[2]*A Short Account of . . . Esther Hayden . . .* , p. 11.

[3]*A Short Account of . . . Esther Hayden . . .* , p. 11.

[4]Probably "whither."

Abigail Colman Dennie

[1]Thomas Milner, *The Life, Times, and Correspondence of the Rev. Isaac Watts* (London: Simpkin and Marshall, 1834), p. 559.

[2]Ebenezer Turell, *The Life and Character of the Reverend Benjamin Colman* (Boston: Rogers and Fowle, 1749), p. 212.

[3]Turell, *Life and Character of the Reverend Benjamin Colman*, p. 214.

[4]Abigail Dennie's pseudonym.

[5]Presumably Turell's son.

Deborah Prince

[1]*Dying Exercises of Mrs. Deborah Prince and Devout Meditations of Mrs. Sarah Gill . . .* (Newburyport, Mass.: n. p. 1789), p. 4.

[2]Thomas Prince, *A Sermon Occasioned by the Decease of Mrs. Deborah Prince* (Boston: Rogers and Fowle, 1744), pp. 23, 24-25.

Bridget Richardson Fletcher

[1]Bridget Fletcher, "Hymn LXIII: God's Service More Pleasant to the Saint than His Daily Food," *Hymns and Spiritual Songs* (Boston: Isaiah Thomas, 1773), p. 53.

[2]Editor's "Preface," *Hymns and Spiritual Songs*, p. iii.

[3]Editor's "Preface," *Hymns and Spiritual Songs*, p. iii.

[4]Editor's "Preface," *Hymns and Spiritual Songs*, p. iv.

Sarah Prince Gill

[1]"Extracts from Mr. Hunt's Sermon Upon the Death of Mrs. Gill," *Dying Exercises of Mrs. Deborah Prince and Devout Meditations of Mrs. Sarah Gill . . .* (Newburyport, Mass.: n. p., 1789), pp. 24-25.

[2]"Introduction," *Devout Meditations*, p. 27.

[3][Obituary of Sarah Gill "from the *Boston Evening Post*. August 12, 1771"], *Devout Meditations*, p. 54.

Lucy Terry

[1]George Sheldon, "Negro Slavery in Old Deerfield," *New England Magazine*, 8 (March, 1893), 56. Bernard Katz's plausible but inconclusive argu-

ment is detailed in "A Second Version of Lucy Terry's Early Ballad?" *Negro History Bulletin*, 29 (Fall, 1966), 183-184.

[2]Sheldon, "Negro Slavery in Old Deerfield," p. 56.

[3]"Bars" was a colonial term for "meadow."

[4]Probably "fought."

Rebecca Richardson

[1]Rebecca Richardson, ["Do Thou, O God, In Mercy Help"] , *American Weekly Mercury* (January 10, 1738), p. [3] .

[2]Richardson, ["Do Thou, O God, In Mercy Help"] , p. [3] .

Sarah Parsons Moorhead

[1] [Sarah Moorhead] , "Lines . . . Humbly Dedicated to the Rev. Mr. Gilbert Tennent," *New England Weekly Journal* (March 17, 1741), p. [1] . The poem was reprinted in the *General Magazine and Historical Chronicle* (April, 1741), pp. 281-282.

[2]Perhaps an error for "past" or "haste."

Milcah Martha Moore

[1]A brief letter to the editors of the *Pennsylvania Chronicle* introduces "The Female Patriots": "Gentlemen, I send you the inclosed female performance for a place in your paper, if you think it may contribute any thing to

the entertainment or reformation of your male readers, and am, Yours, &c. Q. R."

Barbara Leininger

[1]George Mason Vaught's new translation takes fewer liberties with the original poem than does the earlier version by Edmund de Schweinitz, *Pennsylvania Magazine of History and Biography*, 29 (1905), 414-415. De Schweinitz alters the stress patterns and "embellishes" the meaning considerably. For example, the de Schweinitz translation has only sixteen lines, while the original poem has seventeen. Vaught's seventeen-line text returns to the stress patterns and simpler diction of the original.

Anna Green Winslow

[1]Anna Green Winslow, *Diary of Anna Green Winslow*, ed. Alice Morse Earle (Boston: Houghton Mifflin and Co., 1895), p. 48.

Jane Dunlap

[1]Jane Dunlap, *Poems Upon Several Sermons Preached by the Rev'd and Renowned George Whitefield While in Boston* (Boston: n.p., 1771), p. 19.

[2]Dunlap, *Poems*, p. ii.

[3]Dunlap, *Poems*, p. ii.

[4]Dunlap refers to Phillis Wheatley's "Elegiac Poem on the Death of . . . George Whitefield" (1770).

Anonymous Poets

[1]*South-Carolina Gazette* (January 22, 1732), p. [4].

[2]"A Lady," "To ********* Desiring To Borrow Pope's Homer," *A Collection of Poems. By Several Hands* (Boston: B. Green and D. Gookin, 1744), p. 44.

[3]"On the Noted and Celebrated Quaker Mrs. Drummond. By a Young Lady," *American Weekly Mercury* (March 16, 1736), p. [2]. The poem is probably of British origin.

[4]The following comments are subjoined to "A Riddle" in the *South-Carolina Gazette:* "We are greatly obliged to the Fair Correspondent, who sent us the above lines; no less for the compliment, she was pleas'd to send with it. But the ladies may be assur'd, that whatever we are favored with, in their hand-writing, may claim a place in our paper, without any other introduction." The last couplet included here appeared only in the *Pennsylvania Gazette* reprint.

[5]Benjamin Franklin's editorial notes for July 3, 1732, list the author as a woman.

[6]Prefacing "Florella to Damon" is a brief letter from "Florella" to the editor of the *South-Carolina Gazette:* "Sir, As the following lines are sent you in a female's handwriting, I shall presume, on that merit only, they'll be indulged with a place in your next. Yours, Florella."

[7]A brief letter to the editor of the *South-Carolina Gazette* introduces "The Maid's Soliloquy": "Mr. Timothy, The following soliloquy, being the performance of a lady in this province, I am persuaded, that, by giving it a place in your Gazette, you will afford some pleasure to your readers, as it will also show that the muses have had their seat in Carolina as well as in other parts remote from us. I am, Yours, &c. S. B."

[8]In 1756, Admiral John Byng was sent from England with a fleet to relieve the British garrison at Port Mahon on Minorca. A French squadron blocked his passage; Byng's fleet was unable to penetrate their defenses. Unable to fulfill his mission, Byng returned to England, where he was court-martialed and convicted of failing to do his utmost. On March 17, 1757, he was executed by a firing squad on the quarterdeck of his own flagship. Like many anonymous

poems, "On a Late Representation . . ." is difficult to assign a national origin. The subject matter may indicate that it is British, but as the only text I have been able to locate is American, I include it here.

9The editor attaches an explanatory note to the poem: "The ancient poets divided the duration of the world into four ages, or periods; the first they called the golden age, the second the silver age, the third the brazen age, the fourth the iron age; alluding to the different purity and value of those metals; and though we now live in an iron age, that metal is certainly the most useful and necessary to mankind."

10The piece which drew this response from H. W. has not been identified.

11The headnote to the poem reads: "Newport (Rhode Island), February 14. Last Friday morning a countryman stepping out of a sloop, at Brown's wharf, with a small bag of the accursed East India tea in his hand, fell into the dock, and had like to have been drowned; the tea was entirely ruined. Be cautious how you travel with the baneful article about you, for the salt water seems of late to attract it as a lodestone attracts iron."

Checklist of Poetry By Women In Pre-Revolutionary America

Checklist of Poetry By Women In Pre-Revolutionary America

     The following checklist collects references to verse by women who began writing before 1775 in what became the United States, even if the verse was published much later. Anthologized reprints, especially common in the early nineteenth century, have been omitted. Women who may have begun writing in pre-Revolutionary America, but for whom no pre-1775 poetry is extant have been excluded. (See the "Note on the Selection and Presentation of the Texts," pages 25-26, for allusions to some of these post-Revolutionary poets.) Prose works with even a few lines of verse have been cited, as have works by men that include verse by women. Entries are arranged alphabetically by poet; chronological order has been followed within entries. Anonymous and pseudonymous listings complete the checklist.

Ann Eliza Bleecker

Bleecker, Ann Eliza. "Thaumantia and Fame." *New-York Magazine; or, Literary Repository*, 1 (February, 1790), 118.

—. "Recollection." *New-York Magazine; or, Literary Repository*, 1 (February, 1790), 118.

—. "To Miss M. V." *New-York Magazine; or, Literary Repository*, 1 (February, 1790), 118-119.

—. "Written in the Retreat from Burgoyne." *New-York Magazine; or, Literary Repository*, 1 (March, 1790), 184-185.

—. "Lines on a Great Coxcomb Recovering from an Indisposition." *New-York Magazine; or, Literary Repository*, 1 (March, 1790), 185.

—. "The Immensity of Creation." *New-York Magazine; or, Literary Repository*, 1 (June, 1790), 364.

—. "A Thought on Death." *New-York Magazine; or, Literary Repository*, 1 (June, 1790), 364-365.

—. "Elegy on the Death of Cleora." *New-York Magazine; or, Literary Repository*, 2 (May, 1791), 295.

—. "Hope Arising from Retrospection." *New-York Magazine; or, Literary Repository*, 2 (June, 1791), 356.

—. "A Complaint." *New-York Magazine; or, Literary Repository*, 2 (July, 1791), 417.

—. "An Evening Prospect." *New-York Magazine; or, Literary Repository*, 2 (August, 1791), 475-476.

—. "On Seeing Miss S----- T- E---," *New-York Magazine; or, Literary Repository*, 2 (October, 1791), 607.

—. "Lines on Reading Dryden's Virgil." *New-York Magazine; or, Literary Repository*, 2 (November, 1791), 670.

—. "A Complaint." *New-York Magazine; or, Literary Repository*, 2 (December, 1791), 734-735.

—. *The Posthumous Works of Ann Eliza Bleecker in Prose and Verse* .... Ed. Margaretta V. Faugeres. New York: T. and J. Swords, 1793.

Bathsheba Bowers

Bowers, Bathsheba. *An Alarm Sounded To Prepare the Inhabitants of the World to Meet the Lord in the Way of His Judgments.* [New York: William Bradford (?), 1709].

Elizabeth Bradford

Bradford, Elizabeth. "To the Reader, in Vindication of this Book." *War with the Devil* ... By Benjamin Keach. 12th ed. [New York: William Bradford, 1714].

Anne Bradstreet

Bradstreet, Anne. Manuscripts. Stevens Memorial Library, North Andover, Massachusetts.

—. *The Tenth Muse Lately Sprung Up In America* .... London: Stephen Boutell, 1650.

—. *Several Poems Compiled with Great Variety of Wit and Learning, Full of Delight* .... Boston: John Foster, 1678.

—. *Several Poems Compiled with Great Variety of Wit and Learning, Full of Delight* . . . . Boston: n. p., 1758.

—. *The Works of Anne Bradstreet in Prose and Verse.* Ed. John Harvard Ellis. Charlestown, Mass.: Abram E. Cutter, 1867; rpt. New York: Peter Smith, 1932; Gloucester, Mass.: Peter Smith, 1962.

—. *The Poems of Mrs. Anne Bradstreet Together with her Prose Remains.* Ed. Frank E. Hopkins. [New York?] : The Duodecimos, 1897.

—. *A Dialogue Between Old England and New, and Other Poems.* Old South Leaflets, General Series, VII, No. 159. Boston: Directors of the Old South Work, 1905.

—. *The Tenth Muse (1650) and, From the Manuscripts, Meditations Divine and Morall Together with Letters and Occasional Pieces by Anne Bradstreet.* Ed. Josephine K. Piercy. Gainsville, Fla.: Scholars' Facsimiles & Reprints, 1965.

—. *The Works of Anne Bradstreet.* Ed. Jeannine Hensley. Cambridge, Mass.: Harvard University Press, 1967.

—. *Poems of Anne Bradstreet.* Ed. Robert Hutchinson. New York: Dover, 1969.

Martha Brewster

Brewster, Martha. *Poems on Divers Subjects* . . . . New London, Conn.: John Green, 1757.

—. *Poems on Divers Subjects* . . . . Boston: Edes and Gill, [1758] .

Abigail Dennie

Dennie, Abigail. "Lines by Mrs. Abigail Dennie." *New England Historical and Genealogical Register*, 14 (April, 1860), 170.

"Mrs. Jane Turell." *North American Review*, 93 (July, 1861), 32-33.

Elizabeth Drinker

Drinker, Elizabeth. Manuscript Diary in thirty-six volumes. Historical Society of Pennsylvania, Philadelphia.

—. *Extracts from the Journal of Elizabeth Drinker from 1759 to 1807.* Ed. Henry Drinker Biddle. Philadelphia: J. B. Lippincott Co., 1889.

—. "Verses by Elizabeth Drinker." *Pennsylvania Magazine of History and Biography*, 15 (1891), 246.

—. *Not So Long Ago, A Chronicle of Medicine and Doctors in Colonial Philadelphia.* Ed. Cecil K. Drinker. New York: Oxford University Press, 1937.

Jane Dunlap

Dunlap, Jane. *Poems, Upon Several Sermons, Preached by the Rev'd, and Renowned, George Whitefield, While in Boston.* Boston: n. p., 1771.

Mary English

English, Mary. ["May I With Mary Choose the Better Part"]. "A Sketch of Philip English ..." By George F. Chever, *Essex Institute Historical Collections*, 1 (1859), 164.

Elizabeth Graeme Fergusson

Fergusson, Elizabeth Graeme. Manuscript correspondence, papers and poems. Historical Society of Pennsylvania, Philadelphia.

—. Two manuscript poems. Princeton University Library, Princeton, New Jersey.

—. Manuscript poem. The Charles Patterson Van Pelt Library, University of Pennsylvania, Philadelphia.

—. Manuscript commonplace book. Dickinson College Library, Carlisle, Pennsylvania.

—. Manuscript commonplace book. Privately owned by Mrs. Welsh Strawbridge of Pennsylvania.

—. Three poems. *Poems on Several Occasions*. By Nathaniel Evans. Philadelphia: John Dunlap, 1772.

—. "Ode to Spring." *Pennsylvania Magazine*, 2 (April, 1776), 191. (Attribution by Lyon Richardson.)

—. "On the Death of Leopold, Hereditary Prince of Brunswick. . . ." *Columbian Magazine*, 1 (December, 1786), 198.

—. "Nathan's Parable, Paraphrased From the 12th Chapter of the 2d Samuel." *Columbian Magazine*, 1 (September, 1787), 667.

—. "Lines by a Friend, on Reading Mrs. M. Moore's Printed and Unprinted Extracts for the Use of Schools." *Columbian Magazine*, 2 (June, 1788), 350.

—. "III. Chapter of Job Paraphrased." *Columbian Magazine*, 3 (February, 1789), 127-128.

—. "On a Beautiful Damask Rose; Emblematical of Love and Wedlock." *Columbian Magazine*, 3 (May, 1789), 312.

—. "On the Mind's Being Engrossed by One Subject." *Columbian Magazine*, 3 (July, 1789), 437-438.

—. "A Song." *Columbian Magazine*, 3 (December, 1789), 746.

—. "Lines on Five Modern Evangelical Characters." *Universal Asylum and Columbian Magazine*, 5 (September, 1790), 188.

—. "Friendship Preferable to Love." *Universal Asylum and Columbian Magazine*, 5 (September, 1790), 188.

—. "On the Importance of Time. Addressed to Youth." *Universal Asylum and Columbian Magazine*, 5 (September, 1790), 188.

—. "The Rosebush an Emblem of Life." *Universal Asylum and Columbian Magazine*, 5 (October, 1790), 267-268.

—. "On Reading the Sorrows of Werter." *Universal Asylum and Columbian Magazine*, 5 (October, 1790), 269.

—. "A Paraphrase on Augur's Prayer. Prov. XXX. 7, 8, and 9 Verses." *Universal Asylum and Columbian Magazine*, 6 (February, 1791), 118.

—. "Ode, to Summer and Solitude." *Universal Asylum and Columbian Magazine*, 6 (April, 1791), 255-256.

—. "A Hymn to the Beauties of Creation." *Universal Asylum and Columbian Magazine*, 6 (April, 1791), 256.

—. "Addressed to Mrs. F-----r of Amwell, New Jersey, On the Death of Her Son, a Child of 15 Months Old." *Universal Asylum and Columbian Magazine*, 6 (June, 1791), 410-411.

—. "The Rose and Lily, a Tale: Addressed to the Fair." *Universal Asylum and Columbian Magazine*, 6 (June, 1791), 412-413.

—. "On the Re-Perusal of [Sylvia's 'Lines Occasioned by . . . Walking . . . in the Grave-yard of the Church of Wicacoe . . .'], When Their Writer Was No More." *Universal Asylum and Columbian Magazine*, 7 (August, 1791), 123.

—. "Ode to Sensibility (Written by a Lady, in 1770)," *Universal Asylum and Columbian Magazine*, 9 (July, 1792), 46-47.

—. "Ode to Autumn and Humanity." *Universal Asylum and Columbian Magazine*, 9 (July, 1792), 47.

—. "A Paraphrase on the 16th Chapter of St. Luke's Gospel, from the 19th Verse to the End." *Universal Asylum and Columbian Magazine*, 9 (September, 1792), 189-191.

—. Holograph insert of John Young's epitaph. *Compendium of Ancient Geography*. By Monsieur D'Annville. Trans. John Young. London: n. p., 1791. (The attribution, which is for a single quatrain only, remains uncertain because the insert is not in Fergusson's hand, though the book once belonged to her.)

Gratz, Simon. "Material for a Biography of Mrs. Elizabeth Fergusson, née Graeme." *Pennsylvania Magazine of History and Biography*, 39 (1915), 408; 41 (1917), 390.

Bridget Fletcher

Fletcher, Bridget. *Hymns and Spiritual Songs*. Boston: I. Thomas, 1773.

Mary French

French, Mary. ["A Poem Written by a Captive Damsel . . ."]. *Good Fetch'd Out of Evil. . . .* Ed. Cotton Mather. [Boston: n.p., 1706]; rpt. [Boston]: n. p., 1783.

—. ["A Poem Written by a Captive Damsel . . ."]. *Narratives of North American Indian Captivities.* Vol. IV. Ed. Wilcomb E. Washburn. New York: Garland Publishing, 1975.

Sarah Gill

Gill, Sarah and Deborah Prince. *Dying Exercises of Mrs. Deborah Prince and Devout Meditations of Mrs. Sarah Gill . . . .* Edinburgh: D. Paterson for W. Martin, 1785; rpt. Newburyport, Mass.: John Mycall, 1789. (The Edinburgh edition is signatured with *Six Sermons by the Late Thomas Prince*, Ed. John Erskine.)

Sarah Goodhue

Goodhue, Sarah. *The Copy of a Valedictory and Monitory Writing . . . .* Cambridge, Mass.: James Allen, 1681; rpt. New-London, Conn.: n. p., 1773.

—. *The Copy of a Valedictory and Monitory Writing . . . . Ipswich in the Massachusetts Colony.* By Thomas F. Waters. Ipswich, Mass.: Ipswich Historical Society, 1905-1917. II, 519-524.

Hannah Griffitts

Griffitts, Hannah. Manuscript poems and correspondence. Historical Society of
Pennsylvania, Philadelphia.

Anna Hayden

Hayden, Anna. "Upon the Death of . . . Elizabeth Tompson" and "Verses on
Benjamin Tompson." *Handkerchiefs from Paul, Being Pious and Con-
solatory Verses of Puritan Massachusetts . . . .* Ed. Kenneth Murdock.
Cambridge, Mass.: Harvard University Press, 1927.

Esther Hayden

Hayden, Esther. ["Verses . . . Composed About Six Weeks Before Her Death"].
*A Short Account of the Life, Death and Character of Esther Hayden
. . . .* Boston: Fowle and Draper, 1759.

Sarah Kemble Knight

Knight, Sarah Kemble. *The Journals of Madam Knight and the Rev. Mr. Buck-
ingham . . . .* Ed. Theodore Dwight, Jr. New York: Wilder and Campbell, 1825.

—. [Handwritten insert by Hannah Mather Crocker containing four lines of verse
bound into the American Antiquarian Society copy of Knight's *Journal*
(1825 edition).] Printed in *The Historical Magazine*, 1st series, 9 (1865),
93-94.

—. "Journal of Madam Knight." Ed. William R. Deane. *Littel's Living Age*, 3rd series, 1 (June 26, 1858), 962-980.

—. *The Private Journal of a Journey from Boston to New York in the Year 1704. Kept by Madam Knight*. Ed. William Law Learned. Albany, N. Y.: F. H. Little, 1865.

—. *The Private Journal of Sarah Kemble Knight* . . . . Norwich, Conn.: The Academy Press, 1901.

—. *The Journal of Madam Knight*. Ed. George Winship. Boston: Small, Maynard and Co., 1920; rpt. New York: P. Smith, 1935. Upper Saddle River, N. J.: Literature House, 1970; St. Clair Shores, Mich.: Scholarly Press, 1970.

—. *The Journal of Madam Knight*. New York: Garrett Press, Inc., 1970.

—. *The Journal of Madam Knight*. Boston: D. R. Godine, 1972.

Barbara Leininger

Leininger, Barbara and Marie Le Roy. *Die Erzehlungen von Maria Le Roy und Barbara Leininger, welche vierthalb Jahr unter den Indianern gefangen gewesen*. Philadelphia: Miller u. Weiss, 1759, rpt. in *Narratives of North American Indian Captivities*. Vol. VIII. Ed. Wilcomb E. Washburn. New York: Garland Publishing, 1975.

—. *The Narrative of Marie Le Roy and Barbara Leininger, Who Spent Three and One Half Years As Prisoners Among the Indians* . . . . Harrisburg, Pa.: n. p., 1878.

—. "The Narrative of Marie Le Roy and Barbara Leininger, For Three Years Captive Among the Indians." Trans. Edmund de Schweinitz. *Pennsylvania Magazine of History and Biography*, 29 (1905), 407-420; rpt. Lebanon County (Pa.) Historical Society. *Historical Papers and Addresses*, 3 (1905), 235-248.

Milcah Martha Moore

Moore, Milcah Martha. Manuscript commonplace book and letters. Privately
owned by Sarah A. G. Smith, according to Whitfield J. Bell, Jr., who
last saw the manuscripts in 1967.

—. "The Female Patriots. Address'd to the Daughters of Liberty in America,
1768." *Pennsylvania Chronicle*, 3 (December 18-25, 1769), 392. (Uncertain attribution.)

—. (comp.). *Miscellanies, Moral and Instructive, in Prose and Verse*. Philadelphia:
James, 1787. (This title also appeared under three other American
imprints.)

Sarah Moorhead

Moorhead, Sarah. ["Lines . . . Humbly Dedicated to the Rev. Mr. Gilbert Tennent . . ."]. *New England Weekly Journal* (March 17, 1741), p. [1];
rpt. *General Magazine and Historical Chronicle*, 1 (April, 1741), 281-
282.

—. *To the Reverend Mr. James Davenport on his Departure from Boston, by Way
of a Dream* . . . . Boston: Charles Harrison, 1742.

Sarah Wentworth Morton

Morton, Sarah Wentworth. Manuscripts. Huntington Library, San Marino,
California.

—. "Invocation to Hope." *Massachusetts Magazine*, 1 (July, 1789), 449.

—. "Philander. A Pastoral Elegy." *Massachusetts Magazine*, 1 (September, 1789), 583.

—. *Ouâbi: Or the Virtues of Nature. An Indian Tale.* Boston: Thomas and Andrews, 1790.

—. "Lines to Euphelia." *Massachusetts Magazine*, 2 (January, 1790), 58.

—. "Elegiac Lines to the Memory of Mrs. Abigail Jones." *Massachusetts Magazine*, 2 (March, 1790), 183; rpt. *Federal Orrerry*, 1 (October 27, 1794), 10.

—. "To Constantia." *Massachusetts Magazine*, 2 (May, 1790), 309-310.

—. "Lines to Euphelia." *Massachusetts Magazine*, 2 (June, 1790), 372.

—. "Ode Inscribed to Mrs. M. Warren." *Massachusetts Magazine*, 2 (July, 1790), 437.

—. "Lines Addressed to the Inimitable Author of the Poems Under the Signature of Della Crusca." *Massachusetts Magazine*, 2 (December, 1790), 761; rpt. *New-York Magazine*, 2 (March, 1791), 176.

—. "Sonnet to General Lincoln." *Massachusetts Magazine*, 3 (January, 1791), 50.

—. "To Alfred." *Massachusetts Magazine*, 3 (March, 1791), 183.

—. "The Death Song of an Indian Chief. Taken from *Ouâbi* . . . . Set [to Music] by Hans Gram." *Massachusetts Magazine*, 3 (March, 1791). (The "Death Song" appears in the table of contents without pagination; it was apparently omitted from the magazine erroneously.) Also printed separately, [Boston, 1791].

—. "To Alfred." *Massachusetts Magazine*, 3 (June, 1791), 374-375.

—. "The Tears of Humanity. Occasioned by the Loss of the Question for the Abolition of the Slave Trade, in the British Parliament." *Massachusetts Magazine*, 3 (July, 1791), 442-444; rpt. *Columbian Centinel* (August 3, 1791).

—. "The Retrospect. A Sonnet. Written in Declining Health." *Massachusetts Magazine* , 3 (October, 1791), 637.

—. "Monody, To the Memory of the Young Heroes, Who Fell at the Miami, under General St. Clair." *Massachusetts Magazine*, 3 (December, 1791), 765-766.

—. "Reanimation. A Hymn for the Humane Society." Broadside. [Boston: n. p., 1791?]; rpt. *Massachusetts Magazine*, 7 (June, 1795), 185; *The Tablet* (July 21, 1795), pp. 39-40; *Monthly Anthology*; or, *Massachusetts Magazine*, 1 (June, 1804), 377; *Boston Weekly Magazine*, 2 (June 16, 1804), 136; Broadside, [Boston? 1811?]; *Order of Performances on the 22d Anniversary of the Massachusetts Humane Society*, n. p., n. d.

—. "Midnight Invocation to Sleep." *Massachusetts Magazine*, 4 (May, 1792), 326.

—. "The African Chief." *Columbian Centinel* (June 9, 1792).

—. "To Pollio." *Massachusetts Magazine*, 5 (January, 1793), 52; rpt. *Massachusetts Mercury*, 1 (February 16, 1793), [4].

—. "Stanzas to Myra." *Massachusetts Magazine*, 5 (February, 1793), 118.

—. "Marie-Antoinette." *Columbian Centinel* (January 18, 1794). Inaccurate text reprinted correctly in *Columbian Centinel* (January 25, 1794).

—. "Stanzas Respectfully Inscribed to Antonia." *Federal Orrerry*, 1 (November 10, 1794), 25.

—. *Beacon Hill. A Local Poem*. Boston: Manning and Loring, 1797.

—. *The Virtues of Society*. Boston: Manning and Loring, 1799.

—. "Dedicatory Hymn. Composed for, and to be Sung at the Opening of the West-Boston Meeting House ... November 27, 1808." Broadside. Boston: n. p., 1808.

—. *My Mind and Its Thoughts, in Sketches, Fragments, and Essays*. Boston: Wells and Lilly, 1823; rpt. Delmar, N. Y.: Scholars' Facsimiles & Reprints, 1975.

Judith Sargent Murray

Murray, Judith Sargent. "An Hymn on Colossians I.19." *Some Deductions from the System Promulgated in the Page of Divine Revelation* .... Norwich: Trumbull, 1782; rpt. Portsmouth, N. H.: n. p., 1782, but without the poem.

—. "Desultory Thoughts Upon the Utility of Encouraging a Degree of Self-Complacency, Especially in Female Bosoms." *Gentleman and Lady's Town and Country Magazine* (October, 1784), pp. 251-253.

—. "Reverie, Occasioned by Reading the Vision of Mirza." *Boston Magazine* (June, 1785), pp. 203-206; (July, 1785), pp. 254-256.

—. "Lines Occasioned by the Death of an Infant." *Massachusetts Magazine* 2 (January, 1790), 57-58.

—. "Verses, Wrote at a Period of the American Contest, Replete with Uncertainty." *Massachusetts Magazine*, 2 (February, 1790), 120.

—. "New Epilogue to *The Recruiting Officer.*" *Massachusetts Magazine*, 2 (March, 1790), 186.

—. "On the Equality of the Sexes." *Massachusetts Magazine*, 2 (March, 1790), 132-135; (April, 1790), 223-226.

—. "Lines to Philenia." *Massachusetts Magazine*, 2 (April, 1790), 248-249.

—. "Epilogue to *Variety*, a Comedy." *Massachusetts Magazine*, 2 (April, 1790), 251-252.

—. "On the Domestic Education of Children." *Massachusetts Magazine*, 2 (May, 1790), 275-277.

—. "Frologue to *Variety.*" *Massachusetts Magazine*, 2 (June, 1790), 371.

—. "Apostrophe to the Shade of the Justly Celebrated Founder of Pennsylvania." *Universal Asylum and Columbian Magazine*, 5 (August, 1790), 121-128.

—. "Prologue to *The West Indian.*" *Massachusetts Magazine*, 3 (March, 1791), 181-182.

—. "Apology for an Epilogue." *Massachusetts Magazine*, 3 (May, 1791), 307.

—. "Valedictory Epilogue." *Massachusetts Magazine*, 3 (May, 1791), 307-308.

—. "The Gleaner" Essay Series. *Massachusetts Magazine*, 4-6 (February, 1792-August, 1794).

—. "Occasional Epilogue to *The Contrast.*" *Massachusetts Magazine*, 6 (March, 1794), 179-180.

—. "A Solution to the Rebus in the February Magazine." *Massachusetts Magazine*, 6 (March, 1794), 182-183.

—. "The Reply." *Massachusetts Magazine*, 6 (April, 1794), 146-147.

—. "Rebus." *Massachusetts Magazine*, 6 (April, 1794), 249-250.

—. "Lines Written December Thirty-first, 1794." *Massachusetts Magazine*, 6 (December, 1794), 758-760.

—. *The Gleaner.* 3 vols. Boston: I. Thomas and E. T. Andrews, 1798.

—. Letter to Winthrop Sargent, August 30, 1802. Massachusetts Historical Society, Boston.

—. "Lines Written While Rocking a Cradle." *Boston Weekly Magazine,* 1 (November 6, 1802), 8.

—. "Birth-Day Invitation." *Boston Weekly Magazine*, 1 (November 20, 1802), 16.

—. "Lines Occasioned by the Much Opposed Departure of a Friend, Upon a Long and Hazardous Voyage." *Boston Weekly Magazine*, 1 (December 4, 1802), 24.

—. "Christmas Day, 1802." *Boston Weekly Magazine*, 1 (December 25, 1802), 36.

—. "Lines Inscribed to an Amiable and Affectionate Mother Upon the Death of her Eldest Son, Who Fell a Victim to the Yellow Fever." *Boston Weekly Magazine*, 1 (January 15, 1803), 52.

—. "Lines, On the Birth of an Infant Who, By the Flatteringly Expressed Sanction of Mrs. Martha Washington, Received the Illustrious Name of George Washington." *Boston Weekly Magazine*, 1 (February 5, 1803), 64.

—. "Expiring Amity." *Boston Weekly Magazine*, 1 (February 26, 1803), 76.

—. "On Blending Spirit with Matter." *Boston Weekly Magazine*, 1 (March 5, 1803), 80.

—. "An Hypothesis." *Boston Weekly Magazine*, 1 (March 19, 1803), 88.

—. "A Rebus." *Boston Weekly Magazine*, 1 (April 2, 1803), 96.

Mary Nelson

Nelson Mary. "Forty Shillings Reward." *Pennsylvania Chronicle*, 2 (January 9-16, 1769). 439; rpt. *Pennsylvania Chronicle*, 2 (January 23, 1769), postscript.

Deborah Prince

Prince, Deborah. ["Go Careless Mortal"]. *A Sermon Occasioned by the Decease of Mrs. Deborah Prince*. By Thomas Prince. Boston: Rogers and Fowle for T. Rand, 1744.

Rebecca Richardson

Richardson, Rebecca. ["Do thou, O God, in Mercy help"]. *American Weekly Mercury* (January 10, 1738), pp. [2-3].

Susanna Rogers

Rogers, Susanna. "The Mournful Elegy of Mr. Jona[than] Frye, 1725." *New England Historical and Genealogical Register*, 15 (January, 1861), 91.

Anna Young Smith

Smith, Anna Young. Manuscript poems in Elizabeth Fergusson commonplace book. Dickinson College Library, Carlisle, Pennsylvania.

—. "An Elegy to the Memory of the American Volunteers Who Fell in the Engagement at Lexington on the 19th of April, 1775." *Pennsylvania Magazine*, 1 (June, 1775), 278-279; rpt. *Universal Asylum and Columbian Magazine*, 6 (March, 1791), 186-187; *Memoirs of the Historical Society of Pennsylvania*. Ed. Edward Armstrong. Philadelphia: J. B. Lippincott and Co., 1864. I, 461-463.

—. "On Reading Swift's Works." *Universal Asylum and Columbian Magazine*, 5 (September, 1790), 185.

—. "Ode to Liberty." *Universal Asylum and Columbian Magazine*, 6 (February, 1791), 113-114.

—. "Good-Natured Wit." *Universal Asylum and Columbian Magazine*, 6 (February, 1791), 114.

—. "To the Memory of General Warren, Who Fell at the Battle of Bunker's Hill, June 24th, 1776." *Universal Asylum and Columbian Magazine*, 6 (May, 1791), 340-341.

—. "Epistle from Sylvia to Damon." *Universal Asylum and Columbian Magazine*, 6 (June, 1791), 411-412.

—. "Lines Occasioned by the Writer's Walking One Summer's Evening in the Grave-yard of the Church of Wicacoe, in the Southern Environs of the City of Philadelphia, on the Bank of the Delaware." *Universal Asylum and Columbian Magazine*, 7 (August, 1791), 121-123.

—. ["Hail, Honored Wedlock!"] *Universal Asylum and Columbian Magazine*, 9 (July, 1792), 45-46.

Grace Smith

Smith, Grace. *The Dying Mother's Legacy* .... Boston: Timothy Green, 1712.

Annis Boudinot Stockton

Stockton, Annis Boudinot. Manuscript poetry and correspondence. Princeton University Library, Princeton, New Jersey.

—. Manuscript poetry and correspondence. Historical Society of Pennsylvania, Philadelphia.

—. Manuscript poems and letters to George Washington. Washington Papers, Library of Congress, Washington, D. C.

—. Two poems copied into Esther Burr Journal. Beinecke Library, Yale University, New Haven, Connecticut.

—. "To the Honorable Col. Peter Schuyler." *New York Mercury* (January 9, 1758), p. [1]; rpt. *New American Magazine*, 1 (January, 1758), 16.

—. "By a Lady in America to her Husband in England." *Pennsylvania Magazine*, 1 (June, 1775), 280-281.

—. [Untitled poetic dialogue]. *New Jersey Gazette,* 4 (November 21, 1781), [4].

—. "On Hearing of the News of the Capture of Lord Cornwallis and the British Army by Gen. Washington." *New Jersey Gazette* (November 28, 1781), p. [2].

—. Poems appended to *A Funeral Sermon on the Death of the Hon. Richard Stockton, Esq. . . .* By Rev. Samuel Stanhope Smith. Trenton, N. J.: Isaac Collins, 1781.

—. "A Poetical Epistle, Addressed by a Lady of New Jersey, to her Niece, upon her Marriage . . . . *Columbian Magazine*, 1 (November, 1786), 145.

—. "Addressed to General Washington, in the Year 1777, after the Battles of Trenton and Princeton." *Columbian Magazine*, 1 (January, 1787), 245.

—. "On the Celebration of the Birth of the Dauphin of France." *Columbian Magazine*, 1 (February, 1787), 295.

Butterfield, Lyman H. "Morven: A Colonial Outpost of Sensibility. With Some Hitherto Unpublished Poems by Annis Boudinot Stockton." *Princeton University Library Chronicle*, 6 (November, 1944), 1-16.

Butterfield, Lyman H. "Annis and the General: Mrs. Stockton's Poetic Eulogies of George Washington." *Princeton University Library Chronicle*, 7 (November, 1945), 19-39.

Lucy Terry

Terry, Lucy. "Bars Fight." *History of Western Massachusetts.* By Josiah G. Holland. 2 vols. Springfield, Mass.: Samuel Bowles and Co., 1855. II, 360; rpt. George Sheldon. "Slavery in Old Deerfield." *New England Magazine*, 8 (March, 1893), 56.

Consider Tiffany

Tiffany, Consider. *Relation of the Melancholy Death of Six Young Persons Who Were Kill'd by Lightning . . . June, 1767 . . . .* Broadside. [n. p., 1767].

Jane Turell

Turell, Jane. [Selected Poems]. in *Reliquiae Turellae, et Lachrymae Paternae: . . . Two Sermons Preach'd at Medford, April 6, 1735, by Benjamin Colman, D. D., The Lord's Day After the Funeral of His Beloved Daughter, Mrs. Jane Turell. To Which Is Added, Some Large Memoirs of Her Life and Death by her Consort, the Reverend Mr. Ebenezer Turell . . . .* Boston: S. Kneeland and T. Green, 1735.

—. [Selected Poems]. in Ebenezer Turell's *Memoirs of the Life and Death of . . . Mrs. Jane Turell . . . Collected Chiefly From Her Own Manuscripts. To Which is Added, Two Sermons Preached at Medford . . . After Her Funeral by . . . B. Colman, D. D.* London: n. p., 1741.

Mercy Otis Warren

Warren, Mercy Otis. Manuscript poetry, correspondence and papers. Massachusetts Historical Society, Boston.

—. Manuscript poetry and correspondence. Houghton Library, Harvard University, Cambridge, Massachusetts.

—. "The Massachusetts Song of Liberty." *Bickerstaff's Boston Almanack for . . . 1770.* Ed. Benjamin West. Boston: Mein and Fleeming, [1770]. (Uncertain attribution.)

—. *The Adulateur, a Tragedy. Massachusetts Spy,* 2 (March 26, 1772) 15; rpt. Boston: n.p., 1773; *Magazine of History with Notes and Queries.* Extra Number 63 (1918), 225-229; Tarrytown, N. Y.: W. Abbott, 1918.

—. "Extracts from *The Defeat." Boston Gazette* (May 24, 1773), p. [2]; (July 19, 1773), p. [2].

—. ". . . A Squabble Among the Celestials of the Sea, Arising From a Scarcity of Nectar and Ambrosia." *Boston Gazette* (March 21, 1774), p. [1].

—. "To a Gentleman Who Requested a List of those Articles which Female Vanity has Comprised under the Head of Necessaries." *Royal American Magazine,* 1 (June, 1774), 233-234.

—. [Extract from *The Group]. Boston Gazette,* (January 23, 1775), pp. [2-3].

—. [Extract from *The Group]. Massachusetts Spy,* 4 (January 26, 1775), [2].

—. ["A Political Reverie"]. *Boston Gazette* (February 13, 1775), p. [4].

—. *The Group, a Farce.* Boston: Edes and Gill, 1775; rpt. New York: John Anderson, [1775]; Philadelphia: James Humphreys, Jr., 1775; Ann Arbor, Mich.: University of Michigan Press, 1953.

—. *The Blockheads: or, The Affrighted Officers, a Farce.* Boston: [John Gill], 1776.

—. "O Tempora! O Mores!" *Boston Gazette* (October 5, 1778), p. [1].

—. "On the Death of the Hon. John Winthrop, Esq." *Independent Chronicle* (October 21, 1779), p. [1].

—. *The Motley Assembly, A Farce* . . . . Boston: Nathaniel Coverly, 1779.

—. *Poems, Dramatic and Miscellaneous.* Boston: T. Thomas and E. T. Andrews, 1790.

—. "To Mr. Adams." *Warren-Adams Letters.* Massachusetts Historical Society *Collections*, 73 (1925), 402-403.

Phillis Wheatley

Wheatley, Phillis. Manuscript poetry. Massachusetts Historical Society, Boston.

—. Manuscript poetry. Historical Society of Pennsylvania, Philadelphia.

—. Manuscript poem. Houghton Library, Harvard University, Cambridge, Massachusetts.

—. Manuscript poetry. American Antiquarian Society, Worcester, Massachusetts.

—. Manuscript poetry. Dartmouth College Library, Hanover, New Hampshire.

—. Manuscript poetry. Bowdoin College Library, Brunswick, Maine.

—. "On Messrs. Hussey and Coffin." *Newport Mercury* (December 21, 1767), p. [3]; rpt. Carl Bridenbaugh. "The Earliest-Published Poem of Phillis Wheatley." *New England Quarterly*, 42 (December, 1969), 583-584.

—. *An Elegiac Poem, on the Death of . . . George Whitefield . . .* Boston: Ezekiel Russell and John Boyles, [1770]. (Numerous Boston, Newport, New York, Philadelphia and London reprints.)

—. "To Mrs. Leonard, on the Death of Her Husband." Broadside. [Boston: n. p., 1771].

—. "To the Rev. Mr. Pitkin, on the Death of his Lady." Broadside. [Boston: n. p., 1772].

—. "A Poem on Providence, written by a Young Female Slave." [Boston (?): n.p., 1772 (?)]; rpt. as "A Beautiful Poem on Providence, Written by a Young Female Slave . . . ." Halifax: E. Gay, 1805.

—. "To the Hon'ble Thomas Hubbard, Esq., on the Death of Mrs. Thankfull Leonard." Broadside. [Boston: n. p., 1773].

—. "An Elegy to Miss Mary Moorhead. . . ." Broadside. [Boston]: M'Alpine, [1773].

—. *Poems on Various Subjects, Religious and Moral.* London: A. Bell, 1773. (Numerous reprints.)

—. "Poem Addressed by Philis . . . to a Gentleman of the Navy, with his reply." *Royal American Magazine*, 1 (December, 1774), 473-475.

—. "Philis's Reply to the Answer in our Last by the Gentleman in the Navy." *Royal American Magazine*, 2 (January, 1775), 34-35.

—. [Letter and Poem . . . to "His Excellency Gen. Washington."] *Virginia Gazette.* Ed. Dixon and Hunter (March 30, 1776), p. [1]; rpt. *Pennsylvania Magazine* 2 (April, 1776), 193.

—. "To Mr. and Mrs. ------ on the Death of their Infant Son." *Boston Magazine* (September, 1784), p. 488.

—. *Liberty and Peace, a Poem.* Boston: Warden and Russell, 1784.

—. *An Elegy, Sacred to the Memory of that Great Divine, the Reverend and Learned Dr. Samuel Cooper . . . .* Boston: E. Russell, 1784.

—. "An Ode, On the Birth Day of Pompey Stockbridge." Broadside. [n. p., n. d.].

—. *Memoir and Poems of Phillis Wheatley.* Boston: George W. Light, 1834; rpt. Boston: Light and Horton, 1835; Boston: Isaac Knapp, 1838, with poems by George Moses Horton added. Facsimile reprint of 1838 edition, Miami: Mnemosyne Publishing Co., 1969. (Numerous other editions of Wheatley's poems appeared throughout the nineteenth and twentieth centuries.)

—. *Poems and Letters by Phillis Wheatley.* Ed. Charles F. Heartman. New York: Charles Heartman, 1915; rpt. Miami: Mnemosyne Publishing Co., 1969.

—. *The Poems of Phillis Wheatley.* Ed. Julian D. Mason, Jr. Chapel Hill, N. C.: University of North Carolina Press, 1966.

Kuncio, Robert C. "Some Unpublished Poems of Phillis Wheatley." *New England Quarterly*, 43 (June, 1970), 287-197.

Robinson, William H. *Phillis Wheatley in the Black American Beginnings.* Detroit: Broadside Press, 1975.

Mercy Wheeler

Wheeler, Mercy. *An Address to Young People . . . .* Boston: n. p., 1733.

Lydia Willis

Willis, Lydia. *Rachel's Sepulchre; or, A Memorial of Mrs. Lydia Willis, Taken, Chiefly, from her Letters to Friends. . . .* [Boston? Coverly? 1767?].

—. *Madam Willis's Letters and Her Character. With Some Strictures of Madam Ann Stockbridge's, and the Character of Madam Sarah Page . . . .* Boston: Nathaniel Coverly, 1788.

Anna Winslow

Winslow, Anna. *Diary of Anna Green Winslow: a- Boston School Girl of 1771.*
Ed. Alice Morse Earle. Boston: Houghton Mifflin Co., 1895; rpt. Detroit:
Singing Tree Press, 1970.

Susanna Wright

Wright, Susanna. Manuscript poems and correspondence. Historical Society of
Pennsylvania, Philadelphia.

Anonymous and Pseudonymous Poets

"Amelia." "A Reply, in Doggerel Rhime, to . . . Caution to Bachelors." *New
England Courant* (September 25-October 2, 1721), p. [1].

"Renuncles." "Reply to Lucilius, for his Caution to Bachelors." *New England
Courant* (October 2-9, 1721), p. [1].

"Widow R–lt." "A Dream." *American Weekly Mercury* (May 27, 1724), p. [2].

"A Lady." "The Answer." *American Weekly Mercury* (May 27, 1724), p. [2].

"A Female Hand." "The Progress of Life." *New England Weekly Journal* (August 23, 1731), p. [1]; rpt. *South-Carolina Gazette* (June 22-29, 1734),
p. [1]; *American Magazine and Historical Chronicle*, 2 (March, 1745),
128.

"A Fair Correspondent." "A Riddle." *South-Carolina Gazette* (January 15-22,
1732), p. [4]; rpt. *Pennsylvania Gazette* (June 15-19, 1732), p. [4].

"Lucretia." "The Seventh Chapter of the Proverbs, in a Poetical Dress, Being the Description of a Harlot." *South-Carolina Gazette* (February 5-12, 1732), p. [2].

"Belinda." "Since th' Am'rous Bard Has Thus Essay'd." *South-Carolina Gazette* (February 19-26, 1732), p. [3].

"Dorinda." "To Belinda." *South-Carolina Gazette* (March 18-25, 1732), p. [3].

"Louisa." "O Thou Eternal Power." *South-Carolina Gazette* (May 6-13, 1732), p. [1].

"Florella." "Florella to Damon." *South-Carolina Gazette* (June 10-17, 1732), p. [3].

"A Female Hand." "The Pow'r of Letters Can't Be Weak." *Pennsylvania Gazette* (June 19-26, 1732), p. [4].

"A Young Lady of 12 Years Old." "Oh, Spotless Paper . . . ." *South-Carolina Gazette* (April 7-14, 1733), p. [3]; rpt. *Pennsylvania Chronicle*, 6 (June 8-15, 1772), 88.

"Sally's Answer to the Poem on Similes." *South-Carolina Gazette* (August 4-11, 1733), p. [3].

"Virgin's Prayer." *South-Carolina Gazette* (June 22-29, 1734), p. [1].

"A Lady of Superior Genius." "Hail Capt. Slayton . . . ." *Boston Gazette* (December 23-30, 1734), p. [3].

"A Young Lady." "On the Noted and Celebrated Quaker Mrs. Drummond." *American Weekly Mercury* (March 16, 1736), p. [2].

"E. R." "The Lady's Complaint." *Virginia Gazette*, Ed. Parks (October 15-22, 1736), p. [3]; rpt. *South-Carolina Gazette* (August 15, 1743), p. [3]; as "The Maiden's Complaint." *Essex Almanack, for . . . 1773*. Salem: S. and E. Hall, [1773].

"Helena Littlewit." "Hor. Ode IX. Cormin. 1.3. Dial. Hor. and Lydia." *Virginia Gazette*, Ed. Parks (July 15-22, 1737), p. [1].

"A Lady." "Written Under a Libel upon a Deceased Gentleman." *Virginia Gazette*. Ed. Parks (July 15-22, 1737), p. [2].

"Sylvia to Philander." *American Weekly Mercury* (February 19, 1741), p. [2].

"Flavia Complains of Dull Restraint." *General Magazine and Historical Chronicle*, 1 (April, 1741), 278-279. (The editor notes that this poem was taken from the *Virginia Gazette*, though I have been unable to locate it there.)

"An Answer to the Riddle for the Ladies." *American Magazine and Historical Chronicle*, 1 (October, 1743), 80.

"Verses Written by a Young Lady, on Women Born to be Controll'd!" *South-Carolina Gazette* (November 14-21, 1743), pp. 2-3; rpt. *American Magazine and Historical Chronicle*, 1 (June, 1744), 435; *American Magazine, or General Repository* (August, 1769), pp. 271-272.

"A Young Lady." "A Riddle." *American Magazine and Historical Chronicle*, 1 (December, 1743), 168.

"A Young Lady," "A Song." *American Magazine and Historical Chronicle*, 1 (February, 1744), 259.

"A Young Lady." "A Song." *American Magazine and Historical Chronicle*, 1 (August, 1744), 523.

"A Lady." "To the Memory of Archibald Home, Esq. . . ." *Pennsylvania Gazette* (August 9-16, 1744), p. [2]; rpt. *American Magazine and Historical Chronicle*, 1 (August, 1744), 520-521.

"A Lady." "To ********* Desiring to Borrow Pope's Homer." *A Collection of Poems. By Several Hands*. Boston: B. Green and D. Gookin, 1744.

"A Lady's Lamentation for the Loss of her Cat." *American Magazine and Historical Chronicle*, 2 (January, 1745), 36.

"Eugenia." "An Epigram on a Religious but Censorious Lady." *American Magazine and Historical Chronicle*, 2 (January, 1745), 35.

"Miss Jacobiton." "A Ballad, To the Tune of Chevy Chase." *Virginia Gazette*. Ed. Parks (August 21-28, 1746), pp. [2-3].

"Eugenia." "A Hymn; or, an Attempt to Versify the 104th Psalm." *American Magazine and Historical Chronicle*, 3 (October, 1746), 470-471.

"Carolina." "On her Father Leaving, Desired her to Forbid all Young Men the House." *South-Carolina Gazette* (July 27-August 3, 1747), p. [2].

"By a Lady on the Loss of her Son at Sea." *Independent Advertiser* (June 12, 1749), pp. [1-2].

"The Dying Mother's Advice." Broadside. [New London, Conn.: n. p., 1749].

"A Lady in this Province." "The Maid's Soliloquy." *South-Carolina Gazette* (February 25-March 4, 1751), p. [1]; rpt. *Virginia Gazette.* Eds. Purdie and Dixon (September 20, 1770), p. [4].

H–S––. "To the Memory of a Much Lov'd Friend, Mrs. Hannah Dale . . . ." *South-Carolina Gazette* (April 29-May 6, 1751), p. [1]. Corrected text printed in *South-Carolina Gazette* (May 6-13, 1751), p. [3].

"A Lady in New England." "The Spouse of Christ Returning to her First Love. An Hymn." *Boston Gazette* (July 9, 1751), p. [2].

W. K. "My Son, th' Instruction that my Words Impart . . . ." *Boston Gazette* (June 2, 1755), p. [2].

"A Young Lady of Fifteen." "On a Late Representation." *Virginia Gazette.* Ed. Hunter (April 22, 1757), p. [2].

"A Young Lady." "On the Liberties of the Nation." *New York Mercury* (July 4, 1757), p. [1].

"Amelia." "A Rebus." *American Magazine and Monthly Chronicle*, 1 (December, 1757), 129.

"A Female." "On Marriage." *New American Magazine*, 1 (January, 1758), 13.

"Philandreia." "A Pindaric Ode." *American Magazine and Monthly Chronicle*, 1 (February, 1758), 240-242.

"A Female Hand." "On the Evil of Pride." *Pennsylvania Journal* (April 27, 1758), p. [1].

"An Epitaph by a Young Lady, Design'd for Herself." *New American Magazine*, 1 (April, 1758), 80.

"Sophia Meanwell." "The Withered Rose." *New American Magazine*, 1 (June, 1758), 141.

"A Young Lady in a Neighboring Government." "Roxana to Alexander at the Siege of Tyre." *American Magazine, or Monthly Chronicle*, 1 (October, 1758), 645-648.

"A Lady of New-York." "Golden Age Fabulous." *New-England Magazine*, 1 (October, 1758), 56-57.

"A Lady of New-England." "The Rake." *A Collection of Poems in Six Volumes by Several Hands.* Ed. Robert Dodsley. London: J. Hughs, 1758. IV, 318.

"A Lady." "Upon General Amherst's leading his troops from Boston, after the Conquest of Louisbourg, to Join our Army that had been Repulsed at Ticonderoga." *New American Magazine*, 2 (January, 1759), 333-334.

"Fil. Nass. Ale--s." "A Night Piece." *New American Magazine*, 2 (January, 1759), 332.

—. "The Solemn Pensive." *New American Magazine*, 2 (March, 1759), 406-407.

—. "True Politeness." *New American Magazine*, 2 (May, 1759), 467-468.

"The Choice of a Husband. In a Letter to a Friend." *New American Magazine*, 2 (August, 1759), 588-589.

"Fil. Nass. Ale--s." "Louisburg Taken: An Ode." *New American Magazine*, 2 (September, 1759), 621-622.

"Black ey'd Susan's lamentation for the Departure of her Sweet William, who was Impress'd to go to Sea . . . ." Broadside. Boston: [T. and J. Fleet. 176?].

"Clorinda Cora." "Lines in Answer to Those of Esop Coon." *New American Magazine*, 2 (February, 1760), 69.

H. W. *An Answer to a Piece, Entituled a Line Drawn Between Christ, and Anti-Christ.* Providence? William Goddard? 1765.

"Lines, Wrote by a Young Lady in this City." *Pennsylvania Chronicle*, 1 (March 16-23, 1767), 36.

"Lucretia." "The Dry, Dull, Drowsy Bachelor Surveys . . . ." *Pennsylvania Chronicle*, 1 (November 2-9, 1767), 168.

Miss S. P. "A Soliloquy on Death." *Virginia Gazette*. Eds. Purdie and Dixon (March 10, 1768), p. [2].

"To the Visitant, from a Circle of Ladies, on Reading his Paper, No. 3. . . ." *Pennsylvania Chronicle*, 2 (March 7-14, 1768), 50; rpt. *American Museum*, 4 (December, 1788), 491.

"A Young Lady." "Aenigma." *Pennsylvania Chronicle*, 2 (March 14-21, 1768), 58.

"Amanda." "Propitious Solitude, Thou Kind Retreat." *Pennsylvania Chronicle*, 2 (March 14-21, 1768), 58.

"Published at the Request of an Amiable Young Lady." *Virginia Gazette*. Eds. Purdie and Dixon (March 17, 1768), p. [3].

Miss S. R. "Paradox in the Last *Gazette* Answered . . . ." *Virginia Gazette*. Ed. Rind (May 12, 1768), p. [1].

"A Lady." "Few Happy Matches." *Virginia Gazette*. Eds. Purdie and Dixon (July 7, 1768), p. [2].

"A Young Lady's Complaint on the Death of her Squirrel." *Virginia Gazette*. Eds. Purdie and Dixon (December 15, 1768), p. [4].

"Amanda." "When All Was Hush'd Profoundly Calm." *Pennsylvania Chronicle*, 3 (February 6-13, 1769), 18.

"Florella." "A Song." *American Magazine, or General Repository* (February, 1769), p. 56.

"A Lady." "A Wish." *Virginia Gazette*. Eds. Purdie and Dixon (July 13, 1769), p. [4].

"Eliza." "Another." *Virginia Gazette*. Ed. Rind (September 21, 1769), p. [1].

"A Lady." "A Thought on Autumn." *Virginia Gazette*. Eds. Purdie and Dixon (December 21, 1769), p. [4].

"Chloe's Noble Choice." *Virginia Gazette.* Eds. Purdie and Dixon (January 18, 1770), p. [4].

"A Lady." "An Epigram on a Late Marriage." *Pennsylvania Chronicle,* 4 (April 9-16, 1770), 46.

"Sophrona." "Edmund and Catherine. An Epigram." *Pennsylvania Chronicle,* 4 (July 16-23, 1770), 104.

"A Young Lady." "Contentment." *Pennsylvania Chronicle,* 4 (November 26-December 3, 1770), 181.

"A Lady." "A Request to the Divine Being." *Virginia Gazette.* Eds. Purdie and Dixon (October 3, 1771), p. [4].

"The Art to Please." *Pennsylvania Chronicle,* 6 (October 10-17, 1772), 160.

"A Lady." "Impromptu, on Reading an Essay on Education." *Virginia Gazette.* Eds. Purdie and Dixon (February 11, 1773), p. [4].

"Rebecca L——, an Old Maid." "On Hearing an Amiable and Virtuous Young Lady's Reputation Made Too Free With." *Pennsylvania Chronicle,* 7 (June 28-July 5, 1773), 96.

"A Female." "The Death of the Fox." *Pennsylvania Chronicle,* 7 (December 20-27, 1773), 196.

"A Lady's Adieu to her Tea Table." *Virginia Gazette.* Eds. Purdie and Dixon (January 20, 1774), p. [2]; rpt. *Pennsylvania Gazette* (January 26-February 2, 1774), p. [3].

"A Lady of Wit, Sense, and Accomplishments, but Neither Young nor Handsome." "The Complaint, an Ode to Cupid." *Virginia Gazette.* Eds. Purdie and Dixon (February 3, 1774), p. [4].

"Verses Addressed by the Ladies of Bedford, at their Meeting to Resolve Against Tea . . ." *Virginia Gazette.* Eds. Purdie and Dixon (March 17, 1774), p. [2].

"Sylvia." "To the Editor." *Royal American Magazine,* 1 (April, 1774), 154.

"A Mother to a Young Child, Smiling in a Dream." *Royal American Magazine,* 1 (April, 1774), 154.

"A Lady to her Daughter with a Present of a Watch." *Virginia Gazette.* Eds. Purdie and Dixon (May 19, 1774), p. [4].

"A Lady." "On Receiving a Handsome Set of Tea China." *Virginia Gazette.* Eds. Purdie and Dixon (June 16, 1774), p. [4] ; rpt. *Virginia Gazette.* Ed. Clementina Rind (June 16, 1774), p. [1] .

"The Lady's Choice." *Royal American Magazine*, 1 (July, 1774), 268.

"Lucinda." "A Rebus." *Royal American Magazine*, 1 (November, 1774), 433-434.

"Daughter of Liberty." "An Address to New-England . . . ." Broadside. [Boston: Nathaniel Coverly, 1774] .

"A Lady." "Happiness." *Royal American Magazine*, 2 (January, 1775), 34.

"Amanda." "Poem on Christmas Day." *Pennsylvania Magazine*, 1 (January, 1775), 41-42.

"—." "Come Sweetly Pleasing Solitude." *Pennsylvania Magazine*, 1 (February, 1775), 86.

"Delia." "Ode to Charity." *Pennsylvania Magazine*, 1 (February, 1775), 87.

"Daphne." "Gentle Cupid." *Pennsylvania Evening Post*, 1 (February 2, 1775), 20.

"A Very Young Lady." "A Winter Scene in the Country." *Virginia Gazette.* Ed. Pinkney (February 9, 1775), p. [3] .

"Daphne." "I'm a Girl (If My Glass and My Lovers Told True)." *Pennsylvania Evening Post*, 1 (Februry 21, 1775), 52.

"A Lady." "The Confession." *Virginia Gazette.* Eds. Dixon and Hunter (March 11, 1775), p. [4] .

"A Young Lady of this City." "On the death of Miss R---- D--- . . . ." *Pennsylvania Magazine*, 1 (March, 1775), 134- 135.

"Delia." "To a Young Lady." *Pennsylvania Magazine*, 1 (April, 1775), 183.

"A Lady." "On Gathering a Snow-Drop in the Garden of her Lover." *Virginia Gazette.* Eds. Dixon and Hunter (May 6, 1775), p. [4] .

"A Young Lady." "On the Death of her Husband." *Virginia Gazette*. Ed. Pinkney (June 8, 1775), p. [4].

"Mira." "The Complaint." *Pennsylvania Magazine*, 1 (June, 1775), 281.

"A Letter from Miss ***** to her God Mother." *Pennsylvania Magazine*, 1 (August, 1775), 374.

"On Reading an Invitation to the Spinners in the *Pennsylvania Gazette*, Number 2433." *Pennsylvania Gazette* (August 16, 1775), p. [3].

"On the Death of a Young Lady's Squirrel." *Virginia Gazette*. Ed. Pinkney (October 19, 1775), p. [4].

"An Epistle from a Lady to her Husband, who Embarked at Plymouth, on the American Expedition." *Virginia Gazette*. Eds. Dixon and Hunter (November 4, 1775), p. [4].

"A Lady." "Answer to the Riddle in the Last Magazine." *Pennsylvania Magazine*, 1 (November, 1775), 527.

POEMS INDEX, TITLES

POEMS INDEX, FIRST LINES

GENERAL INDEX